American Writers and the Picturesque Tour
The Search for National Identity, 1790–1860

Beth L. Lueck

Garland Publishing, Inc.
New York and London
1997

PS366
.T73
L84
1997

Library of Congress Cataloging-in-Publication Data

Lueck, Beth Lynne.
      American writers and the picturesque tour : the search for national iden-
tity, 1790–1860 / by Beth L. Lueck.
            p.   cm. — (Garland studies in nineteenth-century American litera-
ture ; vol. 7)   (Garland reference library of the humanities ; vol. 1967)
      Includes index.
      ISBN 0-8153-2285-2 (alk. paper)
      1. Travelers' writings, American—History and criticism.   2. American
prose literature—19th century—History and criticism.   3. Americans—
Travel—United States—History—19th century.   4. National characteristics,
American, in literature.   5. Picturesque, The, in literature.   6. Group
identity in literature.   7. Landscape in literature.   8. Travelers in literature.   9. Travel in literature.   I. Series.   II. Series: Garland reference
library of the humanities ; vol. 1967.
PS366.T73L84   1997
810.9'355—dc21   97-19947
                                                                                        CIP

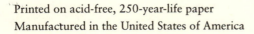

Printed on acid-free, 250-year-life paper
Manufactured in the United States of America

For my parents

Contents

Series Editor's Preface

Specialists in nineteenth-century American literature will find
much to digest in this book, a critical survey of the picturesque tour in
our national literature from Charles Brockden Brown to writers of the
American Renaissance. American literary nationalism is no new
concern in cultural issues, but Beth Lueck's approach to it is.
Customarily critiques of the picturesque have dwelt upon what I'd call
the more grave aspects that, for many, were thought to be inherent in
the subject matter. Accounts of the picturesque and the picturesque
tour, particularly those established by William Gilpin and others in
Great Britain, could be calculated to elicit awe and its ramifications
among most readers. Lueck details how American writers' attitudes
toward this European aesthetic and its discourse occasioned interesting
strategies in adaptations. These alterations were aimed at promoting
interests of American literary nationalism. As was typical of his outlook
toward European literary traditions in other respects, Charles Brockden
Brown, her first exemplar of an American who ventured to handle
picturesqueness, cast a wary eye upon the picturesque. He discerned the
pitfalls awaiting Americans who too unheedingly tried to view their
own landscapes through Old World lenses, so to speak. With the
faddishness that rapidly came to be associated with American travelers
in search of such stimuli, however, and because of the frequent
dependence of such travelers upon a small number of quickly emerging
"standard" guidebooks to spots of the picturesque to be encountered in
American travel, satiric-parodic reactions sprang up from those who
detected an increasing ridiculousness in the overarching American yen
to take a picturesque tour, but without sufficient spontaneity within the
tourist(s) to engage landscape with any really original intuitive
impulses. To an eye taking a long view, large numbers of travelers
who quested after the picturesque depended too emphatically and
facilely on what amounted to how-to-do-it manuals of limited, and
limiting scope; therefore they might as well not have taken efforts to
undertake such travel in the first place.

Beth Lueck is no stranger to American authorship and the picturesque tour, having contributed to a significant study of Hawthorne's ventures into that kind of travel writing, and her survey provides insights into the aims and methods of several American authors whose art involves in some one way or another an engagement with the picturesque. The names of Irving, Parkman, and Thoreau, along with those of Hawthorne and Melville, are certainly no surprise in such contexts. The inclusion of Brown, Paulding, and Poe may, however, not initially seem to fit into the same mosaic as these others. Lueck's chapters nonetheless suffer no annoying wrenchings in theme or placements as she leads us from one to another of these writers. From Brown's questioning the value of European conceptions of picturesqueness and the picturesque tour for American culture, on to Melville's far more grim handling of the picturesque, we learn in these pages, is no obstructed pathway. In terms of political ideals and the practicalities of coping with the American frontier, Brown's *Edgar Huntly* stands as a warning signal against too easily yielding to artificialities potentially in picturesqueness.

Moving outside of the sobriety that characterized *Edgar Huntly* (and Brown's other novels), writers like Paulding, Poe, and Melville exercised their propensities for parody and satire on what they envisioned as the extravagances and lopsided thinking to which writings about the picturesque were prone. Lueck's chapter on Paulding alone should be required reading for Americanists, among whom his stock has remained undervalued for many years. This section of Lueck's book makes an excellent compliment for Leland S. Person's critique of Paulding in *Western American Literature* (1981), and it also supplements Larry J. Reynolds's Twayne series book on Paulding. As with his handling of literary Gothicism, Paulding's treatments of the picturesque are varied, fairly straightforward in *Letters from the South*, comic in a story like "Childe Roeliff's Pilgrimage" or *The New Mirror for Travellers; and Guide to the Springs*. Lueck's chapter also amplifies much that has already been published on the intertwinings of the Hudson River school of painters with American literature and nationalistic impulses in the arts during the era.

Likewise, the name of Edgar Allan Poe does not spring immediately to mind in discussions of the picturesque, but Lueck's placement of him as one whose talents encompassed the western tour and other aspects of picturesqueness, and who should thus not be ignored in such contexts, illuminates several of his fictions that have not been done to death by Poe specialists, e.g., *The Journal of Julius Rodman*, "Morning on the Wissahiccon, ""Landor's Cottage," and "The Domain of Arnheim." Poe, too, could not seem to resist comic presentations of materials of picturesqueness, as is evident in these pieces, and Lueck's work enriches our perceptions of Poe's successes as a humorist. Thus her Poe chapter makes good companion reading for that excellent book on Poe's landscape aesthetics, Kent Ljungquist's *The Grand and the Fair*. A near kinsman in terms of registering possible flaws in unheeding acceptance of the picturesque, Hawthorne also hit at travellers who depended too unthinkingly upon guidebooks' canned picturesqueness. Lueck's critiques of Hawthorne's landscape techniques remind us that he wrote much else, and that of high artistic worth, in addition to *The Scarlet Letter* or "Young Goodman Brown." The achievements of Poe and Hawthorne in the art of the short story were in part enhanced by their adapting elements of the picturesque tour to bolster such successes.

Dovetailing neatly with Lueck's assessments of these authors' achievements in characterization by means of the picturesque tour are those concerning Irving and Parkman on the western tour as a barometer to issues of American manhood, and that on Thoreau's works, in which the picturesque tour (in northeastern environs) symbolizes moral and spiritual growing. Parkman in particular transforms the conventional picturesque tour by his implications about its outcome not in consequence of the individual only, but in the greater context of the nation overall. Reading these chapters may prompt us to see some origins for heroes in twentieth-century western fiction and films. Lueck's presentation of manliness in *The Oregon Trail* could plausibly figure into discussions of the Lone Ranger character (although film fans may recall that the actor who, for many, was "The" Lone Ranger, Clayton Moore, also appeared as a bad guy in films from time to time) or that of a host of other cowboy stars. Knowing that Parkman in his book did not dwell upon his own extended illness during his western travel, we might think of his being a relative to Poe's Julius Rodman, who was not really what he seemed to be (and, of course, both works in their method of omitting important information pave the way for a similar lacuna in *The Education of Henry Adams*). And these ambiguities bring us full circle. By the mid-nineteenth century, fashionable picturesque touring had run its course, and Melville could fashion dark parody of it in *The Piazza Tales*.

In sum, Lueck's book extends the work of such scholars as Benjamin T. Spencer, Blake Nevius, Kent Ljungquist, Dennis Berthold, and others, who have mapped courses in landscape aesthetics as American literature emerged during its formative years. Lueck's assessments of individual primary texts remind us that considerations of so-called "major" texts may not always give us all we might profitably learn or know about any given author or cultural movement. Not only do Lueck's readings of individual texts themselves reveal a keen ability in literary analysis, but they offer all sorts of implicit outreaches to other texts by their own creators and to other writers and the other arts as well. For one example, the comments by the narrator in "The Fall of the House of Usher," concerning how rearrangement of landscape-pictorial details could change emotional responses, offers perspectives for approaching the Poe texts included in this book, and for may others in his canon. For another example, many features of the picturesque in William Cullen Bryant's poems also may stand out in more sharply etched detail and with more sophisticated suggestions, once one reads Lueck's pages. *American Writers and the Picturesque Tour* ought to enjoy a long shelf life for what it establishes and for what it implies in regard to additional prospects into territories of the American literary picturesque.

Benjamin F. Fisher

Acknowledgments

I am grateful to my colleagues in the Department of Languages and Literatures at the University of Wisconsin--Whitewater for their support and encouragement, especially Mary Pinkerton, Larry Schuetz, DeWitt Clinton, Mary Emery, John Fallon, Rebecca Hogue, and Geneva Cobb Moore. I also would like to thank Howard L. Ross, Dean of the College of Letters and Sciences, for his financial support for the index.

I wish to thank the University of Wisconsin--Whitewater for a Summer Faculty Enhancement Grant, 1995.

I also want to thank the University of Wisconsin--Milwaukee for its Graduate School Research Fellowship, 1986-87, and for the Committee on Institutional Cooperation's Summer Research Opportunity Grant for the summer of 1987. The late Howard Deller provided expert assistance with the travel guides and maps in the American Geographical Society Collection in the Golda Meir Library at the University of Wisconsin--Milwaukee. Donna Schenstrom, of the university's Cartographic Services Laboratory, also deserves recognition for the three maps she created for this book.

This book started as a dissertation at the University of North Carolina more than a decade ago. For their advice and encouragement, I want to acknowledge the late Robert Bain, the late C. Hugh Holman, Joy S. Kasson, Richard D. Rust, and John Seelye, who pointed me towards Gilpin in America.

I also wish to thank my former colleague Ralph M. Aderman for his generous help and encouragement, particularly for the Paulding and Irving chapters. In addition, my conversations with Dennis Berthold on American travel writing in general and on Hawthorne in particular helped clarify my thinking. Both colleagues exemplify humane scholarship.

Finally, I want to thank my children, Benjamin and Daniel, for being so patient and keeping a sense of humor throughout the long history of this book.

Earlier versions of the chapters on Brown and Paulding appeared in *Studies in American Fiction* (1987) and *University of Mississippi Studies in English* (1991). I am grateful to the editors for permission to reprint here.

I wish to thank University Press of New England for permission to reprint "Hawthorne's Ironic Traveler" from *Hawthorne's American Travel Sketches* (1989).

American Writers and the Picturesque Tour

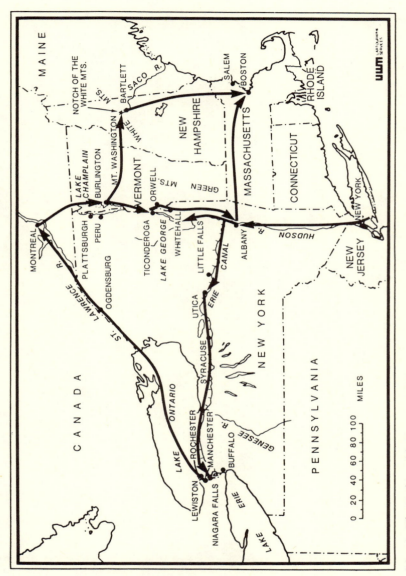

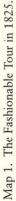

Map 1. The Fashionable Tour in 1825.

Chapter 1

Introduction

In 1855, writing about travelers of various nations, a critic for *Putnam's Monthly* compared British, French, and American travelers and made the following observations about his fellow countrymen: "The American," he wrote, "has a pleasure in foreign travel, which the man of no other nation enjoys. With a nature not less romantic than others; with desires and aspirations for the reverend and historically beautiful, forever unsatisfied at home, fed for years upon the splendid literature of all time, and the pompous history of the nations that have occupied and moulded the earth, and yet separated from those nations and that history, not only by space and the total want of visible monuments, but by the essential spirit of society around him; born with poetic perception amid the stateliest natural forms--forests, mountains, rivers, and plains--that seem to foreshow a more imperial race, and results more majestic than are yet historical, but with none of that human association in the landscape, which gives it its subtlest beauty and profoundest influence, the American mind is solicited by Europe with unimagined fascination." The American traveler, he concludes, "goes out [to Europe] to take possession of his dreams, and hopes, and boundless aspirations."[1]

He was wrong. For at least a half-century before this essay appeared Americans had been traveling in their native land, their routes expanding ever westward. During this same period dozens of travel books had appeared by recognized writers, by minor writers, and by people without the least pretense to this title. Contrary to this critic's observation, the great majority of these travelers found plenty to satisfy them on the American continent, both landscapes and history. Even though Washington Irving complained early in the century about the dearth of historical associations in the American landscape, he was finding and exploiting dozens of historical and geographic sites in early sketches such as "Rip Van Winkle" and "The Legend of Sleepy Hollow" and, later on, in tales such as "The Devil and Tom Walker" and "Kidd the Pirate."[2] Americans, including Irving and most other major writers, did travel to Europe in great numbers, often paying lip service to the complaint that the American landscape lacked the associations and history necessary for a vital, indigenous literature. Nevertheless, many of these same writers found enough to write about and produced hundreds upon hundreds of travel books, sketches, tales, and novels.

These works of travel literature constitute the material of this study. Although critical interest has been stirred in recent years by the extraordinary volume of travel literature written in the eighteenth and nineteenth centuries, and an occasional work has appeared that links the interest in particular landscapes with people traveling to view such scenery, no one has examined the broader issues that arose when Americans in increasing numbers traveled in pursuit of scenic beauty in the first half of the nineteenth century.[3]

American travelers' passion for picturesque beauty was fostered by various accounts of landscapes worth viewing, by artists' renderings of scenery that appeared in periodicals in the form of woodcuts and engravings, as well as in paintings, and by the nationalistic fervor following the War of 1812. With peace newly returned to the country, with prosperity, and with leisure time at hand, people increasingly sought out well known landscapes and traveled in search of landscape beauty. Picturesque travel led to the development of the American picturesque tour, a written version of the popular British tour. But what was most significant about this phenomenon, in which almost every major author of the first half of the nineteenth century participated, was the role it played in shaping the literature of the new nation. Critics have assumed that, by and large, American writers borrowed British literary conventions and used them relatively uncritically to present native materials to their American and European audiences. In sharp contrast to this view, it is clear that American authors did not feel at all confined by some literary forms. Instead, they adapted these conventions for a national literature, keeping elements that seemed essential and abandoning those that appeared irrelevant. In the case of the picturesque tour, American writers seized upon an essentially British form that originated in the late eighteenth century and modified it for their own use.

Right from the beginning, with Charles Brockden Brown's *Edgar Huntly* (1799), the American tour took off in a direction scarcely suggested by the British original. From Brown's picturesque tourist, asleep and stumbling through a dark landscape, to James Kirke Paulding's later satires on tourism, to Poe's parodies of the genre, American writers transformed the picturesque tour, recognizing its extraordinary adaptability in tone and its particular usefulness as a means of expressing their nationalistic sentiments. In addition, picturesque discourse offered a flexible series of conventions that enabled American writers to celebrate verbally the unique landscapes and associated legends and peoples that set their nation apart from the rest of the world. Its many variations in tone, from straightforward description to irony and satire, also allowed writers to adapt the picturesque for various kinds of writing, including nonfictional forms such as tours and essays and fictional forms such as sketches, tales, and novels. How these writers took the conventions of the picturesque tour and adapted them to help shape the nation's identity through literature is the focus of this book.

Most of the leading writers of the period between 1790 and 1860 showed familiarity with picturesque travel and used at least some of its conventions in their writing. Some writers borrowed the picturesque tour and its literary conventions wholesale from English models and adapted them to the realities of the American landscape. Brown's picturesque tourist in *Edgar Huntly,* for example, explored the wilderness landscapes of Norwalk, and Paulding's tourists traveled throughout the South and New York. Later Washington Irving and Francis Parkman adapted the modes of picturesque discourse to the prairies and mountains of western America. Other writers dealt with the divergences between English conventions and American realities by introducing new tonal qualities into the picturesque tour. Thus Hawthorne created an ironic tourist who satirized the pretensions of other travelers, while Poe employed comic and parodic strategies in his travel writings. Thoreau also responded creatively to the problem of adapting the British model to American landscapes, employing picturesque discourse in a wide range of tones and forms, ranging from irony to awe, and from description to meditation.

In this study I propose to define the picturesque tour both as a form of travel and literature, and to examine the national and cultural background that led to the popularity of picturesque travel. Then I will explore the ways the major writers between 1790 and 1860 adapted the existing conventions of picturesque travel to American locales and shaped the tour for their own needs in both fictional and nonfictional narratives. Focusing on the writings of seven major authors whose work reflects a knowledge of and interest in picturesque travel--Brown, Irving, Paulding, Hawthorne, Parkman, Poe, and Thoreau--I will examine the varying modes of picturesque discourse that resulted in their work.

The conventions of the picturesque tour date back to the 1780s and '90s in England, or even earlier, if one considers the continental grand tour a forerunner of picturesque travel. During this period William Gilpin, an English clergyman, traveler, and writer, emerged as the chief advocate and practitioner of the picturesque tour. His published tours of Great Britain introduced the upper ranks of British society to the pleasures of touring. These tours also established the format for the picturesque tour for the next half-century, both in England and America, and set the standard for travel books that featured the picturesque tour.

Gilpin's influential essay "On Picturesque Travel" (1792) defined the conventions of this form of travel, even as his essay "On Picturesque Beauty" (1792) initiated a prolonged debate about this form of landscape beauty. According to Gilpin, the picturesque tour was a tour in search of picturesque beauty, which he defined as the kind of landscape beauty that would be suitable in a picture. Travelers searched for landscapes featuring contrasts in light and shadow; rough textures, or "ruggedness" (as opposed to smoothness, which was associated with the beautiful); compositional unity within the varied elements of a scene, sometimes achieved through the unifying light of the sun or moon on a landscape; and historical, legendary, literary, or other associations.[4] Contemporary critics such as Uvedale Price and Richard Payne Knight debated Gilpin's definition of picturesque beauty. More recently, modern critics such as Martin Price argue for both a more complex and less stable definition of this aesthetic category. But because the term "picturesque beauty" was most widely understood in America as embracing the qualities listed here, and because Gilpin's works were most frequently cited and read by American writers, I will use the term in this sense throughout this study.[5] Several examples will illustrate the first three elements in picturesque description as American writers used them in the art of the verbal sketch; the issue of associations and landscape will be taken up later.

Washington Irving, one of the most enthusiastic picturesque travelers in America and abroad, offers an excellent example of the verbal sketch in a scene from *A Tour on the Prairies* (1835), as he and his fellow tourists pause to view a river valley in what is now Oklahoma. Irving's highly trained picturesque eye appreciates the scene before him, and he creates the following sketch of the view:

> A beautiful meadow about half a mile wide, enameled with yellow autumnal flowers, stretched for two or three miles along the foot of the hills, bordered on the opposite side by the river, whose banks were fringed with cotton wood trees, the bright foliage of which refreshed and delighted the eye, after being wearied by the contemplation of monotonous wastes of brown forest.
>
> The meadow was finely diversified by groves and clumps of trees, so happily disposed that they seemed as if set out by the hand of art. As we cast our eyes over this fresh and delightful valley we beheld a troop of wild horses quietly grazing on a green lawn about a mile distant to our right, while to our left at nearly the same distance, were several buffaloes . . . The whole had the appearance of a broad beautiful tract of pasture land, on the highly ornamented estate of some gentleman farmer, with his cattle grazing about the lawns and meadows.[6]

The entire scene provides a refreshing contrast to the "monotonous wastes" of forest through which the company has just ridden. Within this scene the smooth meadowland contrasts effectively with the rougher textures of the trees, just as the meadow is "diversified" by "clumps" of cottonwoods. (These terms originate with Gilpin, who had defined the usage of such terms for picturesque discourse in *Remarks on Forest Scenery* [1791].[7])

Irving provides the requisite variety for a picturesque composition with the river, meadow, trees, flowers, and animals, and although the unifying touch of the sun is absent here, his focus on the valley, with its surrounding hills, helps to frame the scene for the reader. Directional references also help the reader picture the scene. Water, whose changeable quality Gilpin admired in the picturesque landscape, is present in the river.[8] The grazing buffalo and wild horses give rough texture to the composition, an element Gilpin often included by means of sheep or other rough-coated animals, and add a pastoral element that softens the wildness of the western landscape.[9] At the end of the verbal sketch Irving's comparison of the river valley to a gentleman farmer's estate domesticates the landscape even further and suggests its future potential as farmland for the pioneers who would one day settle here. This reference also introduces the element of class to the sketch, an element that plays an indirect role in landscape appreciation for many picturesque tourists. For the upper-middle class or upper-class traveler in America or abroad, the act of categorizing landscapes as picturesque often involved class distinctions since farmers--real ones, not "gentleman farmers"--who actually tilled the soil, shepherds, and similar figures often appeared in picturesque sketches, verbal or otherwise. Such figures were often sentimentalized by the very nature of the tourist's viewing them as "picturesque"; indeed, a later American traveler, Francis Parkman, distinguished between such persons (Indians, for example) seen at close range and at a distance. In the foreground, they and their dwellings are merely ugly or dirty, but with the softening effect of distance they become picturesque. Prosperous figures, whether businessmen or middle-class tourists, lack the roughness and quaintness of humbler persons and rarely appear in the picturesque sketch until the late 1820s, when they enter the scene as objects of the author's irony or satire. Paulding frequently satirizes the tourists at popular Virginia and New York watering places, and Hawthorne occasionally features such characters in his American travel sketches.

While Irving celebrated western scenery in the example from *A Tour on the Prairies*, Hawthorne's travel sketches from the 1830s illustrate the usefulness of picturesque discourse for depicting the scenery of eastern America and reflect, like Irving's description, Gilpin's compositional principles at work in the verbal sketch. "A Night Scene" provides an excellent example of how contrast and unity can function in picturesque composition. Although most picturesque scenery is viewed in the daytime or during the early morning or evening hours, in this sketch Hawthorne finds visual excitement in the strong contrasts created by a bonfire on a riverbank, which he views from a steamboat at night:

As the evening was warm, though cloudy and very dark, I stood on deck, watching a scene that would not have attracted a second glance in the day-time, but became picturesque by the magic of strong light and deep shade. Some wild Irishmen were replenishing our stock of wood, and had kindled a great fire on the bank, to illuminate their labors. It was . . . blazing fiercely, spouting showers of sparks into the darkness, and gleaming wide over lake Erie-- a beacon for perplexed voyagers, leagues from land. All around and above the furnace, there was total obscurity. No trees, or other objects, caught and reflected any portion of the brightness, which thus wasted itself in the immense void of night, as if it quivered from the expiring embers of the world, after the final conflagration. But the Irishmen were continually emerging from the dense gloom, passing through the lurid glow, and vanishing into the gloom on the other side. Sometimes a whole figure would be made visible . . . ; others were but half seen, like imperfect creatures; many flitted, shadow-like, along the skirts of darkness, tempting fancy to a vain pursuit; and often, a face alone was reddened by the fire.[10]

In a twist on the typical picturesque scene, darkness and not light provides the unifying element in the composition, and the sharp contrast between the gloomy night and the glare of the bonfire attracts the observer's eye. Hawthorne's interpretation of the scene, and perhaps even his attraction to it, owes more than a little to the popularity of Salvator Rosa's paintings in nineteenth-century America. The seventeenth-century Italian artist's work had become synonymous with the savage aspect of picturesque beauty since before Gilpin's time,[11] and in this verbal sketch the writer's depiction of "wild Irish" provides the visual equivalent of Rosa's banditti in the Italian countryside for the relatively tame American landscape. Unlike Irving's work, however, in which picturesque description orders and civilizes the western landscape and the author's tone remains the smoothly admiring voice of a gentleman-tourist, Hawthorne's sketch suggests some of the diverse tonal qualities possible in picturesque discourse. "A Night

Scene" glows in an apocalyptic light that distorts rather than illuminates
the scene, and the narrator's tone is one of awe or even horror at the
supernatural, almost magical quality of the picture created by the
bonfire's lurid blaze.

The picturesque principle of unity in variety can be illustrated
by Edgar Allan Poe's description of a prospect near the Missouri River
in *The Journal of Julius Rodman* (1840). From high grounds Rodman
and his fellow explorers viewed the "extensive prospect" that follows:

> We saw here an immense and magnificent country
> spreading out on every side into a vast plain, waving
> with glorious verdure, and alive with countless herds
> of buffaloes and wolves, intermingled with occasional
> elk and antelope. To the south the prospect was
> interrupted by a range of high, snow-capped
> mountains . . . Behind these again was a higher
> range, extending to the very horizon in the north
> west. The two rivers presented the most enchanting
> appearance as they wound away their long snake-like
> lengths in the distance.

The composition centers on the "vast plain," within which various
elements such as the prairie verdure and wild animals provide interest
for the observer. The scene is framed by mountains, and the rivers,
which "vanished in the shadowy mists of the sky,"[12] add depth to the
landscape, beckoning the observer into the distance like the golden light
in the background of a painting by Claude. The meandering rivers also
add the curved lines that are a common feature of picturesque beauty
in the verbal sketch.

One question that arises in reading picturesque discourse
concerns the combination of aesthetic categories in natural landscapes.
Nature, of course, seldom provided pure examples of each aesthetic for
the picturesque tourist, and travelers took it upon themselves to try to
describe, and sometimes to label, the various landscapes they observed.
Gilpin himself acknowledged that the traveler rarely found "perfectly
pure" examples of the grand (a synonym for sublimity[13]) or the
beautiful, and in practice he often mixed the various modes of
landscape beauty, particularly the picturesque and the sublime.[14] An
example from *Remarks on Forest Scenery* illustrates these mixed
modes. Gilpin describes "a very grand, and picturesque forest view"

that included clumps of wood and areas of pasturage, which create contrast and variety (elements of the picturesque), and a vast expanse of wood (the sublime).[15]

American writers offer numerous examples of the mixed mode of the picturesque and sublime, which was sometimes called picturesque sublimity.[16] For various reasons, this mixed mode appealed to Hawthorne and Poe in particular, although Parkman and Thoreau were also attracted to various combinations of the picturesque and the sublime; the travel writings of these writers will be discussed later. An anonymous "traveller in search of the picturesque," writing in *The Knickerbocker Magazine* in 1835, offers a glimpse of picturesque sublimity in his description of the Connecticut River Valley. Here the Vermont mountains, he suggests, "if not so grand as . . . the White Hills," offer "beauty, verdure, romantic vallies, secluded nooks" for the tourist. "When wearied with clambering among the hills of this charmingly picturesque country, with its immense belt of ever-greens, and its cool, mountain trout streams," the picturesque traveler might turn to "the beautiful shores of Lake Champlain" for relief.[17]

According to Gilpin's essay "On Picturesque Travel," the pleasures of the tour centered on the anticipation and discovery of picturesque beauty, as well as the later recollection of the scenery by sketching or writing about it. Since one of the primary "amusements" of picturesque travel, as Gilpin describes it, is the pursuit of landscape beauty, one of the special pleasures of this form of travel is "the expectation of new scenes." Stating that the "love of novelty" motivates the lover of picturesque beauty to explore unknown landscapes, Gilpin argues that unexplored country is the ideal setting for the tourist.[18] This laid the groundwork for the New World's preeminence as a location for picturesque travel. Even in the early nineteenth century parts of the Eastern Seaboard and vast territories both east and west of the Mississippi River remained largely unexplored, if not actually undiscovered by whites. The excitement generated by vast tracts of unknown and potentially beautiful landscapes cannot be overstated. It left travelers eager to win recognition for discovering particular areas of great beauty, and they laid claim to this distinction in periodicals and travel books. Occasionally this led to accounts of so-called undiscovered territory that had not only been discovered by earlier travelers, but had even been described at length in published travel narratives. Not unexpectedly, the need for unknown landscapes also inspired some travel writers to create wholly imaginary landscapes for readers hungry for new picturesque and sublime views.[19]

Throughout the essay "On Picturesque Travel," Gilpin emphasizes the relationship between traveler and landscape; the observer's response to the landscapes through which he or she traveled is as important as the terrain itself. The traveler, Gilpin suggests, takes pleasure in examining scenery according to the rules of picturesque beauty or in comparing one scene to another. But the main pleasure of picturesque travel lies in the power of landscape beauty to affect the observer emotionally. When a "grand scene" suddenly bursts upon the traveler's view, it "strikes us beyond the power of thought," Gilpin states, marveling at the "enthusiastic sensation of pleasure" that fills the soul. "We rather *feel*, than *survey*" such a scene, he concludes.[20] For example, in *Observations on the Western Parts of England* Gilpin describes the beauties of the Isle of Wight and explains the influence of picturesque beauty on the observer:

> The beauteous forms of nature and art thus impressed on the mind, give it a disposition to happiness, from the habit of being pleased, from the habit of seeking always for pleasing objects, and making even displeasing objects agreeable by throwing on them such colours of imagination, as improve their defects; and if a *love for beauty* is not immediately connected with *moral* ideas, we may at least suppose that it softens the mind, and puts it in a frame to receive them.[21]

As a result of Gilpin's emphasis on the tourist's response to landscape and the prominence given to such first-person reflections in his published tours and those of other travelers, in the decades that followed travel books often combined straightforward descriptions of scenery with reflections about its effect on the writer.[22] This set the stage for much later romantic writing about landscape that was devoted almost exclusively to the traveler's subjective rather than objective response to nature.

In addition, published tours such as Gilpin's often included historical anecdotes, local legends, and accounts of colorful personalities encountered on the tour, all of which contributed to the associations that were necessary for true picturesque beauty in a landscape.[23] Such digressions, according to Gilpin, offered "occasional relief" from "travelling continually among rocks, and mountains; hills, and vallies; and remarking upon them." "Therefore," he noted, speaking of himself as a writer of tour books, "when any observations, anecdote, or history, grew naturally from his subject, he was glad to take the advantage of it; and draw the reader a little aside, that he might return to the principal object with less satiety." Although Gilpin considered his use of digressions in the tours "poetic license," few readers would argue with him about including such material.[24] Such digressions satisfied a wider audience by creating a much more varied, entertaining, and informative travel book than otherwise would exist in a tour offering only landscape description. Since the favored location for picturesque travel was wholly unknown or relatively untraveled lands, digressions provided travelers with an opportunity for commenting on local inhabitants, customs, politics, legends, and history. Travelers in America--and Americans in particular--found digressions especially useful because they could then feel free to expatiate upon whatever subjects or ideas were suggested by the lands through which they traveled, yet still keep to the basic structure of the picturesque tour. For this reason, Francis Parkman comments at length upon Native American customs and society, in addition to describing landscape beauty in the West. Exciting tales of buffalo hunts and encounters with colorful trappers and hunters enliven sections of *The Oregon Trail* that otherwise might make dull reading.

Whether picturesque travel had a moral impact on the traveler is a question that, though rarely considered in debates on aesthetics, is relevant to any discussion of the meaning and significance of these travel narratives. Gilpin addressed this issue in his original essay on the subject. "A search after beauty," he wrote, "should naturally lead the mind to the great origin of all beauty." But, he added, it is unlikely that "every admirer of *picturesque beauty*, is an admirer also of the *beauty of virtue*."[25] Certainly travelers and readers had, by the end of the eighteenth century, grown accustomed to finding evidence of God's glory and power as creator in sublime landscapes, particularly mountains, yet no equivalent moral impact had been discerned for picturesque beauty.[26] Gilpin, however, made the best effort possible towards arguing for such a relationship: "If however the admirer of nature can turn his amusements to a higher purpose; if it's great scenes can inspire him with religious awe; or it's tranquil scenes with that complacency of mind, which is so nearly allied to benevolence, it is certainly the better. " He concluded that although picturesque travel may have a "moral tendency," for most people it would remain nothing more than an "agreeable amusement."[27]

The moral effect of picturesque travel, a relatively unimportant issue for most European tourists, assumed greater significance for Americans. Determined to demonstrate the superiority of their nation, sometimes by arguing for the superiority of its landscape beauty, American travel writers could easily turn a picturesque or sublime scene into a metaphor for national supremacy. This occurred frequently with regard to Niagara Falls, where travelers debated the relative superiority of the American Falls over the Canadian Falls and commented upon the falls as evidence of God's power.[28] Certainly Margaret Fuller found picturesque travel to have a "moral tendency," for she was moved to reverence for God on viewing Niagara Falls in *Summer on the Lakes in 1843*: "There arose in my breast a genuine admiration, and a humble adoration of the Being who was the architect of this and of all."[29] And for a writer such as Thoreau, accustomed to moving from specific natural phenomena to general observations about nature and mankind, picturesque travel offered the opportunity for discussions of the moral impact of landscape scenery, whether picturesque or sublime.

Tours of Great Britain and the European continent influenced both the development and popularity of picturesque travel in America. Writers such as James Fenimore Cooper, who traveled abroad extensively after his writing career had begun, acquired their enthusiasm for the picturesque and shaped their taste for landscape scenery in England, France, Switzerland, Germany, and Italy.[30] Similarly, Francis Parkman, who was sent to Europe in 1843 to recover his health before completing his senior year at Harvard College, filled his European journal with comments on the scenery he admired and had learned to appreciate there, though what he saw frequently reminded him of American landscapes. Whether viewing the softened Italian landscapes of Lake Como or wilder scenes along the Rhine, he often imagined himself back home again, enjoying the wild beauties of New York's Lake George or the rough pleasures of the American woods, and sometimes expressed a preference for the landscapes of his homeland.[31] Fired with a love of the picturesque and sublime, he returned to America, where he delivered an oration entitled "Romance in America" at his Harvard commencement. Parkman's speech reveals the influence of his European travels in its comparison of American and European landscapes, his emphasis upon scenery as a topic worthy of literary treatment, and his expectations for romance in the American landscape, notably at Lake George.[32] His travels abroad and at home profoundly influenced both *The Oregon Trail* and his multivolume history *France and England in North America*, and, through these works, generations of readers.

By the second decade of the nineteenth century, picturesque travel and the picturesque perspective on landscape were both familiar to and popular with educated men and women in Great Britain and America.[33] As the popularity of picturesque travel soared in England, it became ripe for satire. For example, in *The Tour of Doctor Syntax in Search of the Picturesque* (1812) William Combe satirized Gilpin's theory and tours with an eye for wit and profit. Working with caricaturist Thomas Rowlandson, who provided the aquatints that inspired the poem, Combe created the unforgettable Doctor Syntax.[34] As a poor schoolmaster and clergyman, much like Gilpin, Doctor Syntax decided to improve his fortunes by traveling and writing a tour book:

> "*I'll make a* TOUR--*and then I'll* WRITE IT.
> You well know what my pen can do,
> And I'll employ my pencil too:--
> I'll ride and *write*, and *sketch* and *print*,
> And thus create a real mint;
> I'll *prose* it here, I'll *verse* it there,
> And *picturesque* it ev'rywhere:
> I'll do what all have done before;
> I think I shall--and somewhat more.
> At Doctor *Pompous* give a look;
> He made his fortune by a book;
> And if my volume does not beat it,
> When I return I'll fry and eat it."[35]

Picturesque travel took hold more slowly in the United States, for a second war with Great Britain had to be fought, leisure time had to become available, and transportation innovations would have to be introduced before the tour could become the fashionable pastime it already was in England. Once the fashion for picturesque touring did catch hold in the United States in the 1820s, James Kirke Paulding, who had first treated the phenomenon in *Letters from the South* (1817), was quick to satirize the convention in *The New Mirror for Travellers* (1828). Poking fun at the "gentleman of taste" as a man interested only in his next meal, Paulding waxes poetic over the mouth-watering foods available on the fashionable tour and ignores, as much as possible, the delights of picturesque scenery. Although he could describe a picturesque landscape as well as anyone, in *The New Mirror* Paulding preferred satirizing picturesque travelers and the guidebooks they carried. This suggests that this form of travel had become so popular and well known by the late 1820s that writers who satirized picturesque travel and tourists in their work expected their readers to recognize-- and join in laughing at--the miscellaneous types one encountered on the tour and their various foibles.[36]

American tourbooks and travel guides provide insights into the way picturesque travel developed in the United States. The very existence of travel guides, which first appeared during the 1820s, suggests the increasing popularity of picturesque travel and the tourist's need for help with travel routes, transportation schedules and prices, accommodations along the way, and, frequently, suggestions about which sites to visit for scenes of historical and picturesque interest. Because tourists increasingly relied upon such books, major routes began to be established, and what came to be known as the American Grand Tour began to evolve, particularly during the 1830s and '40s. Variously described as the "Fashionable Tour," the "Northern Tour," or simply the "Grand Tour," it initially comprised several different routes through the northeastern United States, though by the third quarter of the century it encompassed areas located farther south and west. In fact, as land and water transportation improved and westward expansion became a reality, the Grand Tour came to include more western sites and to focus almost as much on the exciting scenes of prairie and Indian country as on the more domesticated landscapes of the Northeast.

A typical route of the early nineteenth century is described by Gideon Miner Davison in *The Traveller's Guide*, a popular travel book published in 1825. The changing subtitle of the work in its early editions suggests the evolving route of the American tour. In its first edition Davison's guide was called *The Fashionable Tour, in 1825. An Excursion to the Springs, Niagara, Quebec and Boston.*[37] By the time the fifth edition was published less than ten years later, the book had expanded to become *The Traveller's Guide: Through the Middle and Northern States, and the Provinces of Canada.*[38] The original route began in the central Atlantic states, at Philadelphia, and made its way first to New York City, collecting travelers along the way who might have come from farther south or from neighboring states such as New Jersey and Maryland or Delaware. From New York tourists traveled to Albany, following the recommended route up the Hudson River by steamboat. From Albany tourists might detour north by stagecoach to visit the celebrated watering places, including Saratoga Springs, and from there they could travel by coach to picturesque Lake George. Returning through the springs, tourists would travel to Utica, New York, to take passage on an Erie Canal packet almost the entire way west to Niagara Falls, stopping en route, if they liked, at any number of minor attractions such as scenic Genesee Falls or the growing commercial port of Buffalo. After a short trip by stagecoach tourists would reach Niagara Falls, the sublime wonder of the New World and the climax of most eastern tours. They might then travel across Lake Ontario by steamboat and head north on the St. Lawrence to Montreal and Quebec. From there they could take a stagecoach to Burlington, Vermont, the "inland port" filled with immigrants, sailors, soldiers, and colorful characters by the 1830s. On this final leg tourists might head south to Albany and thence to Boston. Or if they preferred to explore more of New England first, they could instead go through the White Mountains, including the celebrated--and often painted--Notch, and on to Boston. (See Map 1.)

So goes the "Fashionable Tour" in 1825. But if one reads the travel guides carefully, it becomes clear that the route of the Grand Tour changed almost annually as new places were discovered and advertised to would-be tourists. Consider Theodore Dwight's *The Northern Traveller*, a popular travel guide similar to Davison's, that appeared in 1825 with 213 pages. By the following year, its second edition had swelled to 382 pages; when the sixth edition appeared in 1841, it had grown to well over 400 pages, adding many new places for the tourist to explore.[39]

Why was America's Grand Tour constantly expanding? Two obvious reasons were the addition of new territory and settlements to the west and south and some key breakthroughs in transportation development. To take one state, New York, as an example, dramatic improvements in overland and water transportation were introduced in a matter of years. In 1825, the first year of publication for both Dwight's and Davison's guides, the Erie Canal was completed with great fanfare. Tourists who earlier had had to make their own difficult pilgrimage west from the Hudson River to Niagara Falls--frequently by stagecoach, on horseback, or even on foot--could now sail smoothly along the canal. Six years later, the state's first railroads were completed. Guidebooks increased in size again to describe the newer, easier routes, and by the early 1840s, when railroads covered the state's major routes fairly completely, tourist traffic--and guidebooks--expanded accordingly.

Even literature and contemporary events influenced travel routes. Dwight's *The Northern Traveller*, for example, recommends Sleepy Hollow, "rendered interesting by Mr. Irving," as a site worth visiting on the Hudson River route.[40] The great avalanches in the White Mountains attracted further attention, especially after the Willey disaster of 1826, when an entire family was wiped out by mudslides. *The Traveller's Guide* notes that this disaster attracted more tourists than ever and recommends various places where evidence of the slides might be seen.[41] A tragedy of another sort also attracted tourist attention. In a description of the scenic beauties of the falls on the Genesee River near Rochester, guides note the place where "the celebrated *Sam Patch*" made his fatal jump in 1829.[42]

Guidebooks clearly demonstrate the rapidity with which picturesque travel caught on in the United States in the 1820s and '30s, with the American tour's routes expanding from year to year and edition to edition, and tourists reporting their journeys more and more frequently in periodicals and travel books. At the same time, the variety of places recommended as locales for picturesque travel suggests that in the United States the tour expanded from a focus on natural landscapes to include artificial landscapes such as urban scenes, agricultural scenery, and watering places. The frequent inclusion of colorful local characters such as Ethan Crawford in Hawthorne's "Our Evening Party Among the Mountains," however, follows the British tradition of commenting on noteworthy locals in the context of a picturesque tour. Gilpin himself was fond of describing and evaluating landscape paintings he admired in the noble houses he visited during his tours.[43] From the beginning, the picturesque tour covered more than just landscape scenery.

To highlight the difference between ordinary travel books and picturesque tours, it will be helpful to compare a group of writers whose works did not use the conventions of picturesque travel, although they often admired landscape scenery, and two popular writers--Nathaniel Parker Willis and Augustus E. Silliman--whose works exemplified the picturesque tour. St. Jean de Crèvecoeur, William Bartram, and Timothy Dwight all traveled and wrote during the period when picturesque travel was just becoming popular, but aesthetically speaking all belong to the eighteenth century. None used the new perspectives of landscape appreciation sufficiently to qualify his works as picturesque tours, and none traveled with a primary object as the search for picturesque beauty. Even so, each of these travelers frequently mentioned attractive landscapes and described them in terms that suggest his familiarity with the various categories of aesthetic beauty.

Crèvecoeur, for example, wrote one major travel book, *Journey into Northern Pennsylvania and the State of New York* (1801),[44] and at least one of his essays, "On the Susquehanna," focuses on his travels in Pennsylvania along the Susquehanna River and features his observations on its people and landscapes. In the first work the author travels with a companion up the Hudson River. Both travelers comment frequently on the beauty of the landscapes through which their boat passes. The companion, who speaks in what were even then cliches, exclaims: "'How beautiful and impressive all this is! What grandeur! What majesty nature imprints on her works!'" The author more often interprets the landscape, admiring what one might call the "future picturesque," that is, evidence in the present-day landscape of its future development and glory. For instance, when Crèvecoeur comments upon a "new vista" of the river that is "more pleasant, more picturesque, and more varied" than the last one, the boat captain remarks at length upon its potential:

> 'In the course of time, when farming, trade, and industry have accumulated riches in our coastal cities, and our population is increased, it is here where luxury and the arts will build homes of elegance, direct and harness these fine waters, seize the most advantageous sites, convert these deserts, today so arid, into healthful, happy and delightful homes . . . Never do I go upstream or downstream without my imagination involuntarily entertaining itself in exploring these delightful sites, so numerous and so varied. Here in the shadow of fine oaks planted by nature on the banks of this roaring river, my imagination can already see a spacious and attractive

home. There on the western slope . . . it can already see a little farm.'[45]

Crèvecoeur's descriptions of Niagara Falls reveal his appreciation of natural beauty, though even here his companions comment upon the rapid changes already taking place in the surrounding towns and the future development of this area.[46] This work, however, does not qualify as a picturesque tour because its emphasis is not on landscape beauty, but rather on history, recent events, anecdotes of settlers, and descriptions of local Indian tribes and their customs. "On the Susquehanna" contains similar comments both on the landscapes encountered during Crèvecoeur's trip and on the settlers he visited. Here, too, the traveler thinks more often of the area's economic and social potential than of its present-day condition. In describing one large area, he states: "When the age, the wealth, the population of this country will be arrived to such a pitch as to be able to clear this immense tract; what a sumptuous, what a magnificent sight will it afford! . . . Here imagination may easily foresee the immense agricole richesses which this great country and this spot in particular contain. I never travell anywhere without feeding in this manner on those contemplative images. "[47]

Where Crèvecoeur, traveling in the Northeast, fed on "contemplative images" of the future greatness of his adopted country, William Bartram, traveling south, more often took pleasure in the present state of the land. Between observations on natural history, Indians, and the relationship between nature and its creator, he made frequent comments on the beauties of the southern landscape in the *Travels*. Combining the perspective of an eighteenth-century rationalist with that of an early Romantic writer,[48] Bartram admired the natural world as both scientist and poet. Yet though his descriptions of scenic beauty are interpretive and not just objective, his focus remains on the discovery of new forms of plant life, animals and their habits, and Indians, making it clear that Bartram is not a proto-picturesque traveler in the New World. For example, he comments upon the following scene of "unlimited savannas and plains": "How happily situated is this retired spot of earth! What an elisium it is!" Though he describes himself as "seduced by these sublime enchanting scenes of primitive nature, and these visions of terrestrial happiness," the emphasis is on the "wandering Siminole" and the ideal world he appears to inhabit, not solely on the beauties of this world.[49]

Even Timothy Dwight, a later writer of the period who would certainly have had access to Gilpin's works and thus could have become one of the nation's first picturesque travelers, maintains a strongly eighteenth-century perspective in his travels, eschewing any emphasis on the appreciation of landscape beauty. Dwight traveled between 1796 and 1815 while president of Yale College; his journals were later edited and published in 1821-22 as *Travels in New England and New-York.* Although this clergyman-traveler resembles Gilpin in background, Dwight feels obliged to defend his occasional descriptions of landscapes and criticizes several unnamed "modern travelers" who have "carried to excess" their love of such description. Yet since American scenery is "very fine" and "so many individuals converse on the scenes of nature with so much pleasure," he decided to appeal to such readers by including scenes of landscape description in his *Travels.*[50] Although the volumes that follow are filled with such descriptions, the emphasis again remains on history, society, and, in Dwight's case, on "one of the most delightful prospects which this world can afford." The "succession of New England villages" suggests to him the successful "*conversion of a wilderness into a desirable residence for man*" (Dwight's emphasis), a theme strongly reminiscent of his Puritan forebears and their errand into the wilderness.[51]

The travel writings of two minor but popular nineteenth-century writers illustrate the difference between travel works such as those by Crèvecoeur, Bartram, and Dwight, which include landscape scenery but emphasize history, geography, and natural history, and those that employ the conventions of the picturesque tour and focus on landscape beauty. Nathaniel Parker Willis, a writer as well known for his poetry and plays as for his travel writings, and Augustus E. Silliman, a less popular writer, both published works during the 1830s and '40s that featured the picturesque tour, whether of Europe or America. Willis's "The Four Rivers," included in *Loiterings of Travel* (1840), is a classic example of the midcentury sketch featuring picturesque travel, and Silliman's *A Gallop among American Scenery* (1843) is a typical book-length treatment of the American picturesque tour of this period.

In "The Four Rivers" Willis explores four of the most scenic waterways in the eastern United States: the Hudson, Mohawk, Chenango, and Susquehanna Rivers. Considering the discovery of a "noble river" as one of the greatest pleasures in the world, he extols the beauties of these New York rivers, with the Hudson taking the prize for most scenic, though "there are sweeter rivers to live upon."[52] Along with complaints about bordering railroads and "extras" that turned out to be the regular stagecoach, Willis celebrates the "glorious scenery" of the Mohawk and the beauties of the Chenango. He speaks most highly of the Susquehanna, commending its scenery for the unique mixture of "the grand and the beautiful," the most glorious in the world. Like Gilpin, who had a special fondness for river scenery, Willis loves the changing scenes that are part of river views, "giving a perpetual refreshment, and an hourly-changing feast to the eye." Yet Willis, like Crèvecoeur and countless other American tourists, wishes to domesticate the landscape. At the end of his sketch he celebrates, not the wildness of river scenery, but its potential for domestication. At the same time that he praises the "romantic" views of river and valley, he longs to build a cottage by one of these rivers, effectively taming the "glory of Nature" that he commemorates.[53] Regardless of Willis's purpose in praising river scenery, his appreciation for landscape beauty and description of it in the sketch, as in most of his European and American travel writings, emphasize the nature of his work as a picturesque tour. Indeed, his focus on landscape scenery even in the humorous sketches for which he was famed suggests that this writer was both fond of picturesque travel and aware that at midcentury this was the kind of writing that sold well in America and abroad.[54]

Silliman's *Gallop among American Scenery; or Sketches of American Scenes and Military Adventure* features, as its title suggests, a fast-paced tour of various scenes in the eastern United States, some memorable as the sites of great battles and others simply for their picturesque scenery. Only a few of the pieces focus on people rather than landscapes. "Hudson River," a typical example of Silliman's style and subject matter, describes a trip by steamboat up that river in colloquial language that alternates with the poetic diction he uses for describing landscapes. His descriptions of river scenery are commonplace, if not outright trite: "How beautifully the Narrows and the Ocean open to our view, and the noble bay, studded with its islands, and fortresses, and men-of-war, 'tall, high admirals,' with frowning batteries and chequered sides. . . . The dark pallisades above us, with fringed and picturesque outline, are reflected on its polished surface; and the lordly sloops, see how lazily they roll and pitch on the long undulating swell made by our progress."[55] Silliman's fondness for poetic language sometimes overwhelms his travel sketches, but it was popular with his audience. In "Lake George and Ticonderoga" he begins: "The Sun of Morning hurls himself in blazing splendour o'er thy crystal waters, beautiful Horicon! as we float upon thy placid bosom, not as of yore, in feathery canoe, but in gaily-coloured bark, drawn by Steam Spirit."[56] The narrator imagines Fort Ticonderoga at different times in the past, in the midst of battles fought by the French, Indians, British, and colonists, all with a fast-paced though archaic style. Other pieces feature sketches of Montreal, Niagara, the White Mountains, Mount Vernon, Newport, and Mount Holyoke, making the book read like a catalog of the fashionable tour at the middle of the nineteenth century.

Both Willis and Silliman, popular writers in the picturesque mode, use the picturesque tour frequently and straightforwardly in their travel writings. It took the creative impulse of more imaginative writers, beginning as early as the last decade of the eighteenth century, to break with the notion that the only way to use the picturesque tour in fiction or nonfiction was to portray one's characters taking such a tour. An imaginative writer such as Charles Brockden Brown viewed picturesque travel in the New World as a means of criticizing his protagonists for not understanding themselves or the wilderness landscape of this early period. James Kirke Paulding, taking advantage of the craze for picturesque touring in the late 1820s, satirized both tours and tourists in his fiction and nonfiction, suggesting that the fashion for the picturesque had already peaked by this time. Washington Irving and Francis Parkman, after embarking upon their own travels in the West, returned to write up tours of adventure that included a heavy proportion of landscape appreciation, too. Still to come were Hawthorne, Poe, and Thoreau, who treated the picturesque tour as a serious means of exploring new territory--geographical, intellectual, and spiritual--and of shaping both the structure and meaning of a narrative. In the hands of such masters, picturesque travel became more than a passing fashion. Instead, the picturesque tour influenced American literature during its formative decades and contributed to the development of a national identity during the first half of the nineteenth century.

Notes

1. George William Curtis, "American Travelers," *Putnam's Monthly Magazine* 5 (1855): 563-64.

2. Washington Irving, "The Author's Account of Himself," *The Sketch Book of Geoffrey Crayon, Gent.*, ed. Haskell Springer (Boston: Twayne, 1978), p. 9.

3. General studies of nature, art, and aesthetics, and studies of individual places and authors include Hans Huth, *Nature and the American: Three Centuries of Changing Attitudes* (Berkeley: University of California Press, 1957); Barbara Novak, *Nature and Culture: American Landscape and Painting, 1825-1875*, rev. ed. (New York: Oxford University Press, 1995); Elizabeth McKinsey, *Niagara Falls: Icon of the American Sublime* (Cambridge: Cambridge University Press, 1985); Blake Nevius, *Cooper's Landscapes: An Essay on the Picturesque Vision* (Berkeley: University of California Press, 1976); and Kent Ljungquist, *The Grand and the Fair: Poe's Landscape Aesthetics and Pictorial Techniques* (Potomac, Maryland: Scripta Humanistica, 1984).

4. Gilpin, "On Picturesque Travel," *Three Essays: On Picturesque Beauty; On Picturesque Travel; and On Sketching Landscape: to which is added a poem, on Landscape Painting*, 2nd ed. (London: R. Blamire, 1794; repr. Westmead, England: Gregg International, 1972), p. 42. For a complete discussion of the causes and effects of picturesque beauty, see Gilpin's "On Picturesque Beauty," *Three Essays*, pp. 3-33. For the best study of Gilpin's life and works, see William D. Templeman's *The Life and Work of William Gilpin (1724-1804), Master of the Picturesque and Vicar of Boldre*, Illinois Studies in Language and Literature, vol. 24, nos. 3-4 (Urbana: University of Illinois, 1939).

5. Uvedale Price, *An Essay on the Picturesque, As Compared with the Sublime and the Beautiful, and on the Use of Studying Pictures, for the Purpose of Improving Real Landscape*, 2 vols. (London, 1794, 1798); Uvedale Price, *Essays on the Picturesque*, 3 vols. (London, 1810); Richard Payne Knight, *An Analytical Inquiry into the Principles of Taste* (London, 1805). For a full discussion of the picturesque, see Christopher Hussey's *The Picturesque: Studies in a Point of View* (London: G. P. Putnam, 1927); for further reading on the three aesthetic categories see Walter John Hipple, Jr., *The Beautiful, The Sublime, & The Picturesque in Eighteenth-Century British Aesthetic Theory* (Carbondale: Southern Illinois University Press, 1957). Martin Price's study focuses almost exclusively on British uses of picturesque beauty rather than American interest in this aesthetic category, but it remains one of the first and best brief studies of the history of picturesque theory and its influence on literature ("The Picturesque Moment," *From Sensibility to Romanticism*, ed. Frederick W. Hilles and Harold Bloom [New York: Oxford University Press, 1965], pp. 259-92). See pp. 260-62 in particular for what Price considers the distinguishing characteristics of picturesque beauty.

6. Washington Irving, *A Tour on the Prairies*, in *The Crayon Miscellany*, ed. Dahlia Kirby Terrell (Boston: Twayne, 1979), pp. 83-84.

7. William Gilpin, *Remarks on Forest Scenery*, 2nd ed., 2 vols. (London: R. Blamire, 1794), 1: 180-211.

8. Gilpin, *Remarks on Forest Scenery*, 1: 198-99.

9. Gilpin comments on the picturesque qualities of rough-coated animals in "On Picturesque Beauty," *Three Essays*, pp. 14-15.

10. Nathaniel Hawthorne, "A Night Scene," *Hawthorne's American Travel Sketches*, ed. Alfred Weber, Beth L. Lueck, and Dennis Berthold (Hanover, New Hampshire: University Press of New England, 1989), p. 48.

11. For further reading on Salvator Rosa's influence on English aesthetics see Elizabeth Manwaring, *Italian Landscape in Eighteenth-Century England: A Study Chiefly of the Influence of Claude*

Lorrain and Salvator Rosa on English Taste, 1700-1800, Wellesley Semi-Centennial Series (New York: Oxford University Press, 1925).

12. Edgar Allan Poe, *The Journal of Julius Rodman*, in *The Imaginary Voyages*, ed. Burton R. Pollin (Boston: Twayne, 1981), p. 575.

13. Throughout this work the term "sublimity," sometimes called grandeur, refers to the Burkean sublime, or the qualities of obscurity, power, privation (darkness and solitude, for example), vastness, infinity, magnitude or infinity, and magnificence in a landscape that cause the observer to experience awe or terror (Edmund Burke, *A Philosophical Enquiry into the Origin of our Ideas of the Sublime and Beautiful*, ed. J.T. Boulton [New York: Columbia University Press, 1958], pp. 57-79).

14. William Gilpin, "Instructions for Examining landscape" (c. 1789-94), quoted and discussed in Carl Paul Barbier, *William Gilpin: His Drawings, Teaching, and Theory of the Picturesque* (Oxford: Clarendon Press, 1963), p. 112.

15. William Gilpin, *Remarks on Forest Scenery*, 2: 63-64. For examples of picturesque sublimity in art, see Gilpin's sketches in Barbier, plates 4e, 11c, 16 XXII, and 16 XXIV, in which sublime mountains and cliffs mix with picturesque trees, woods, and lakes.

16. The language is confusing sometimes because few attempts were made by British or American writers to codify the separate categories of the beautiful, picturesque, and sublime, much less to codify the various ways these categories could combine in a landscape.

17. "Sketches of Travel," *The Knickerbocker Magazine* 5 (1835): 243-44.

18. William Gilpin, "On Picturesque Travel," pp. 42-48.

19. See chapter six on Poe's *The Journal of Julius Rodman* and "The Domain of Arnheim."

20. Gilpin, "On Picturesque Travel," pp. 48-50.

21. William Gilpin, *Observations on the Western Parts of England* (London: T. Cadell and W. Davies, 1798; repr. Westmead, England: Richmond Publishing, 1973), p. 320.

22. Charles L. Batten, Jr., *Pleasurable Instruction: Form and Convention in Eighteenth-Century Travel Literature* (Berkeley: University of California Press, 1978), pp. 112-13. See also ch. 3 in general, "Descriptive Conventions in Eighteenth-Century Travel Literature" (pp. 82-115).

23. See William Gilpin, "On Picturesque Travel," pp. 41-58. For a typical example of one of Gilpin's highly influential tours, see *Observations on the River Wye, and several parts of South Wales, &c. relative chiefly to picturesque beauty; made in the summer of the Year 1770* (London: R. Blamire, 1782).

24. William Gilpin, *Observations, related chiefly to picturesque beauty, Made in the Year 1772, On several parts of England; particularly the Mountains, and Lakes of Cumberland, and Westmoreland*, 3rd ed., 2 vols. (London: R. Blamire, 1792), 1: xxiii.

25. Gilpin, "On Picturesque Travel," pp. 46-47.

26. Marjorie Hope Nicolson, *Mountain Gloom and Mountain Glory: The Development of the Aesthetics of the Infinite* (Ithaca: Cornell University Press, 1959).

27. Gilpin, "On Picturesque Travel," p. 47.

28. Elizabeth McKinsey, *Niagara Falls: Icon of the American Sublime* (New York: Cambridge University Press, 1985), pp. 104-07, 52.

29. Margaret Fuller, *Summer on the Lakes in 1843*, ed. Madeleine B. Stern (1844; repr. Nieuwkoop: B. De Graaf, 1972), p. 13.

30. Blake Nevius notes that Cooper's travels abroad (1826-1833) "provided a kind of postgraduate course in aesthetics" for him. He discusses Cooper's travels and their effect on his writings in

Cooper's Landscapes, pp. 33-63.

31. *The Journals of Francis Parkman*, ed. Mason Wade, 2 vols. (New York: Harper, 1947), 1: 209, 212.

32. Parkman's oration is reprinted by Wilbur R. Jacobs in "Francis Parkman's Oration 'Romance in America,'" *American Historical Review* 68 (1963): 696-97.

33. Christopher Mulvey, *Anglo-American Landscapes: A Study of Nineteenth-Century Anglo-American Travel Literature* (New York: Cambridge University Press, 1983), p. 253.

34. See Harlan W. Hamilton, *Doctor Syntax: A Silhouette of William Combe, Esq. (1742-1823)* (Kent: Kent State University Press, 1969), pp. 243-55, for a discussion of the inception of this poem and of its satire on Gilpin's works. The comic poem originally appeared in Ackermann's *Poetical Magazine* as "The Schoolmaster's Tour" (1809-11).

35. [Combe, William], *Doctor Syntax: His Three Tours In Search of the Picturesque, of Consolation, of a Wife* (New York: Frederick Warne, 1890), p. 7 ("In Search of the Picturesque," Canto I).

36. James Kirke Paulding, *The New Mirror for Travellers; and Guide to the Springs* (New York: G. & C. Carvill, 1828), pp. 11-12, 90, 114-15.

37. Gideon Miner Davison, *The Fashionable Tour* (Saratoga Springs: G.M. Davison, 1825).

38. Gideon Miner Davison, *The Traveller's Guide* (Saratoga Springs: G.M. Davison and G. & C. & H. Carvill, 1833).

39. Theodore Dwight, *The Northern Traveller; containing the routes to Niagara, Quebec, and the Springs* (New York: Wilder & Campbell, 1825); Dwight, *The Northern Traveller; containing the routes to Niagara, Quebec, and the Springs, with the Tour of New-England, and the Route to the Coal Mines of Pennsylvania*, 2nd ed.

(New-York: A.T. Goodrich, 1826); Dwight, *The Northern Traveller; containing the routes to the Springs, Niagara, Quebec, and the Coal Mines; with the Tour of New-England, and a Brief Guide to the Virginia Springs, and Southern and Western Routes*, 6th ed. (New-York: J.P. Haven, 1841.

40. Theodore Dwight, *The Northern Traveller*, 4th ed. (New-York: J. & J. Harper, 1830), p. 24.

41. G.M. Davison, *The Traveller's Guide*, 5th ed. (1833), pp. 359-61.

42. See, for example, Davison, 5th ed. (1833), pp. 245-46.

43. Barbier suggests that Gilpin's interest shifted from both landscape scenery and art--paintings and prints--in the early tours to an emphasis on natural landscapes in the later works (*William Gilpin*, p. 49).

44. This work by St. Jean de Crèvecoeur appeared originally as *Voyage dans la Haute Pensylvanie et dans l'Etat de New-York* (1801), 3 vols., and has been translated by Clarissa Spencer Bostelmann (Ann Arbor: University of Michigan Press, 1964).

45. *Journey Into Northern Pennsylvania*, pp. 119-21.

46. *Journey Into Northern Pennsylvania*, pp. 290-91.

47. Crèvecoeur, "On the Susquehanna," *Letters from an American Farmer and Sketches of Eighteenth-Century America*, ed. Albert E. Stone (New York: Penguin Books, 1981), p. 363.

48. Hugh Moore, "The Southern Landscape of William Bartram: A Terrible Beauty," *Essays in Arts and Sciences* 10 (May 1981): 41-42.

49. William Bartram, *The Travels of William Bartram*, ed. Francis Harper (New Haven: Yale University Press, 1958), p. 69.

50. Timothy Dwight, *Travels in New England and New York*, ed. Barbara Miller Solomon with Patricia M. King, John Harvard Library, 4 vols. (Cambridge, Mass.: Belknap Press of Harvard University Press, 1969), 1: 3.

51. Dwight, 1: 7.

52. Nathaniel Parker Willis, "The Four Rivers," "Sketches of Travel," *The Prose Works of N.P. Willis* (Philadelphia: Henry C. Baird, 1854), pp. 574-75.

53. Willis, pp. 575-76.

54. See, for example, "Incidents on the Hudson" and "Niagara--Lake Ontario--the St. Lawrence," in "Inklings of Adventure," *Prose Works*, pp. 366-72, 410-12.

55. Augustus Ely Silliman, *A Gallop among American Scenery; or, Sketches of American Scenes and Military Adventure* (New York: D. Appleton, 1843; repr. Freeport, New York: Books for Libraries Press, [1970]), p. 109.

56. Silliman, p. 131.

Chapter 2

Charles Brockden Brown's *Edgar Huntly*: The Picturesque Traveler as Sleepwalker

Charles Brockden Brown's *Edgar Huntly; or, Memoirs of a Sleep-Walker* (1799) stands as an early landmark in American literature for its original use of the picturesque traveler convention to characterize the protagonist, to develop theme, and to comment upon the American borrowing of European literary conventions. Although Brown's borrowing of British aesthetics for landscape description, notably the picturesque and the sublime, is not original in American literature at this date, he is one of the first American writers to place himself consciously within the British aesthetic tradition. More important, he is the first American to employ the conventions of picturesque travel in a full-length novel. This use of the picturesque tourist not only as subject, but also as a narrative device and as a form of cultural commentary in the novel, is strikingly original in Brown's writing and creates a fictional work of depth and complexity.

In Edgar Huntly's repeated excursions into the wilderness Brown attempts to relocate the picturesque tourist onto American soil. But the protagonist's imitating the picturesque tourist is unsuccessful and even ludicrous. The resulting disjunction between picturesque conventions and American landscape suggests that, without some sacrifice of credibility or without a consideration of the potentially dangerous New World landscape, the picturesque tour as it was known in Great Britain could not be readily transplanted to America. Critics such as Dennis Berthold, Jane Tompkins, and Robert Lawson-Peebles have argued that Brown's work must be read within its historical context for its social and cultural commentary to be understood. Viewed in this context, Brown's criticism of the picturesque traveler in

America takes on new meaning, suggesting another way this writer contributed to the nation's search for a distinct political and literary identity in the years following the Revolutionary War. Just as *Wieland, Ormond,* and *Arthur Mervyn* attack Jeffersonian agrarianism, *Edgar Huntly* takes on a European landscape aesthetic and a form of travel-- the picturesque and the picturesque tour--and criticizes the wholesale application of these concepts to the American landscape and experience.[1] What is equally important is how Brown's use of the picturesque in *Edgar Huntly* responds to concerns about Americans' relationship to the environment, particularly the wilderness. In Huntly's mistaken notions about the nature of the territory that borders the frontier community in which he lives the author reveals the distorted perceptions of some Americans about the wilderness they both fear and admire and suggests how such distortions may get individuals, and even the nation itself, into trouble.

Brown was familiar with British uses of the picturesque and sublime and was interested in adapting these conventions as ways of looking at and appreciating American landscapes. His knowledge of aesthetics is clear from articles he wrote or edited for *The Monthly Magazine, and American Review* (1799-1800), and *The Literary Magazine, and American Register* (1803-08), both of which he edited. Articles in both periodicals attest to their editor's continued interest in aesthetics.[2] In one essay that appeared the year after *Edgar Huntly's* publication, Brown recommends "'the pleasure which the beauties of nature afford'" to persons of a cultivated mind. For those ignorant souls whose poverty of imagination and vocabulary brings them to call every scene merely "pretty" or "fine," he enthusiastically recommends the study of picturesque beauty in the works of William Gilpin, who is "eminent for displaying the principles of landscape," particularly in his *Remarks on Forest Scenery* (1791). Brown also advises that the landscape enthusiast read Ann Radcliffe's novels and those of other "commentators upon Gilpin" who travel in search of picturesque beauty.[3]

Brown only alludes to picturesque travel in this early article, but he devotes a later essay in *The Literary Magazine* to the subject, an article which has been ignored by most critics.[4] "Men of true taste," according to Brown, appreciate all kinds of beauty in nature, including picturesqueness and sublimity. "In a word," he concludes, "they reverence and admire the works of God, and look with benevolence and pleasure on the works of men." Brown's article concentrates on those in search of the picturesque: "Of all kinds of travellers, or pedestrian hunters, those that travel in search of the pleasure of the picturesque are the fewest in number, particularly in America, but perhaps they are the most judicious in their choice of an object of pursuit." From this point on, Brown lets "a great traveller of this kind," William Gilpin, speak in favor of picturesque travel. Indeed, most of the article quotes verbatim from Gilpin's essay "On Picturesque Travel" (1792).[5] Brown comments upon Gilpin's writings and cites the master of the picturesque frequently in his articles published between 1800 and 1806, quoting freely to convey the British traveler's theories of this aesthetic.[6]

The author's journals attest to his pursuit of picturesque beauty in his personal life, too. According to journal entries quoted by William Dunlap in *The Life of Charles Brockden Brown*, Brown enjoyed traveling in search of natural beauty both as a youth and as a mature man.[7] His solitary excursions even caused his family an occasional alarm, just as Edgar Huntly's nightly wanderings would later disturb both his uncle and his tutor, Sarsefield. Dunlap writes that Brown's walks led to an abstracted mind, which "caused, from a total unconsciousness of what was passing about him, or of the flight of time, or the progress of his feet, such unseasonable rambles as often to excite great uneasiness in the different members of his family."[8]

When Brockden Brown was in his late twenties, at about the same time he began writing and publishing his major novels, including *Edgar Huntly*, he began to make summer excursions to the New England states. In an article describing a trip to Rockaway, New York, the author disclaims any talent for close observation of scenery. This has led at least one critic to assume that Brown was incapable of such observations as would befit the picturesque traveler.[9] But Brown's journal entries on excursions into New England suggest otherwise. During a tour of Connecticut in 1799, the same year *Edgar Huntly* was published, Brown writes in a journal entry: "'I had a vigilant eye for passing objects, roads, dwellings and passengers. My curiosity was awakened by the intention I had formed of describing what I saw. In this respect my mind has undergone a sudden and memorable revolution. Instead of being as I used to be, sluggish, torpid and inattentive, my eye was watchful and my mind busy in arranging and comparing objects.'"[10] Thus writes the picturesque traveler. Brown reveals his ability for description and his affinity for the picturesque in numerous journal entries that attest both to his knowledge of the picturesque and to his love of picturesque travel.[11]

Charles Brockden Brown's picturesque travels served to inform his fourth novel, *Edgar Huntly*, in spirit and in detail. Like Brown, the protagonist in this novel is also a picturesque traveler, fond of searching out natural scenes of picturesque beauty to enjoy and reflect on. In some ways Brown follows Gilpin's conventions for the picturesque traveler remarkably closely, but the author's attempts to apply these conventions result in a critical disjunction: the picturesque traveler appears to be more out of place than at home in the American wilderness, and as a result the conventions of picturesque travel brought from England seem absurdly inappropriate on the frontier.

For almost the first half of the novel, Edgar Huntly appears to be a fairly conventional picturesque traveler. He loves to tramp in the woods in search of wild scenery, he enjoys such landscapes, and he reflects on the scenery afterwards. Very early in the narrative, Huntly tells his correspondent, Mary Waldegrave, who is his fiancee and the sister of Huntly's murdered friend, "A nocturnal journey in districts so romantic and wild as these . . . was more congenial to my temper than a noon-day ramble."[12] (Daytime journeys were more customary for picturesque travelers, but there is nothing too unusual in Huntly's preference for evening expressed here. In fact, Gilpin considered the shadows of nightfall and moonlight to add much interest to a landscape.[13]) Later in the novel, Huntly reveals how he learned to enjoy rambles in the Norwalk wilderness. Although he had explored the area from an early age, his training in philosophy and picturesque beauty began when, as a youth, he came under the tutelage of Sarsefield. Huntly recalls, "I became his favourite scholar and the companion of all his pedestrian excursions. He was fond of penetrating into these recesses [of Norwalk], partly from the love of picturesque scenes, partly to investigate its botanical and mineral productions, and, partly to carry on more effectually that species of instruction which he had adopted with regard to me, and which chiefly consisted in moralizing narratives or synthetical reasonings" (97). Sarsefield's combination of education with the pursuit and enjoyment of picturesque beauty resembles William Gilpin's tours and related works, though Brown does not acknowledge his debt to Gilpin here.[14] Although Huntly does not state outright that Sarsefield taught him to understand and appreciate picturesque beauty during these excursions, the youth seems to have learned these things right along with the moral and natural philosophy his tutor shared with him.

In the tradition of the picturesque traveler, Huntly also learned to enjoy the novelty of unfamiliar landscapes unfolding before his eyes. While walking with Sarsefield, Huntly writes: "Every new excursion, indeed, added somewhat to my knowledge. New tracks were pursued, new prospects detected, and new summits were gained. My rambles were productive of incessant novelty, though they always terminated in the prospect of limits that could not be overleaped" (97). Huntly's recollections of his youthful excursions with Sarsefield characterize him as a picturesque-traveler-in-training, yet they also suggest a symbolic interpretation of these walks, one which will become important later in the book: just as Huntly pursues new tracks in Norwalk and gains novel prospects of scenery there, he pursues new paths to knowledge with Sarsefield and discovers new insights through their conversations. Huntly is, in the process, discovering himself.[15]

Huntly's appreciation for prospect views, along with his appropriate psychological response to the landscape and reflections on it, also suggests that he is modeled on the picturesque traveler. Throughout *Edgar Huntly* the protagonist frequently climbs to the summit of a mountain to admire the view from the top. Early in the book he tells of his youthful love for this perspective. When Huntly steals away at night to Chestnut-hill, he recalls memories of youthful occasions spent in a similar fashion: "Concealed among its rocks, or gazing at the prospect, which stretched so far and so wide around it, my fancy has always been accustomed to derive its highest enjoyment from this spot" (16-17). In the classic fashion of the picturesque tourist, he seeks out the view from the hilltop, responds with pleasure to the prospect, and is moved to imaginative reflection by the scene.

Two key journeys in *Edgar Huntly* reveal the protagonist as a picturesque traveler in the American wilderness, which will dominate the last part of the book in the sleepwalking episode. Both journeys into the Norwalk wilds are characterized as picturesque tours, fulfilling the general conditions of this form of travel: the pursuit, attainment, and enjoyment of picturesque beauty. But neither journey is an ordinary picturesque tour. The first, which includes a sojourn in a dark cavern, parodies the classic daytime picturesque tour. The second features Huntly as a lost and bewildered picturesque traveler, unlike the calm, secure figure of the Gilpin tour books. During both experiences Huntly is repeatedly subjected to the inherent dangers of the American wilderness: storms, pits, caverns, panthers, and Indians. By using these two journeys to characterize Edgar Huntly as a foolhardy picturesque tourist, Brown implies that the British view of picturesque travel is appropriate only when the traveler is merely an observer of landscape scenery. When the traveler must live in the landscape, however, and not just observe it, he should pay attention to wilderness survival rather than contemplate picturesque beauty. A close examination of the two key journeys will substantiate this thesis.

On the first journey, Huntly is ostensibly in search of the lost Clithero, who he fears has committed suicide in the wilderness. Yet the narrator himself suggests that he wishes to explore the Norwalk wilds because, in truth, he wants to view again those scenes he traversed before at night while in pursuit of the sleepwalking Clithero. For example, when Huntly considers his motives for setting forth into the wilderness tract, he states his intentions to explore the cave into which Clithero disappeared, looking for evidence of the man's death. But in the same breath Huntly adds that this exploration also "might lead into spaces hitherto unvisited, and to summits from which wider landscapes might be seen" (98). It is the prospect of new scenes that attracts this picturesque tourist. As Brown's article on picturesque travel states, quoting Gilpin, "The first source of amusement to the picturesque traveller is . . . the expectation of new scenes continually opening and arising to his view." Unexplored country is likely to provide the most unexpected--and therefore pleasing--views.[16] One wonders which motive prevails for Huntly: the search for Clithero or the search for picturesque beauty. But the protagonist is tantalized by a "faint remembrance" of the landscapes he saw during the previous nighttime journey with Clithero, and his resolution seems to answer the question of dominant motive: "One morning I set out to explore this scene" (97-98).

Yet Huntly's picturesque journey, his daylight exploration of the "wider landscapes" promised by his earlier nighttime pursuit of Clithero, could only take place after a dark journey through the cavern into which Clithero had disappeared. This first stage is, perhaps unintentionally, a dark parody of a picturesque journey. Instead of walking or riding, Huntly is reduced to crawling on his hands and knees. And instead of seeing new vistas, Huntly sees nothing, only the "intense dark" that renders him fearful (100). Yet this picturesque journey in the dark is not without its reward. At length, Huntly emerges from the obscurity of the cave into the light of day.

To the "spectacle" of the scene before him, Edgar Huntly responds with "exquisite sensations." Climbing to the summit of the precipice on which he stands, the intrepid picturesque tourist describes the scene before him: "A large part of this chaos of rocks and precipices was subjected, at one view, to the eye. The fertile lawns and vales which lay beyond this, the winding course of the river, and the slopes which rose on its farther side, were parts of this extensive scene" (101-02). Huntly responds with "rapture" to the prospect. He explains why this view is superior to others, especially at this particular moment: "Now my delight [in the scene] was enhanced by the contrast which this lightsome and serene element bore to the glooms from which I had lately emerged. My station, also, was higher, and the limits of my view, consequently, more ample than any which I had hitherto enjoyed" (102). Huntly responds precisely as a picturesque tourist ought, noting the qualities of the scene that enhance its picturesqueness--here, the contrast between light and dark. As Gilpin had written, "We are most delighted when some grand scene, though perhaps of incorrect composition, rising before the eye, strikes us beyond the power of thought . . ." "Every mental operation is suspended," Gilpin added, and "an enthusiastic sensation of pleasure overspreads" the soul.[17] Lost in the picturesque beauty of the scene, Huntly has forgotten Clithero. Instead of searching for the lost man, he writes: "I changed frequently my station in order to diversify the scenery" (102). Surely no picturesque traveler ever followed Gilpin's injunction to enjoy novel views with as much perseverance as Edgar Huntly. In the heart of the wilderness, perched precariously on the summit of a hill, this devotee of the picturesque thinks only of improving his perspective. Sighting a higher position, Huntly ignores the rugged territory he must cross to reach it: "Its greater elevation would extend my view," he explains, "and perhaps furnish a spot from which the whole horizon was conspicuous" (102).

Huntly continues to discover new scenes of "desolate and solitary grandeur" and to admire the "phantastic shapes, and endless irregularities" (103) of the landscape, of which Gilpin, incidentally, disapproved.[18] Although Huntly's single-minded pursuit of scenic beauty is admirable, it is both impractical and dangerous in this situation. For example, while Huntly explores the landscape for ever finer views, he suddenly catches a glimpse of a face (Clithero's) among the rocks across from his position on the summit. Caught off guard, the protagonist is surprised into a complete lapse of judgment. "I forgot for a moment the perilous nature of my situation," he writes (103). Letting go of the branch that steadies him, he nearly tumbles into an abyss. By picturing Huntly's behavior as a picturesque tourist as endangering his life here, Brown suggests that the protagonist's actions are inappropriate for the situation. This scene implicitly criticizes Huntly's zealous dedication to picturesque beauty. The American wilderness is no place for the traveler merely to observe and admire the landscape, as the picturesque convention requires; instead, the New World explorer ought to pay close attention to his situation and its potential dangers.

Huntly's efforts to reach Clithero on this trip are fruitless, and he decides to go home and return later with an ax. With this he can fell a tree and bridge the chasm that prevents him from reaching Clithero (106-07). The expedition to relieve Clithero is successful, though brief (108-11), and Huntly, unarmed, sets out once more to take food to his friend. This journey serves as a transitional episode in *Edgar Huntly*. Earlier, picturesque travel in the book was generally safe and comparatively uneventful, but this journey points up some of the dangers that Huntly has previously ignored and foreshadows some of the problems of picturesque travel in the wilderness that the final journey will explore.

Edgar Huntly sets the scene for his second attempt to relieve Clithero with provisions, characterizing himself at the same time. "The next day was stormy and wet," he writes to Mary Waldegrave. "This did not deter me from visiting the mountain. Slippery paths and muddy torrents were no obstacles to the purposes which I had adopted" (122). Posturing a little to his fiancee, Huntly presents himself as the intrepid traveler, daring to venture forth even in the midst of a storm. His motive this time is less to seek out new scenes of sublimity than to relieve Clithero's suffering, but even so, Huntly remains a picturesque traveler at heart. Just as Gilpin sometimes found that rain conferred "a gloomy grandeur" upon a scene, Huntly considers the storm's value for adding to the sublimity of the Norwalk scenes.[19] In spite of a downpour, he pauses to admire the landscape: "Torrents of rain poured from above, and stronger blasts thundered amidst these desolate recesses and profound chasms. Instead of lamenting the prevalence of this tempest, I now began to regard it with pleasure. It conferred new forms of sublimity and grandeur on this scene" (122).

Brown pictures Huntly as being so submerged in the role of the picturesque traveler that he is oblivious to any real dangers in the landscape. It is as if Huntly views scenery through a Claude glass, the oval, tinted glass carried by Gilpin and other picturesque travelers to frame the scene before them and alter it subtly, as if an artist had painted it. But Huntly's perceptions of the scene do not merely transform it into a more sublime landscape in his eyes; the protagonist's knowledge of the picturesque perspective actually distances him from the landscape, lifting him out of his real situation momentarily to let him stand back and admire the scene. According to the description of the landscape, Huntly could as easily be standing in a picture gallery and admiring a landscape painting as he is, in fact, hesitating on the brink of an abyss before crawling over an unsteady log bridge in a downpour. The distinction here between aesthetic appreciation and real situation becomes clear when the protagonist, creeping along his makeshift bridge, is "nearly whirled . . . into the frightful abyss below" (122). In an instant, the passage has moved from the sublime to the ridiculous: at one moment the picturesque traveler stands heroically surveying the sublime forces of the storm, and in the next he is flattened on a tree trunk, within seconds of being cast into an abyss. Huntly's characteristic understatement, that this near escape "disconcerted and distressed" him (122), reflects his own foolhardiness and the potential dangers of picturesque travel in America. Once again, a scene implicitly criticizes the traveler whose dedication to picturesque beauty renders him oblivious to the real dangers of the American wilderness.

The perils of the wilderness are becoming increasingly evident to the reader, if not to the protagonist, as the next scene in this journey suggests. Having just escaped being hurled into an abyss, Huntly encounters a more horrible fate: to be devoured by a wild animal. But here, too, he acts unlike any sensible woodsman. His attitude toward wild animals is naive, just as his relationship to the landscape--that of the picturesque traveler--is foolish and unrealistic at best. Faced with a bloodthirsty panther, or gray cougar, Huntly embarks on a brief discourse on his love of wildlife, stating that he "never delighted in carnage and blood." In spite of his name, Huntly denies ever taking pleasure in shooting game in the woods. He considers it his "duty" to kill "sanguinary spoilers" of the wilderness such as rattlesnakes and panthers (124).[20] He brags of his "juvenile prowess" in killing many panthers with his tomahawk, but his forgetting to bring a weapon on this excursion into the wilderness speaks volumes more than his excuse that he usually carries some means of defense on such trips (124-25). Once again, Huntly is revealed as the naif foolishly endangering himself by forgetting to take precautions when traveling in the wilds of Norwalk. But neither Huntly's near escape here nor earlier encounters with the wilderness teach him to be more practical, for on his next journey into the wilds of Norwalk, the most perilous one by far, Huntly will not only venture forth alone and unarmed, but fast asleep. The picturesque traveler is now so lost to the perils of the wilderness landscape that he has become a picturesque sleepwalker.

Edgar Huntly discovers himself in the wilderness at the beginning of the last journey in the book, but, interestingly, he has not arrived there of his own volition. Transported mysteriously into Norwalk, Huntly has traveled, apparently, because of some unconscious compulsion he neither recognizes nor understands. No matter how he got there (and it is clear that Huntly has become a sleepwalker like Clithero), what is important is that the protagonist is compelled to travel once again into "the heart of the wilderness" (171). This final journey into the wilderness might have been an ideal picturesque tour, for Huntly is traveling in territory hitherto unknown (259) and thus has a rare opportunity to discover and appreciate countless new vistas. But the perils of such a journey, and indeed the foolhardiness of such a traveler, are obvious to almost everyone except Huntly, who is quite unconscious for its duration.

Because this final journey takes place largely at night, it becomes a parody of a picturesque tour, for no one can appreciate landscape that is obscured by total darkness. Gilpin might have admired the shadowy atmosphere created in a forest by nightfall, but he never recommended a picturesque tour in pitch darkness.[21] Huntly's friends speculate on the reason for his night journey and come close to hitting upon the truth. They suspect, at first, that the young man's "restless and romantic spirit" tempted him from his sleep to explore the Norwalk wilds (248). Sarsefield later comes even closer to the mark: "None but a man, insane or asleep, would wander forth so slightly dressed" and at night (249). Finally, Huntly's former tutor, whose mature presence often gives voice to reason and practicality, sums up the fears he and others had for Huntly's reason and for his safety on such a fool's errand into the wilderness: "You had roved into Norwalk, a scene of inequalities, of prominences and pits, among which, thus destitute of the guidance of your senses, you could scarcely fail to be destroyed, or at least, irretrievably bewildered. I painted to myself the dangers to which you were subjected. Your careless feet would bear you into some whirlpool or to the edge of some precipice, some internal revolution or outward shock would recall you to consciousness at some perilous moment. Surprise and fear would disable you from taking seasonable or suitable precautions, and your destruction be made sure" (249).

Sarsefield's fatherly concerns are not without basis. Not only pits and precipices threaten Huntly. The loss of contact with his family and the proximity to Indian territory also endanger him. In fact, the location of the Norwalk tract in relation to his home and to the Indian-controlled lands beyond plays an important role in his journey. Huntly's first thought upon emerging from the pit and perceiving the Indians at the cavern's mouth reveals his twin concerns: "Had some mysterious power snatched me from the earth, and cast me, in a moment, into the heart of the wilderness? Was I still in the vicinity of my paternal habitation, or was I thousands of miles distant?" (171). First, Huntly fears he may be in the wilderness. Second, he fears separation from his family. This second fear suggests something more: fear of separation from the civilized community. Huntly's twin concerns actually reflect two sides of the same issue. He fears that the territory to which he has mysteriously been transported is neither civilized nor safe for him. Though Huntly has previously considered Norwalk to be safe--indeed, safe enough for a picturesque tour--the fact that it is still a wilderness tract begins to become clear and frightens him. Huntly's confusion and concern about his location is, therefore, significant. His sense of place tells him he is in Norwalk, but he is shaken by the presence of Indians. "How was this opinion," he wonders, "to be reconciled to appearances so strange and uncouth, and what measure did a due regard to my safety enjoin me to take?" (172). Since Norwalk is close to the farms that Huntly considers safe and civilized, he cannot reconcile the appearance of "savages" on the scene.

The protagonist's problem results from his confusing simple geography with a true understanding of the landscape through which he has carelessly wandered. Norwalk, a wilderness tract beginning in Indian country, separates two settlements that are only connected by a few narrow paths (172). Huntly has previously considered this tract as no more than a shortcut between the two communities and a rich source of picturesque beauty on an occasional tour through the area. But his perceptions are grossly inaccurate, particularly since the reader later learns that Indians have used this territory in the past for periodic raids on the white settlements, including one murderous raid on his own family (173). What is worse, the protagonist's misconceptions and naivete have gotten him, once more, into trouble in the wilderness. The landscape he thought was safe has, in a sense, betrayed him. What he considered neutral territory is in truth a borderland more savage than civilized. Behind the sublime prospects lurk Indians anxious to slay him, pits ready to swallow him up, and hidden rocks and roots able to trip him unaware. This is no landscape for a picturesque tour.

Edgar Huntly must come to terms with the uncivilized nature of the wilderness, even more than with the Indians who occasionally inhabit it. Just as he has consistently refused to acknowledge the dark side of human nature, particularly in himself, he has refused to accept the dark side of the landscape in America.[22] Though he imagines himself safe, both from dangers without and within, he is never truly safe and secure. Ignoring this truth has only served to endanger him and others.[23] In the protagonist's last journey into the wilderness, Brown reveals that, in order to become whole and to live realistically in the American wilderness, Huntly must resolve these twin concerns: he must recognize and accept the dark half of himself, and he must acknowledge and learn to live with the dark side of the wilderness. He is, in a real sense, on a romantic quest to resolve the disjunction of his inner and outer worlds.[24]

Huntly's experience in the cavern suggests, as critics have shown, an initiation experience in which the protagonist simultaneously discovers and acknowledges his own feral impulses and realizes the dark side of the wilderness.[25] When Huntly kills and eats a life-threatening panther in the cavern, he acts from instincts of self-preservation, in spite of considering suicide moments before (164-68). He is, however, dead wrong when he says he "subdued the sentiments of nature" to do this (167). Huntly has, in fact, done exactly what nature--both human nature and the wilderness--demands: he has saved his own life by taking the life of the one who threatened him. It is the dictates of reason or sensibility that Huntly must subdue here, not those of nature. This is also a form of initiation into the world of the wilderness. As Ursula Brumm states, "Huntly is initiated into the deepest core of nature as a ferocious, devouring[,] relentless, and at the same time a life-giving force." Brumm considers Huntly's encounter with the Indians and his subsequent murder of them the "ultimate test" of his initiation,[26] but this explanation ignores the equally important role of the landscape in Huntly's progress to a full understanding of himself and the wilderness.

In the Norwalk wilds, Huntly's last journey is as circuitous as the mazy tract he explores. A pattern of approach and withdrawal develops in which the protagonist approaches civilization, usually represented by a habitation of some sort, and then withdraws again into the wilderness. Though Huntly is constantly moving towards civilization, as Norman Grabo has shown, his path is circuitous and long.[27] In some respects this tortuously slow progress suggests both the difficulty of returning to civilization after a total immersion in the wild and Huntly's need for further testing in the wilderness before he can return to the community a whole man, at ease with himself and his environment.

In the protagonist's attitude towards landscape, there are several differences between this journey and earlier ones. For one, Huntly no longer seeks out prospects solely for the picturesque view. If he climbs a mountain, he does so usually because he wants to get to the other side. Also, he does not ignore the perils of the landscape any longer; instead, he assesses the dangers of his situation like a good frontiersman and presses on. Huntly has, of course, a different motive on this journey: he is no longer in search of picturesque beauty. Instead, he is trying to come to terms with the wilderness and to return to civilization. This requires that he immerse himself in the landscape, not just admire it.

For example, early in the last journey Huntly gets directions from a frontier woman and takes a path up over a rocky ridge that leads to the road home along the river. Having proven himself adept at getting lost, Huntly pauses on the summit to collect his wits before pushing on. Gazing at the prospect before him, a sublime view of towering cliffs and thundering river, Huntly writes: "I pondered for a while on these stupendous scenes. They ravished my attention from considerations that related to myself; but this interval was short, and I began to measure the descent, in order to ascertain the practicability of treading it" (214). Earlier in the narrative, Huntly paused to enjoy a similar prospect and, distracted from his concerns, commented at length upon its picturesque beauty. Here the author uses none of the terminology associated with aesthetic appreciation. The "stupendous scenes" may "ravish" Huntly's attention for a moment, but he promptly returns to more practical matters. Later, after climbing another hill, Huntly "sat down upon the highest brow to meditate on future trials." Other than a brief description of the topography, Huntly pays no attention to the scene's beauty (225). These landscapes are more functional than those described on earlier journeys since these scenes depict the territory through which he must travel to reach home. The "ruggedness" and "sterility" of the tract, words which frequently recur on the last journey, emphasize the hostility of the landscape. This is a wilderness that tests the hero and demands to be understood on its own terms rather than in the aesthetic terms Huntly has previously tried to apply to it.

Huntly has previously perceived the wilderness in two different but related ways: wilderness as playground and wilderness as a source of beauty, a place for the picturesque tour. Both interpretations prove woefully wrongheaded, particularly in the final journey into Norwalk. The first view is tested several times in the novel. Earlier, Huntly's fondness for squirrels had to be conquered, and his idea that panthers and rattlesnakes, natural inhabitants of the forest, were "spoilers" of his wilderness playground had to be overcome (124). When he killed first one panther and then another, feeding on the warm blood and body of the second and absorbing its animal strength, Huntly learned to acknowledge their powerful presence. Elsewhere, Huntly discovers that a river perceived earlier as playground is actually hostile territory to man. Diving into a river to escape the pursuit of what seem to be Indians, he is now beaten down by the same element that previously buoyed him up. The river is so hostile, in fact, that it will not let him go, and he must struggle to escape from the watery grave he imagines is waiting for him. Huntly musters the strength to pull himself out of the stream and climb to the nearest summit (224-25).

The landscape that Huntly had once found so inviting is now hostile territory, but he only conquers it insofar as he survives it. He is no Natty Bumppo. Unlike Cooper's Leatherstocking, who could follow an invisible trail in the dark, Huntly belies his name once again by continually getting lost, even when he has directions. Trying to follow old cattle trails, Huntly winds up stumbling into pits and thorny bushes. Unlike any frontiersman before or after him in American literature, Huntly persists in thinking that following a straight line in any direction guarantees a route home. Often he simply wanders at random in Norwalk, dragging the helpless girl he rescued from the Indians beside him (181-82). Although not completely without frontier sense and skills (after all, Huntly is handy with both hatchet and gun), he is sadly lacking in most wilderness survival skills. Lawson-Peebles also comments on Huntly's poor frontier skills, observing, "He possesses only negative savagism, not the survival skills of the Coonskinners." Edgar Huntly, he concludes, "represents an absolute rejection of the sentimental savagism occasionally indulged in by Revolutionary writers."[28]

Huntly's foolish actions with regard to Clithero after his return from the last frightening journey into Norwalk suggest that the protagonist learned very little of substance about himself and others from that long sojourn in the wilderness. He makes the same kind of errors of judgment about people and circumstances that led him mistakenly to pursue Clithero in an attempt to solve Waldegrave's murder in the first place. And since he did not learn how to understand and deal with the dark side of people, it is unlikely that he learned anything about the wilderness either. Indeed, if we consider Huntly's responses to the landscape on the last journey, it is clear that the protagonist has not yet understood--and perhaps never will--the true nature of the American wilderness: its inherent hostility to civilized people and the necessity of knowledge and precaution when setting forth into the wilds.

Part of the problem in discerning whether Huntly has learned anything from his experience lies with the author. Had Brown understood his own achievement in the novel more clearly, perhaps he would have clarified his protagonist's experience in the wilderness.[29] The best clue to the author's intentions in the novel lies in the preface, which states that "the perils of the Western wilderness, are far more suitable" for an American novelist than the "puerile superstition and exploded manners" of European gothics. He argues that the New World should furnish new "themes to the moral painter." In America, he writes, there are "sources of amusement to the fancy and instruction to the heart" that are "peculiar" to its people and landscape, sources for the writer of native fiction to explore (3). According to Brown, the novel's purpose is twofold: to entertain and to teach. *Edgar Huntly's* sensationalism guarantees its entertainment value, both for contemporary audiences and today. As Lawson-Peebles points out, this is Brown's "only novel to go into a second edition in his lifetime."[30] As for the work's didactic value, the author's comments elsewhere help to clarify his purpose in this regard. In his article on picturesque travel, for instance, he notes, "Of all kinds of travellers, or pedestrian hunters, those that travel in search of the pleasure of the picturesque are the fewest in number, particularly in America,"[31] suggesting that the author was indeed weighing the potential for picturesque travel in the New World. In *Edgar Huntly* Brown presents readers with an original American novel that vividly illustrates the failure of picturesque travel in the New World wilderness, revealing its many failures and dangers by characterizing the protagonist, a "pedestrian hunter" of the picturesque, as naively ignorant of the real dangers of the American wilderness. Lawson-Peebles argues that Brown's "fiction provided his peers with an omen about the gap between their perceptions of the terrain and its reality." I would state this even more strongly: In *Edgar Huntly* Brown warns his countrymen about the dangers of blindly applying European values to the New World, the wilderness in particular. Very few, however, as Lawson-Peebles wryly observes, paid much attention to the warning.[32]

In addition to arguing the impracticality and danger of picturesque travel in America in *Edgar Huntly*, Brown suggests that this kind of travel in the native wilderness is incongruous through his portrait of the picturesque tourist as sleepwalker. Unlike the conventional traveler, for whom the primary model is William Gilpin, Edgar Huntly cannot simply enjoy the landscape's beauties. While the picturesque tourist should respond with pleasure to the scene, tensions are always present in Huntly's response to the landscape, for Huntly is actually threatened by the very wilderness he admires. While Gilpin could calmly ride through the peaceful English countryside, pointing out its finer perspectives, Huntly struggles on foot through the tangled brush and stony ground of Norwalk. Gilpin's worst danger is from an occasional drizzle; Huntly's is from a torrential downpour. At best, Gilpin may fear the antics of a skittish horse, but Huntly is stalked by a vicious panther. Not surprisingly, Brown comments on this predicament of his picturesque traveler, albeit indirectly. Huntly is often seen naively enjoying a particularly spectacular view and commenting on its sublimity; while lost in thought he is suddenly recalled to his danger, shaken back to reality by a panther's cry or the wind's shriek. Daydreaming, Brown suggests, is out of place in the American wilderness. This is not the place for the picturesque tourist. Huntly is not, of course, bent solely on enjoying prospects in the Norwalk wilds; he is ostensibly in search of Clithero. But he forgets his mission repeatedly, pausing dreamily to admire the scenery. There is both a feeling of tension and an unintended humor in these scenes because Huntly is a picturesque tourist out of his natural element, a safe English countryside. For although the American landscape is picturesque in conventional terms, it is much more than that. One important facet of the experience of both the picturesque and the sublime is the safety of the observer. A landscape that threatens the observer either physically or psychologically is dangerous and terrifying, not sublime. Huntly cannot come to terms with the fact that the American wilds are at once dangerous and wildly beautiful any more than he can understand how he himself can be both good and evil. He no more understands contradictions in the landscape than he understands contradictions in human nature.

In *Edgar Huntly* Brown's use of the conventions of picturesque travel implicitly criticizes the protagonist's position in relation to the wilderness in the New World. Intrigued with the picturesque point of view and the idea of picturesque travel, Brown explores its potential in America in his numerous articles on the subject, but his depiction of Edgar Huntly's experiences in the wilderness suggests that only with great difficulty and with some sacrifice to the truth can these conventions be adopted without modification by American travelers and writers. Some European conventions cannot be transferred wholesale to America and made to work without regard for the change in setting. Picturesque and sublime scenery does exist in America, but one cannot enjoy it as easily as Gilpin does, and as Brown himself might wish.

In truth, the American wilderness is dangerous, not peaceful and safe for travelers and those who dwell in it. Not only panthers and Indians are harmful, but the land itself is potentially dangerous. There are tangled roots to trip the hero in blind pursuit of a good view; the protagonist may topple off a precipice while admiring a prospect; and he may even lose his way back to civilization. There is no safe road from which to enjoy the scenery, and from within the wilderness itself there is even more danger. Therefore conventions of the picturesque must be adapted, if at all, with careful consideration for the wilderness landscape.

On another level, Brown may well be warning Americans in the post-Revolutionary New World that they are metaphorically sleepwalking in the wilderness, unaware of the dangers that beset them on every side. Although he does not state what the dangers are, there are two strong possibilities: first, the political dangers of independence and an untried political path, and second, the dangers lurking in the dark, unexplored side of the human psyche, as represented by Clithero, Huntly's doppelganger. Brown warns Americans to know where they are headed politically and, most of all, to know themselves. Be cautious, he advises, about the wholesale adoption of imported aesthetics or literary forms. Be wary about making broad, often naive assumptions about the nature of people and about the environment.

Provided with guides and prepared for danger, later writers such as Washington Irving and Francis Parkman would more successfully adapt the picturesque tour to the American West. In the eastern United States, on the other hand, where much of the land had already been tamed and transportation to scenic areas had improved by the 1820s, touring became so popular that a writer such as James Kirke Paulding could satirize the hordes of tourists eager to view picturesque America as he turned to the conventions of the tour to comment upon contemporary fashions, mores, and more important issues of national concern.

Notes

1. Dennis Berthold, "Charles Brockden Brown, *Edgar Huntly*, and the Origins of the American Picturesque," *William and Mary Quarterly*, 3rd series, 41 (1984): 62-84. Jane Tompkins discusses *Wieland* and *Arthur Mervyn* in *Sensational Designs: The Cultural Work of American Fiction, 1790-1860* (New York: Oxford University Press, 1985), chs. 2 and 3. In *Landscape and Written Expression in Revolutionary America: The World Turned Upside Down* Lawson-Peebles discusses the relationship between literary landscapes and political ideology in all of Brown's major novels (New York: Cambridge University Press, 1988), ch. 7.

2. Charles Brockden Brown, "Moral and Physical Sublimity Compared," *Literary Magazine, and American Reg.* 5 (May 1806): 363-64; "Reflections on Taste," *Literary Magazine, and Amer. Reg.* 5 (June 1806): 408-09; "Distinctions Between the Beautiful and the Picturesque," *Literary Magazine, and Amer. Reg.* 5 (June 1806): 439-40. Kenneth Bernard comments on Brown's knowledge and use of the picturesque and sublime in "Charles Brockden Brown and the Sublime," *Personalist* 45 (1964): 235-49. Dennis Berthold discusses this series of articles and the way Brown develops the picturesque for the American landscape in "Brown, *Edgar Huntly*, and . . . the American Picturesque," pp. 62-84.

3. [Charles Brockden Brown], "On a Taste for the Picturesque," *Monthly Magazine, and Amer. Review* 3 (July 1800): 11-13.

4. [Charles Brockden Brown], "On the Picturesque," *Literary Magazine, and Amer. Reg.* 6 (July 1806): 6-8. Kenneth Bernard does not mention this article in his essay "Charles Brockden Brown and the Sublime." Dennis Berthold discusses this article briefly in "Charles Brockden Brown, *Edgar Huntly*, and . . . the American Picturesque" (pp. 66-68).

5. Brown apparently is using Gilpin's original work, "On Picturesque Travel," in *Three Essays: On Picturesque Beauty; on Picturesque Travel; and on Sketching Landscape* (London: R. Blamire, 1792), as his source, for no reprint of Gilpin's essay in America that I have located quotes as much as Brown does here. The *Encyclopedia Britannica* (Philadelphia: n.p., 1798), which Brown may have seen, quotes part of Gilpin's essay "On Picturesque Beauty" (vol. 14, 730-31), but it does not quote from the essay on picturesque travel.

Rees's Cyclopaedia, a "Universal Dictionary of Arts, Sciences, and Literature," a copy of which was found in Brown's library upon his death (David Lee Clark, *Charles Brockden Brown: Pioneer Voice of America* [Durham, N.C.: Duke University Press, 1952], p. 331), contains a three-column article on picturesque beauty. It quotes extensively from Gilpin's essay "On Picturesque Beauty" (Abraham Rees, *Rees's Cyclopaedia*, 1st Amer. ed. [Philadelphia: Samuel F. Bradford, (1805-1825?)], vol. 28). Brown might also have seen an earlier British edition of this encyclopedia.

6. Other than encyclopedia articles, there are several other possible sources for Brown's knowledge of the picturesque. First, he might have read William Gilpin's work firsthand in the collection of the Library Company of Philadelphia, which lists a copy of Gilpin's *Three Essays* in its possession in 1794, when Brown was still living in that city (Clark, p. 332; Janice G. Schimmelman, *A Checklist of European Treatises on Art and Essays on Aesthetics Available in America Through 1815* [Worcester, Mass.: American Antiquarian Society, 1983], p. 187). Brown later became a member of the Library Company in 1809, the year before his death (John C. Van Horne [Librarian, The Library Company of Philadelphia] to author, 26 June 1986).

Other relevant works held by the Library Company before 1799, when *Edgar Huntly* was written and published, include Richard Payne Knight's *The Landscape, A Didactic Poem* (1794) and Uvedale Price's *An Essay on the Picturesque* (1796) (Schimmelman, p. 187), both of which might have contributed to Brown's understanding of the picturesque.

7. According to William Dunlap, Brown's first biographer, Brockden Brown was so studious as a child that his health became impaired. Brown's schoolmaster, Robert Proud, "recommended an abstinence from study, and prescribed relaxation and excursions into the country as indispensable for the re-establishment of his health." Dunlap notes too that Brown became so fond of such excursions on foot "that he continued the practice ever after" (*The Life of Charles Brockden Brown* [Philadelphia: James P. Parke, 1815], 1: 13).

8. Dunlap, 1: 14.

9. [Charles Brockden Brown], "A Jaunt to Rockaway," *Literary Magazine, and Amer. Reg.* 1 (Oct. 1803): 10-14. Kenneth Bernard concludes from the Rockaway article: "It is unlikely, in view of Brown's poor powers of observation, that he could celebrate the American or any other scene very much" ("Brown and the Sublime," p. 236).

10. Quoted in Dunlap, 2: 48.

11. Dunlap, 2: 48, 51.

12. Charles Brockden Brown, *Edgar Huntly; or, Memoirs of a Sleep-Walker*, ed. Sydney J. Krause and S. W. Reid, Bicentennial Edition (Kent, Ohio: Kent State University Press, 1984), p. 7. All subsequent references to this edition appear in the text.

13. For example, the note to plate 20 in *Gilpin's Day* describes evening as "the picturesque time of the Day" (London: Edward Orme, 1810), n.pag.

14. For example, in a book detailing the permissible amusements of gentlefolk, Gilpin recommends riding or walking through the countryside, where nature's continually changing scenery will stimulate thoughtful reflections in the observer. He particularly suggests this form of exercise for clergymen as a means of discovering material for sermons ([Edward Stillingfleet], *On the Amusements of*

Clergymèn, and Christians in General [London: A.J. Valpy, 1820], pp. 128-30).

15. Dieter Schulz points this out in *"Edgar Huntly* as Quest Romance,* " *American Literature* 43 (Nov. 1971): 324.

16. William Gilpin, "On Picturesque Travel," *Three Essays*, quoted by [Charles Brockden Brown], "On the Picturesque," p. 7.

17. William Gilpin, "On Picturesque Travel," *Three Essays*, quoted by [Charles Brockden Brown], "On the Picturesque," p. 7.

18. William Gilpin, "On Picturesque Travel," *Three Essays*, p. 43.

19. William Gilpin, *Observations on the River Wye* (London: R. Blamire, 1782), p. 16.

20. Richard Slotkin has commented most fully on Huntly's attitude towards killing (whether animals or Indians) and on the meaning of the hunt in *Regeneration Through Violence: The Mythology of the American Frontier, 1600-1860* (Middletown, Conn.: Wesleyan University Press, 1973), pp. 384-90.

21. William Gilpin, *Remarks on Forest Scenery*, 2nd ed., 2 vols. (London: R. Blamire, 1794), 1: 254-55.

22. For example, Huntly refuses to acknowledge the violent impulses in himself. When killing the Indians, he rationalizes each shooting and declares that his is a peace-loving nature (193, 200).

23. "We imagined ourselves at an inaccessible distance from the danger" (of Indians), Huntly writes. He continues to fool himself into believing he is safe as long as he stays in the cavern (Freudians love this passage), and only for the sake of warning others of danger does he emerge from the cave (173-74). Later, Huntly will not admit that Clithero is insane or dangerous, and this ignorance of Clithero as a source of danger directly brings about the miscarriage and resulting illness of Sarsefield's wife. Sarsefield's letter to Huntly on the subject confirms our view of him as one who acts precipitously, without

considering the dark side of people (292-93).

24. For a full account of the quest theme, see Schulz, *"Edgar Huntly* as Quest Romance," pp. 323-35. Schulz argues that Huntly's object in the quest is "the gradual release of the irrational and aggressive part of the hero's psyche, of his 'dark self'" (p. 326).

25. See Ursula Brumm, "Nature as Scene or Agent? Some Reflections on its Role in the American Novel," *Vistas of a Continent: Concepts of Nature in America*, ed. Teut A. Riese (Heidelberg: Winter, 1979), pp. 108-09, on Huntly's experience as initiation into nature. See also the Schulz article cited in n. 15.

26. Brumm, p. 108.

27. Norman S. Grabo, *The Coincidental Art of Charles Brockden Brown* (Chapel Hill: University of North Carolina Press, 1981), pp. 62-64.

28. Lawson-Peebles, p. 251.

29. Alan Axelrod argues that Brown "did not understand, consciously let alone self-consciously, the fullest implications of his materials and themes" (*Charles Brockden Brown: An American Tale* [Austin: University of Texas Press, 1983], p. xx).

30. Lawson-Peebles, p. 252.

31. [Charles Brockden Brown], "On the Picturesque," p. 6.

32. Lawson-Peebles, p. 232.

Chapter 3

"Banqueting on the Picturesque": James Kirke Paulding in the 1820s and '30s

At first glance the Paper War and the picturesque tour would seem to have little in common, but for James Kirke Paulding the war of words between American and British writers in the half century after the Revolutionary War would prompt him to defend his country with his pen. What better way to demonstrate America's glory and to show its past greatness than through the medium of the picturesque tour? The focus on landscape beauty in this genre provided a conventional means of celebrating the landscapes of his native country, while at the same time the stops at historical points of interest during a tour enabled him to exploit past moments of glory in battle as a manifestation of America's heroic past and a token of its future greatness. In addition, the popularity of picturesque travel in the 1820s and '30s led Paulding to satirize some of the absurdities and excesses of fashionables who flocked to eastern watering places and, occasionally, to offer more positive models of probity and patriotism in fictional characters. Paulding contributed in an important way to the development of the picturesque tour in America by transforming it into a vehicle for nationalism.

In the first decades of the nineteenth century American writers and critics began increasingly to call for an American literature based on native materials and featuring national themes. As British critics responded to their efforts with increasingly disparaging reviews, the ensuing Paper War between American and British writers threatened to distract patriotic Americans from their stated purpose. But for Paulding and other nationalistic authors, the Paper War not only gave them an impetus to respond to British critics, but also provided an opportunity for them to demonstrate by their imaginative use of Old World literary conventions that the new nation's literary culture was alive and well. In defending American interests, such writers attacked European values and conventions as immoral or outmoded, and, more important, they reassured their American audience that the patriotic values of the previous generation were still vital for their own.

Since much of the criticism and misinformation propagated by British writers was found in travel books from American tours, the travel narrative--this time written by Americans--became a logical outlet for corrective views. Paulding, in particular, favored the travel narrative as a loosely structured genre that enabled him to include whatever information he wished and to adopt the tone he needed in different books. In the first twenty years of his publishing career the Knickerbocker writer turned to the travel narrative again and again to respond to British critics and to present his own nationalistic view of the United States, contributing in this way to the transatlantic debate about the New World's cultural vitality and to the ongoing debate among American writers and social critics concerning the identity of the new nation. Five of the seventeen major works published during this period take the form of travel narratives, including *The Backwoodsman*, a lengthy poem featuring, in part, the protagonist's travels from the Hudson River Valley through New Jersey, Pennsylvania, and west to Ohio; *A Sketch of Old England, by a New-England Man* (1822), a satiric travelogue; and *John Bull in America, or, The New Munchausen* (1825), a burlesque on British travel writers.

Among Paulding's American travel narratives, two books and a tale present interesting studies in the use and modification of the picturesque tour. Beginning with *Letters from the South* (1817), the picturesque tour takes on added importance for Paulding as a means of presenting his increasingly critical view both of British travelers and of American tourists who aped Continental fashions and mores on the picturesque tour. Later works such as *The New Mirror for Travellers; and Guide to the Springs* (1828) and the tale "Childe Roeliff's Pilgrimage" (1832) also use the picturesque tour both to attack critical British travelers in America and to satirize Americans whose travels abroad had corrupted their values. At the same time, Paulding's picturesque tours served to present the beauty of American landscapes to the world--a positive attribute of the United States about which even the most acerbic critics did not argue--and to offer more positive models of American integrity and values. In this respect both his fictional and nonfictional travel writings actively helped shape the national identity: America's greatness became further identified with its scenic marvels and the American reader was advised to take his or her role models not from continental fops but from red-blooded, patriotic natives, with Paulding offering fictional characters as examples and, occasionally, historical figures as role models.

In *Letters from the South, Written during an Excursion in the Summer of 1816*, Paulding reveals a fondness for picturesque landscapes and a knowledge of picturesque travel that suggest not only his familiarity with the conventions of the picturesque but also a distinct pleasure in occasionally using these conventions in unconventional ways. At the same time, he introduces many of the subjects and themes in this travel book which would interest him in future writings: the distorted reports of British travel writers on America, the superficiality of society's fashionables, the questionable value and safety of paper money, plantation life in Virginia, and, of course, the varied beauties of the American landscape, to name just a few of his favorite subjects.

Paulding's *Letters from the South* is based on a tour he made of Virginia during the summer of 1816 to regain his health after a year of working in Washington, D.C., as secretary of the Board of Navy Commissioners, a position he gained partly because of his outspoken patriotism and, more specifically, because of his praise of recent American naval accomplishments, to which President James Madison had responded favorably.[1] The published volume of letters is semi-autobiographical, though no letters have been found on which the book might have been based. Addressed to an apparently fictional person named "Frank," the letters form a travel account of the narrator's tour through Virginia and offer a loose framework for his comments on diverse subjects. Both the content and tone of the letters vary from letter to letter: Paulding offers straight historical narrative in one letter, burlesque in another, and satire in yet a third, ranging from the history of Virginia and rivalry between Virginia Tuckahoes and Cohees, to fashionable life at the springs.[2]

Since picturesque beauty is not the primary object of the narrator's tour in *Letters from the South*, the work cannot be classified as a strictly conventional picturesque tour. But since much attention is paid to various kinds of landscape beauty throughout the *Letters*-- indeed, roughly half of the letters pay some attention or are devoted entirely to the attractions of local landscapes--Paulding's book can be considered a travel narrative that uses several conventions of the picturesque tour: attention to landscape beauty, stories about local history and legends, and anecdotes about various people and social groups encountered on the trip. As other writers had discovered earlier, the loose format of the tour allowed an author to bring much otherwise extraneous material into a travel narrative. Paulding's variations in tone are his own contribution to the nonfictional picturesque tour.

Unlike the two picturesque tours written a decade later, *The New Mirror for Travellers* and "Childe Roeliffe's Pilgrimage," which frequently satirize the picturesque tour and tourist, Paulding's *Letters from the South* generally features straightforward landscape description of the sort any gentleman traveler of the day might record in his travel journal. Accompanied by "Oliver B.----," a former fellow student, the narrator tours Virginia, beginning his "*grand tour*," as he calls it, at Norfolk, traveling through the Chesapeake Bay area and on to Richmond, York, Williamsburg, and Charlottesville (1: Letter #3, 26; #4, 37). He crossed the Blue Ridge of the Allegheny Mountains and explored Weir's Cave. From there he sought out several of the most popular spas in Virginia--White Sulphur, Sweet Springs, and Berkeley Springs--and ended his tour at Harper's Ferry, following the Potomac back to his original starting point, Washington (see Map 2).[3] Traveling through the Allegheny Mountains, Paulding's narrator reveals himself as a picturesque traveler at heart when he gazes on a prospect and comments: "Because I delight to recall and arrange the impressions I derived from the scene, I will sketch a mountain landscape for you, without caring so much to administer to your gratification as to my own" (1: Letter #13, 115). This pleasure in remembering and sketching the elements and impressions of a scene is central to the character of the picturesque traveler. Both the number and quality of the scenes in the *Letters* reveal Paulding, through his narrator, as a sensitive and practiced observer and recorder of the picturesque. His landscape descriptions are detailed and his responses sensitive to the conventions of picturesque description, including the elements of contrast, variety, unity, and, often, association. In addition, he often employs such distinctively American techniques as noting the future value of a scene and recording its moral effect on the observer.

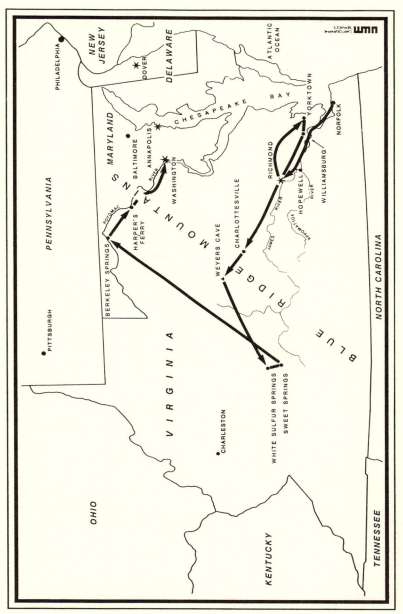

Map 2. James Kirke Paulding's Tour of Virginia in 1835.

For example, Paulding sketches, as he likes to say, the following scene during the narrator's travels in the Allegheny Mountains:

> We saw, what seemed a vast and interminable waste of waters, spreading far and wide, and covering the whole face of the lower world. The vapours of the night had settled in the wide valley, at the foot of the hill, and enveloped it in one unbroken sheet of mist, that in the grey obscurity of the morning, looked like a boundless ocean. But as the sun rose, a gentle breeze sprung up, and the vapours began to be in motion. As they lifted themselves lazily from the ground, and rolled in closer masses towards the mountains, the face of nature gradually disclosed itself in all its varied and enchanting beauty. The imaginary sea became a fertile valley, extending up and down as far as the eye could reach. In the midst of the green foliage of oaks and solemn pines, were seen rich cultivated lands, and comfortable farm-houses, surrounded by ruddy fields of clover, speckled with groups of cattle grazing in its luxuriant pastures, or reposing quietly among its blossoms. Still, as the mists passed silently away, new objects disclosed themselves, with a sweet delay, that enhanced their beauty. Here was seen a little town, and near it a field, animated with sturdy labourers.
>
> (1: Letter #10, 89-90)

Paulding's description reveals a sensitivity to the picturesque and an artist's sense of arrangement in this scene. The obscuring mist unifies the picture, while the trees, fields, and farms add contrast and variety. The presence of cattle and farm workers offers a pastoral element, with the nearby town establishing the location of the scene as Crèvecoeur's middle settlements, the most likely place for the picturesque in America, neither too close to the wilderness nor too near the city.[4] His light touch enables him to sketch in the scene without clumsily underscoring its moral value or its effect on the observer. Instead he simply states: "It seldom falls to the lot of city mortals to see such a scene--and it is seldom, I am told, that it falls to the lot of a traveller to behold it more than once. The impression it made I have since recalled with new delight." He concludes, "I hope to retain the remembrance for a long time, and when at last it fades away in the succession of new scenes, new objects, new enjoyments, and new sufferings, I shall think I have lost a cherished relic of past times" (1: Letter #10, 90-91). Characteristically, Paulding recognizes that the future will change the scene, yet, at the same time, he resists the idea. Oddly, he feels nostalgia for a scene that is not yet lost to progress.

Elsewhere Paulding employs the future picturesque, a picturesque scene whose associations are not in the past, in history, but in the future. Often writers using this kind of associational technique imagine the future glories of a landscape, whether its future role in history (truly a feat of the imagination) or its role as a future site of industry or agriculture. For example, on his way to Richmond, Virginia, the narrator pauses just after the junction of the Appomattox and James Rivers at City-Point and gazes on the prospect. Here the associations with the landscape that he envisions are not only in the future, but also, interestingly, in the past: "Below this, commence those extensive flats where the early settlers first broke the soil of the United States; and where the first sun rose and set on the natives of the eastern hemisphere, pursuing the peaceful occupations of husbandry in this wilderness of the West. It is here then that we see the spot where first was planted the seeds of this great country--mighty in its present vigorous youth, but far mightier in its future destinies. The place, therefore, is one of the most interesting to a reflecting mind . . . of any in this country. To an American it is peculiarly interesting" (1: Letter #8, 79). When Paulding locates the earliest settlements of the first colonists on this spot, he sets up an almost emblematic scene. To the American observer, as he notes, the birthplace of the future nation reverberates with symbolism of past, present, and future glories. The patriotic note on which this descriptive passage concludes is typical of both the historical and the future picturesque of the period, since the picturesque in general was often used by writers as a means of establishing their nation as a worthy seat of literature. In this instance Paulding intensifies the impact of the scene: though his narrator describes his travels in Rome, Smyrna, Constantinople, and elsewhere, he states emphatically that "they excited nothing like the feeling I experienced, on visiting the spot where the first permanent settlement was made by the pilgrims, in this *our* western hemisphere. Nothing now remains . . . but the spot is well known, and every century . . .

will only render it more interesting and illustrious" (1: Letter #8, 81). Like earlier Americans who turned frequently to the Rising Glory theme in their writing, Paulding returns again and again to the notion of the future glory of a nation grounded firmly in its illustrious past, often grounded literally in the soil cultivated by the first colonists.

In addition to being a sensitive observer of landscape and a writer who connects the visible landscape with its past, present, and future potential, Paulding also senses and articulates the moral value of a scene, an ability that William Gilpin had considered rare in the typical picturesque traveler.[5] That one may connect with God through nature--whether in a forest, through a flower, or by means of a prospect--will later become a commonplace among American transcendental and romantic writers from the 1830s through the '50s. But Paulding's sensitivity to the moral value of landscape, particularly picturesque landscape, is noteworthy at this early date. Mountains had been associated with the sublime for more than half a century,[6] but their picturesque qualities and, by extension, their moral value as such were not emphasized until the early nineteenth century by American travelers and writers, who often found America's eastern mountain ranges more picturesque than sublime. For example, in the Allegheny Mountains the narrator finds himself admiring the scenery, with its endless variety of picturesque elements. He recommends the "pure and salutary enjoyment" of the mountain scenery to awaken "the higher powers of the mind." Of the sensitive observer, he states: "He will be led to reflections that, if they do not awaken his mind to the comprehension of new truths, will most likely open new and purer sources of pleasure, and more lofty subjects of contemplation. Activity and noise remind us only of this world: but silence and repose lead us to a world to come" (1: Letter #13, 119).

The narrator's love of solitary walks through romantic scenery (Paulding, like other writers of his time, sometimes used "romantic" and "picturesque" interchangeably) also leads him to comment on a scene's moral value. Strolling in the evening in a meadow through which a stream meandered, with mountains rising in the distance, the narrator reflects: "It is in such scenes and seasons, that the heart is deepest smitten with the power and goodness of Providence, and that the soul demonstrates its capacity for maintaining an existence independent of matter, by abstracting itself from the body, and expatiating alone in the boundless regions of the past and the future" (2: Letter #23, 13). Paulding makes the connection between picturesque landscape, the observer, and God explicit, demonstrating for the reader--and for future Transcendentalists--how a scene may so move the observer that the soul is drawn out of him or her, freed from the limits of time and space, and left to contemplate God's glory or to commune with God in "the only temple worthy of the Deity," Nature itself (2: Letter #23, 13). Scenes such as this also remind the reader that not only the sublime can evoke thoughts of God, but, as Gilpin had found, picturesque beauty, too, could remind the observer of God's hand in creating the natural world.

Paulding also found the loose framework of the picturesque tour ideally suited to bring in the sort of miscellaneous information he delighted in, such as comments on contemporary society, economics, and politics. His frequent forays into local history and legend are, however, an essential part of the tour since these add the requisite associations for picturesque landscapes. Predictably, the narrator of the *Letters* complains at one point about the lack of associations in the American landscape, blaming it here on "this age of stern philosophy" that represses "the sprightly gambols of imagination": fairies, dryads, river-gods, and so forth (1: Letter #12, 100). Paulding's narrator reveals his own affinity for such creatures and connections: "For me," he writes, "I delight in keeping up a good-fellowship with all the airy, fantastic, and indefinite beings of former times. They are to me pleasant sort of people; every beautiful spot of nature derives additional interest from being associated with them; and in the dearth of real sources of pleasure, I am willing to cherish as many imaginary ones as I can." "For the honour of the country," the narrator states his wish "to show that our native solitudes are not so destitute of fairies as some people are pleased to imagine" (1: Letter #12, 100, 103-05).

The author responds to the alleged dearth of landscape associations with an "authentic account" of such imaginary creatures and locates it on the banks of the Musconeconck River in New Jersey, thus establishing the bond between landscape and legend, just as Irving achieved a similar object in "Rip Van Winkle" and "The Legend of Sleepy Hollow," although the latter writer's legends became far more famous than Paulding's ever would be. The fairy story that follows, which is also connected with the War of 1812, doubling its associational value, demonstrates that even "the age of stern philosophy" can produce an imaginative legend and connect it with a particular landscape.[7] Paulding argues that, in spite of America's revolutionary impulse to destroy the past, whether to sever all

connections with an earlier British cultural tradition or to deny the
fanciful and imaginative in its drive to affirm the rule of reason, the
imagination lives on, at least in his writings, bridging the gap between
past and present and helping to create a new literature that draws on the
past without slavishly imitating colonial culture.

Elsewhere in *Letters from the South* the narrator makes an
excursion to York and Williamsburg, Virginia, the former locale
inspiring him to explore the ruins of British fortifications from the
Revolutionary War. The "desolation and decay" appeal to him since
such ruins are "seldom seen in our youthful country" (1: Letter #6,
54), a complaint voiced throughout the early part of the nineteenth
century by other American writers such as Irving and Cooper, who
sought, at the same time, to counter this problem by creating their own
legends and histories from extant Indian or historical ruins. When
Paulding's narrator discovers a cave reputed to have been temporarily
occupied by General Cornwallis during the war, his elation is complete.
Here, at last, is a scene that recalls the triumphant end of America's
War of Independence. Although he downplays the legend's significance
with humor by quoting an old Scotsman who scoffs at the notion of an
English lord hiding in a cave, the ruins at York remain important since
this is where British tyranny in the New World ended, with the
surrender of Cornwallis at York (1: Letter #6, 56). Proud of his
country's triumphs and unconscious of any irony, the narrator looks
forward to the day when American ambition may extend itself to
Europe, founding colonies of its own where once nations sent forth
armies to colonize the New World. He imagines that "the splendours
of the civilized world, which rose in the ruddy east, may set at last in
the glowing west, equally splendid and glorious." Ironically, instead of
predicting that the newly independent United States would become a
symbol of freedom to the rest of the world, and therefore forge its own
identity, Paulding foretells its future evolution into a colonial power
that by the end of the century would imitate European tyranny abroad
rather than condemn it (1: Letter #6, 55). The metaphor of the rising
and setting sun only underscores this irony, for instead of foretelling
the ultimate triumph of western power, it seems to predict its eventual
collapse in the "setting" of the western sun, however "glorious" that
setting might be.

In *Letters from the South* Paulding also uses the format of the
tour to bring in two other favorite themes: the superiority of the
American tour over the European Grand Tour and the problem of

British travelers who misrepresent the United States and its people in their travel books. The first, which will recur in both *The New Mirror for Travellers* and "Childe Roeliffe's Pilgrimage," is a response to the growing popularity of the Grand Tour for Americans in the early nineteenth century. Now, with the conclusion of the recent war between England and America and the Napoleonic wars on the Continent, trade and travel between continents had resumed, and touring England, France, Italy, and other European nations had become popular with those Americans who had both the leisure time and money for touring. Most alarming to writers such as Paulding, it would seem, was the trend for families to send their young men off for the Grand Tour as a finishing touch to their education, for he believed that they returned with a false sense of the inferiority of America, from its fashions and culinary arts to its scenery and institutions. While on tours of their own, whether of the eastern or western United States, other American writers such as Washington Irving and Francis Parkman would later complain of the same problem and offer the same solution as Paulding: the American tour. The picturesque tour, a record of this form of travel, became the logical outlet for such comments.

Paulding comments on the issue through his narrator in *Letters from the South*: "I have often regretted that our young men, whose fortune it is to have leisure, means, and opportunity, instead of gadding into foreign countries, did not sometimes take it into their heads to visit their own. All that is worth knowing of Europe, may be learned from books; and it too generally happens that a visit to the celebrated scenes of antiquity, answers no other purpose than to diminish our enthusiasm, by substituting the impression of a dull insignificant reality, in the place of a glowing picture of the imagination" (2: Letter #31, 82). The narrator recalls the case of one H-----, a parvenu whose son Bobby was sent abroad to acquire the necessary polish of a gentleman. The son returns, having spent all the old man's money, but with nothing more than a superficial sophistication that enables him to become "a person of great distinction in the beau monde." According to the narrator, "So long as this distinction is attained to in society, merely from the circumstance of having been a year or two abroad, it is to be feared that our young men will continue as heretofore, better acquainted with every country than their own; which, of all others, is best worthy of their attention, as of all others it ought to be nearest their hearts" (2: Letter #31, 85-86). On the other hand, one of the advantages foreseen for the "domestic traveller" is, appropriately enough, the discovery of

America's picturesque scenery: "In all the grand and beautiful features of landscape, in variety of scenery, in every thing that constitutes the divinity of nature, this country is equal, and indeed superior, to most; and in no part of the world, perhaps, can the pure admirer of nature be more easily and variously gratified." In this respect the travel book about America written by an American can serve as a corrective to the distorted views reported by foreign travelers and, more important, can give "to his countrymen a picture of themselves" that corrects regional differences based on ignorance and portrays both the "faults" and "virtues" of the American people (2: Letter #31, 87). Paulding himself contributes to this effort in writing *Letters from the South* by offering what he believed was a sympathetic yet clear-eyed view of the South. By recommending domestic rather than foreign travel, he suggested that Americans get to know and love their own country before or instead of going abroad. Both Paulding and other writers who took his advice made a significant contribution towards the creation of a national identity not modeled on that of Europe, nor fragmented by regional differences.

Paulding also takes advantage of the loose format of the picturesque tour and the fact that his narrator in *Letters from the South* is himself on a tour to complain about "the swarms of English tourists that infest our country from time to time" (2: Letter #14, 126). Both British tourists and travelers in general are charged with writing misleading or outright false reports about the United States, a charge he was to repeat and refine upon throughout the next decade, notably in his two major contributions to the Paper War between England and America, *A Sketch of Old England by a New-England Man* (1822) and *John Bull in America* (1825). First, the narrator discusses the general issue of travel writers and travel books both at home and abroad. In a satiric letter on the subject, he tells how a travel writer who knows nothing and has hardly traveled can write a book anyway, padding it out with information culled from encyclopedias. In the "old countries" the "dapper spruce gentleman traveller," as the narrator describes him, has a great advantage over the travel writer in the New World. The first, he argues, "has nothing but what he sees to describe, and nothing but what he thinks and feels to record," whereas someone writing about America "can make a book of travels, good enough for his readers, without either seeing or thinking at all" (2: Letter #25, 36-37). The Knickerbocker writer criticizes British travelers who pretend to write objective reports of their American tours but instead write highly subjective, often disparaging accounts of the New World. "Those literary foreigners who have done us the honour to ride post through our country," he charges, "have supplied the lack of antiquities, and the talent for observation, by resorting to their imagination for facts, and to their memory for good stories and rare adventures" to write highly colored versions of their travels that gullible British readers will snap up and swallow whole (2: Letter #25, 38). Railing at the "ignorance and prejudices" of such writers, he says he would not mind if they pointed out America's faults if they also included her virtues. But they come only to find fault, he writes, and worst of all is their tone: "They begin with a sneer, and end with a calumny." The "consummate arrogance" and "supercilious superiority" of this plague of English tourists is more than he can bear, and Paulding vows "to fire away shot for shot" in this war between English and American writers (2: Letter #33, 107-09).

Finally, in *Letters from the South* Paulding finds a uniquely American use for the picturesque tour when he turns to social criticism to satirize the fashionables at American watering places. Whereas in later works such as *The New Mirror* and "Childe Roeliffe's Pilgrimage" he will satirize both the picturesque tour and tourists headed for the northeastern spas, in this earlier work he skewers only the fashionables themselves. Focusing his satiric eye on Berkeley Springs in Virginia, the narrator notes that this "watering-place" is as fashionable as any, with "almost as great a lack of amusement" as some of the northeastern spas (2: Letter #38, 164). He categorizes the various types of people to be found there, describing each in turn: the belles, among whom he finds the "sentimental lady," the "blue-stocking lady," and the "regular built, systematic, determined, and invincible belles, who go about as roaring lions, seeking whom they may devour"; the matrons, including the "piously scandalous" and those with daughters to offer on the marriage mart; and the few young women whose "exercise of domestic virtues" the narrator admires. Then there are the beaux: gentlemen who neglect the ladies; those who dance attendance on the same; and older men, "spruce bachelors" on the lookout for wives. Paulding adds a few other odd types, but mostly he characterizes the typical fashionables of the spas, satirizing their genteel "airs, graces, paraphernalia, caprices, and elegancies" (2: Letter #38, 164-71). Though the author's satirical tone colors this section of the *Letters*, only in the later works does he sharpen his pen and actually attack what he sees as the vices characteristic of such fashionables when they become picturesque tourists.

Letters from the South offers an early example of Paulding's conventional use of the picturesque tour as a structural device in a travel narrative and as a means of celebrating American landscape. More important, this early work shows the author already experimenting with the genre as a means of correcting distorted foreign views of the United States and of presenting his own ideas about the new nation. *The New Mirror for Travellers* (1828), written over a decade later, presents a more interesting study in his use of this British convention. By the time *The New Mirror* appeared, picturesque travel had become popular in the Northeast among the middle and upper classes, and guidebooks to favorite watering places and tourist attractions proliferated to such an extent that both tourists and guidebooks became ripe targets for satire. Some years later, when Harper was bringing out a collected edition of his works, he described the book as "a quiz on watering places and the Mania for Traveling."[8] Because many readers initially mistook the work for a guidebook, wags christened it *The New Pilgrim's Progress*[9], a nickname suggesting the possibility of reading the book not only as a light-hearted satire on contemporary fashionables but also as a more serious, albeit disguised commentary on the superficial values of this social group.[10] The book evolves from a wickedly funny takeoff on the picturesque tour and tourists of the day to a satire on contemporary social trends.

The New Mirror opens with Paulding calling the reader's attention to new modes of transportation--steamboats, Liverpool packets, and railroads--that have speeded up travel.[11] While decrying the "march of human improvement," he dedicates himself to providing the traveler with instructions on what to take, where to go, and how to behave. But most important of all, he offers "critical and minute instructions, concerning those exquisite delights of the palate, which constitute the principal objects of all travellers of taste" (6). What initially appears to be a straightforward travel guide is revealed in the preface to be aimed, rather, at satirizing the tour guides and tourists themselves. The phrase "gentleman of taste" had become a cliche by this date, referring to a gentleman's exquisite taste in aesthetic matters-- here, scenery. Paulding's work reveals his awareness of the spate of books in the last forty years that had considered the proper education of a man of taste, debated about the various levels of taste, and argued the fine points of defining terms such as "picturesque" and "sublime."[12] But when he promises to instruct readers in "those exquisite delights of the palate," which "constitute the principle objects of all travellers of taste," the reader can expect hilarious results: not content with satirizing the picturesque tour in general terms, Paulding has set out to turn the "gentleman of taste" into a literal gentleman of *taste*. Instead of a scenic tour, then, he produces a gastronomical tour whose noteworthy features will be the foods worth eating and the inns worth patronizing on the "Grand Northern Tour" (8), not the expected scenes of picturesque and sublime scenery of the conventional picturesque tour.

But for what is ostensibly a satire and occasionally a burlesque, a surprising amount of the book involves conventional elements of the picturesque tour, including straightforward description. The contrasting scenes that follow, for example, could be part of any typical tour. Paulding's tourists travel by steamboat up the Hudson River, and after a brief series of anecdotes from the voyages of Hendrick Hudson, ostensibly from the works of "Alderman Janson" (a fictional source much like Irving's Diedrich Knickerbocker), they glimpse the following scenes. The narrator invites the traveler to contemplate "the beautiful world expanding every moment before him, appearing and vanishing in the rapidity of his motion, like the creations of the imagination. Every object is beautiful, and its beauties heightened by the eye having no time to be palled with contemplating them too long." Looking back, the traveler sees the "waters gradually converging to a point at the Narrows," while up ahead, he sees "on one side the picturesque shore of Jersey . . . [and] on the other, York Island with its thousand little palaces." Although there is no evidence that Paulding read Gilpin's works, passages such as this one suggest his familiarity with the English writer's ideas about river travel, as expressed in the *Wye Tour*. Just as Gilpin extolled the "succession of . . . picturesque scenes" presented by the Wye, the traveler in *The New Mirror* admires the scenery along the Hudson River.[13] The various views "by turns allure his attention, and make him wish either that the river had but one side, or that he had more eyes to admire its beauties" (98). Some of this language is fairly hackneyed by the 1820s, but otherwise the writing is accurately descriptive. Certainly the author is attuned to the picturesque point of view that Gilpin had popularized decades earlier.

For example, in a passage following a description of the "sublime bluffs" bordering the Hudson River, Paulding's traveler views the landscape with a well-trained picturesque eye, unconsciously echoing Gilpin's description of the contrasting banks of the Wye: "Contrasting beautifully with this long mural precipice on the west, the eastern bank exhibits a charming variety of waving outline."[14] He admires the "long graceful curving hills," "wood crowned heights," "mingled woods, and meadows, and fertile fields," and "the living emblems of industry; cattle, sheep, waving fields of grain, and whistling ploughmen" (99-100). In these two scenes the use of contrast, an essential element of the picturesque, and the inclusion of domesticated elements such as cattle, sheep, and ploughmen, confirm the picturesque quality of Paulding's description. Significantly, the author advertises the success of American farmers in taming the land and making it productive, thus establishing the pastoral nature of the scene, while at the same time he reassures readers of its picturesqueness. Like other American writers of the time, Paulding finds nothing incongruous about the juxtaposition of farms and scenic beauty. American "industry" recalls the yeoman farmers of Crèvecoeur's and Jefferson's agrarian ideal rather than factories belching smoke. The "march of improvement" Paulding fears and decries is scarcely evident here, except, ironically, in the steamboat on which his narrator travels. To complete the conventional nature of this section of *The New Mirror*, scenes are framed by anecdotes of Hudson's life, as noted earlier, and comments on the region's geology, history, and inhabitants, making this a good example of the kind of material included in a typical picturesque tour of the period.

Elsewhere in *The New Mirror* Paulding satirizes the very elements of the picturesque tour that he takes so seriously in other places, though he generally handles the transition from straightforward narrative to satire deftly enough for the reader to follow his lead comfortably. Skewering guidebooks whose excessive and overbearing descriptions overwhelm the traveler, rendering actual viewing of the scenes almost unnecessary, he recommends that fashionable travelers dispense altogether with scenery and read the guidebook instead, the descriptions of which will be "infinitely superior" to nature's "clumsy productions" (90). Similarly, in "A Tale of Mystery; or The Youth that Died without a Disease," published two years earlier, Paulding satirizes a young gentleman of fashion who consults a guidebook for advice on "reading" the landscape before him.[15] Later in *The New Mirror*, following a lengthy--and generally straightforward--description of various points of interest along the Hudson, Paulding reiterates his advice to the jaded picturesque tourist: "We now approach the

Highlands, and advise the reader to shut himself up in the cabin and peruse the following pages attentively, as it is our intention to give a sketch of this fine scenery, that Nature will not be able to recognise herself in our picture" (114-15). Guidebooks and picturesque tours occasionally exaggerated or rearranged scenery whose composition did not perfectly fit the standards of picturesque beauty. True, William Gilpin had stated that the hand of art could often improve upon nature.[16] But he had never advocated completely ignoring nature in favor of the imaginative verbal or pictorial sketch and would have resisted, as Paulding did, the notion that the picturesque verbal sketch did not need to resemble its original model at all.

In some places Paulding's burlesque of picturesque tourbooks must have struck many a sophisticated traveler--and a few ordinary ones--as very funny, though modern readers may tire quickly of the mock-archaic diction the author affects. In the scene that follows, he begins by invoking the inspiring spirit of the picturesque after the manner of eighteenth-century poets: "Genius of the picturesque sublime, or the sublime picturesque, inspire us! Thou that didst animate the soul of John Bull, insomuch that if report says true, he did once get up from dinner, before it was half discussed, to admire the sublime projection of Antony's Nose [a rock formation in the Hudson Highlands]. Thou that erewhile didst allure a first rate belle and beauty from adjusting her curls at the looking glass, to gaze for more than half a minute, at beauties almost equal to her own. . . . Thou genius of travellers, and tutelary goddess of bookmaking, grant us a pen of fire, ink of lightning, and words of thunder, to do justice to the mighty theme!" (115). By employing inflated language and choosing one of the more absurdly named objects of the traveler on the Northern Tour, Paulding satirizes the jaded picturesque tourist (here, an Englishman) whose appetite for food was stronger than his taste for landscape beauty, and he mocks society women whose egotism leads them to think that their own beauty eclipses that of the passing scenery. He had made the same criticism earlier in "A Tale of Mystery," in which a group of "gay butterflies of fashion" traveling up the Hudson to the springs reveals the same sort of egotism satirized in *The New Mirror*. One spoiled young beauty in particular spends the entire voyage pouting over the unromantic scenes that fail to live up to her inflated expectations.[17]

Elsewhere Paulding satirizes conventions of the picturesque tour by pointing out that it's not always the scenery that draws tourists but the presence of the fashionables who frequent some of the popular stops on the Northern Tour. Of Ballston, a popular spa on the American tour, he writes: "It is very extraordinary, but the first impression derived from the opening scene . . . is that it is the ugliest, most uninviting spot in the universe" (218). Arguing that it is really "beautiful damsels" that attract the eye, Paulding undercuts the reader's expectation of picturesque scenery with the following satirical comment on Ballston's less than scenic views: "If the marshes were only green meadows, dotted with stately elms; the sand hills richly cultivated with fields of golden wheat, and stately corn, waving its green ribbons to the breeze; the muddy brook a pastoral, purling river; the pine trees stately forests of oak and hickory, and their stumps were a little more picturesque, neither Ballston or Saratoga, need be ashamed to show themselves any day in the week, not excepting Sunday" (219). Since travelers are apparently not touring for the sake of the scenery, the author offers some pertinent advice: a ten-chapter "system of rules and regulations" (220) on proper behavior for everyone from young ladies to aging bachelors at the popular watering places on the Northern Tour.

The most obvious and certainly the most humorous way in which Paulding satirizes the conventional picturesque tour is his insistence on picturing "gentlemen of taste" not as tourists whose knowledge of the picturesque is faultless, but as travelers whose pursuit of great culinary experiences is second to none. In the preface to *The New Mirror* the author states that his book will offer detailed instructions on the pleasures of dining on the Northern Tour. Unlike Gilpin, who had described the principal object of the picturesque tour as the discovery and enjoyment of picturesque beauty,[18] Paulding argues humorously that it is really the "exquisite delights of the palate, which constitute the principal objects of all travellers of taste" (6).

Opening the travel book, then, with a few brief comments on sights to see in New York City, the start of the Northern Tour, Paulding gets right down to business and boasts of the city's "consummate institutions for cultivating the noble science of gastronomy." What follows is a mouth-watering catalog of American specialties that rivals some of Washington Irving's feasts: "There too will be found canvass backs from the Susquehanna; venison from Jersey, Long Island and Catskill; grouse from Hempstead Plains; snipe from the Newark meadows; and partridges from Bull Hill; which, if the gourmand hath never eaten, let him despair. Then as for fish! O for a mouth to eat, or to utter the names of the fish that flutter in the markets of New York, silently awaiting their customers like so many pupils of Pythagoras" (11-12). With rhetorical flourishes worthy of Geoffrey Crayon salivating over the joys of a bountiful banquet, Paulding catalogs the many delicious varieties of fish. As his muse inspires him to greater and greater poetic heights, he exclaims, "O most puissant and imperial oyster," concluding that the visitor who leaves New York without sampling these delights "has traveled in vain" (12-13). Later, playing on the accepted theory that one responded to beautiful scenery with pleasure, to the picturesque with delight or astonishment, and to the sublime with awe or terror, the author satirizes the picturesque tourist by describing the effect of a sublime prospect upon his appetite: "The stomach expands with the sublimity and expansion of the prospect, to a capacity equally sublime," he writes. As further evidence of this phenomenon, the narrator cites the case of a "sickly young lady" who learned to "discuss venison for breakfast like an alderman" (145) on her travels. Lest readers take him too seriously, the writer introduces a traveler whose dyspepsia acquired on a recent Grand Tour (of the continent) proves him worthy of emulation as the quintessential "gentleman of taste." The letter that follows, full of references to the most superficial European culture (opera dancers!) and, of course, digestive difficulties resulting from overindulgence, reveals this gentleman traveler as one of the empty-headed, morally deficient sophisticates Paulding abhors (15-21). Even in the most apparently digressive sections of *The New Mirror*, such as this one, the author seldom fails to bring his narrative around to a pointed satire of the fashionables whose aimless, vaguely immoral lives and whose aping of European decadence he deplores.

Paulding also satirizes the fashionables who took up picturesque touring in the 1820s and '30s by focusing on their tendency to praise Europe at America's expense. Just as Colonel Culpeper represents the voice of common sense and conservatism in *The New Mirror*, Stephen Griffen, another member of his traveling party, is the young man whose travels abroad have qualified him as a voice of pseudo-sophistication and modern manners. Called "Signior Maccaroni" by the Colonel (59), Griffen brags that he "got rid of all my home bred prejudices" on the European tour (20). "I brought home a great number of clever improvements," he writes, "to wit, a head enlightened with a hundred conflicting notions of religion, government, morals, music, painting, and what not; and a heart divested of all those vulgarisms concerning love of country, with which young Americans are apt to be impestered at home" (19-20). Lucia Culpeper, the Colonel's niece, criticizes Griffen for his imagined superiority: "He wont let me admire any thing in peace," she complains. "The moment I do so, he comes upon me with a comparison with something in Paris, Rome, or London, which goes near to accuse me of a total want of taste. If you believe him, there is nothing worth seeing here, but what comes from abroad" (57).

Unwarranted criticism of America offends Paulding's pride in the young nation. In the numerous sections of *The New Mirror* in which the narrator's and author's voices are essentially one, he encourages nationalism by highlighting the stops on the northern tour that would appeal to the patriotic tourist. Since the United States fought and won two wars against England, a major world power, in the previous half-century, there were plenty of examples of its people's courage, daring, and fortitude available to the writer. Taking advantage of the tour's emphasis on the associations connected with picturesque beauty in a particular location, Paulding finds in the nexus of landscape and history the means to celebrate America's past military triumphs over a tyrannical foe and offers heroes of earlier wars as models for young Americans growing up in less heroic times. Stops at Tarrytown and Saratoga provide the author with precisely the right materials for achieving these goals. At Tarrytown, where Paulding grew up, "three honest lads of Westchester" (one of whom was Paulding's first cousin) captured the British spy Major André, winning admiration for their courage during wartime. The narrator recounts the story of the spy's capture in detail, emphasizing the Americans' valiance in withstanding the British spy's protestations of innocence and attempts at bribery until he was tried and hanged. In the introductory comments to the story the narrator emphasizes the "romantic interest" attached to the place where Major Andre was captured, recommending Tarrytown as a worthwhile stop on the tour. In spite of the complex nature of the case--and partly in defense of the integrity of his ancestor--Paulding recommends the subject for future poetic and dramatic treatment, lamenting that previous attempts at converting history into literature distorted the heroic nature of the three militiamen involved. With the author's patriotic convictions coloring his own presentation of the story, *The New Mirror* demonstrates how future writers might use the material for shaping the national consciousness by celebrating the heroes of recent conflicts. The length of the story of Major Andre's capture (about half a dozen pages) argues for its importance to the author. Moreover, given the superficial qualities of some of the main characters in *The New Mirror*--notably Stephen Griffen, the much traveled fop--Paulding may well have intended the "three young volunteers" to serve as role models for young Americans who were growing to maturity after similar opportunities for heroism in the wars for independence were past (103-09).[19]

Paulding emphasizes the patriotic value of another stop on the "Grand Northern Tour": Saratoga, a fashionable spa. The narrator suggests numerous excursions in the area for the tourist, particularly "the famous field of Saratoga, on which the key stone of the arch of our independence was raised." Arguing for the historical value of the place, where a major battle with the "English invaders" was fought and won, he recommends that a monument "be erected to commemorate the triumph of free soldiers" (289). Such a monument would attract even more tourists, further establishing Saratoga as a stop worth visiting on the tour of New York and New England described in *The New Mirror*. John Sears has shown that places like Niagara Falls came to represent shrines for travelers on a pilgrimage in search of picturesque beauty, with their aesthetic value transmuted into a quasi-religious experience.[20] So too historical sites from previous wars--the French and Indian War, the Revolution, and the War of 1812--attracted travelers interested in more than just scenic beauty. Places such as Saratoga or, for example, Stony Point, where a British fort was captured by General "Mad Anthony" Wayne, became part of the American tour because of their historical and patriotic associations. Paulding makes this point clear in his comments on the second site. Since the ruins of the fort remain visible, the narrator suggests that readers who wish to appreciate properly the heroism of the general's feat must actually see the site for themselves, thus encouraging tourists to walk in the ghostly tracks of a hero of earlier times and, perhaps, to emulate such heroes. And though the historic field at Saratoga lacks a monument to past heroism, Stony Point has already acquired one: an "ornamental lighthouse" designed "to accommodate the lovers of the picturesque," as the narrator puts it. This "beautiful superfluity" is treated ironically by the narrator, who may consider, however, that half a monument is better than none (113-14).

The New Mirror's inclusion of numerous historical sites on the northern tour and the narrator's comments on their historical significance together argue that Paulding found the picturesque tour a genre well suited for the expression of implicitly political ideas. More important, he clearly considered the tour an appropriate, certainly useful vehicle for the propagation of his patriotic ideals. He could not have found more fertile soil for such seeds, for in spite of the satirical nature of the book, *The New Mirror* would likely encourage further tourism, and enlightened travelers, guidebooks in hand, would in the future see more than an empty field at Saratoga or a ruined fortress at Stony Point. Their imaginations fired by Paulding's patriotic prose, they would see thousands of British soldiers surrendering their flag or a heroic Revolutionary general capturing an enemy fort. Equally important, if these tales of past valor worked their magic, travelers young and old might be inspired to emulate the heroes of an earlier day and maintain the ideals of that first generation of American citizens.

Paulding demonstrated capably in *The New Mirror* that a travel narrative modeled on the picturesque tour could serve several purposes at once. In spite of the occasionally uneven tone of this multi-purpose genre, it successfully described and celebrated the native landscape, urging Americans to visit places important in the nation's history. At the same time, the picturesque tour and guidebook satirized tourists, fashions, and popular spas, and criticized citizens who traveled abroad and then returned to deride others for their outmoded ideas. Even more important to the nationalistic author, these themes were, implicitly or explicitly, patriotic. Tourists visiting places connected with important American victories felt a renewed sense of pride in America's past and faith in her future as a strong, independent nation. Even readers who never left their comfortable firesides could imagine the historic sites Paulding described, often in great detail, and could take pride in the heroic men and women whose stories he told in the book. Yet in spite of the modest popular success of *The New Mirror*, its odd mixture of fiction (the letters of the fictitious Colonel Culpeper and family) and nonfiction, and its references to long-forgotten figures and fashions limit interest in it today. A tale published four years later, however, offers a more successful treatment of similar issues and successfully gains and holds the modern reader's interest. "Childe Roeliff's Pilgrimage" and *The New Mirror* share enough similar characters, scenery, and themes that the earlier work reads almost like a rough draft for the latter.

Written for *Tales of Glauber-Spa*, edited by William Cullen Bryant, "Childe Roeliff's Pilgrimage" is much shorter and more focused than *The New Mirror*. As a result, it is both more successful as a work of literature and better at satirizing its subjects than the earlier work. In this tale Paulding grafted sentimental fiction onto the picturesque tour and produced an occasionally awkward but frequently humorous social satire that only loosely parodied Byron's "Childe Harold's Pilgrimage." The title character is Roeliff Orendorf, who is similar in temperament and conservatism to *The New Mirror*'s Colonel Culpeper. Orendorf is a New Yorker who, "having got rich by a blunder," finds he doesn't know how to spend all his money.[21] He tries spending it on literature, art, and music, but when his wife is seized with a "mania for travelling" the problem of how to spend their money is solved. Although his wife hints that she would really prefer a trip to Paris, she compromises on a tour to Canada after being assured that America's northern neighbor is really a foreign country (115-16). Childe Roeliff's "pilgrimage," then, is not a self-imposed exile from his native land, like the pilgrimage of Byron's poem, but a typical tourist's pilgrimage to the popular sites on the American Grand Tour. Accompanying the Orendorfs on their trip are Minerva, their spoiled, pretty daughter (a character like Lucia Culpeper), and their nephew, Julius Dibdill (like Stephen Griffen), a fop whom Roeliff considers a suitable beau for his daughter and heiress. The family group leaves for Albany by steamboat in the early summer, in the course of their trip frequently encountering Reuben Rossmore, a worthy young man whom Minerva favors.

Traveling by carriage to Saratoga Springs, the family plans to admire picturesque beauty along the way, but as Paulding points out several times, the speed of modern travel prevents them from appreciating the scenery (121). Most of the tale's satire, when not aimed at the foppish Dibdill, who has been corrupted by his European travels, is directed at a group of "picturesque hunters" who travel on board the steamboat with the Orendorfs. These fashionables complain constantly about the slow pace of the boat, wishing they could be at their next destination. In such haste to reach the next stop, they miss its beauties once they do arrive and begin complaining about reaching the next place. Paulding comments: "The day was of a charming temperature; the sweet south wind gently curled the surface of the lake, which gradually expanded to a noble breadth, and all nature invited them to share in her banquet. But they turned from it with indifference, and were continually yawning and complaining of being 'tired to death'" (162-63).

As he implies by his criticism of "picturesque hunters," in "Childe Roeliff's Pilgrimage" Paulding uses the picturesque tour for a

unique purpose, one not seen before in American fiction: The responses
of his characters to picturesque scenery reveal character and, more
important, serve as a measure of their integrity and patriotism. A
classic example of this occurs on the way to Lake George, where the
party encountered "a fine fruitful and picturesque country" along an
untraveled route. The different responses of the main characters serve
to characterize each of them: innocent, forthright Minerva and Reuben
respond to the scenery "with sympathetic delight"; the pseudo-
sophisticated Julius Dibdill "lug[s] in a comparison with some scenery
on the Rhine" and pities "those unlucky wights who . . . could admire
the homely charms of an American landscape"; the self-centered Mrs.
Orendorf chats with other society women; and Childe Roeliff, tired and
bored, "fell fast asleep" (133). Later, confronted with the magnificent
scenery of Lake Champlain, the author is moved to speak of God's
hand in creating the world, an appropriate response to natural
sublimity. In contrast, the unimpressed "picturesque-hunters" are "tired
to death" of the sublime and long for the next stop on their tour,
revealing the shallowness of their character. Unlike those tourists,
Minerva and Reuben respond deeply to the view: They are "abstracted"
from the present and "their spirits communed together in the luxury of
silence" (165).

Sometimes a mutual response to picturesque beauty reveals an
unspoken sympathy between two characters, developing, in this case,
the love relationship between them. The author reveals Minerva and
Reuben's growing love, for example, largely by showing their
sympathetic response to the same scenery. On the way to Lake George
one picturesque view elicits the following comment: "At sight of this
charming scene Reuben and Minerva exchanged looks of mutual
pleasure, indicating that sympathy of taste and feeling which forms one
of those imperceptible ties which finally bind two hearts together, and
constitute the basis of the purest species of youthful love" (134). Few
writers use responsiveness to picturesque scenery as a measure of
character. In examples such as this, it becomes clear how far American
writers have taken what began as a relatively simple love of landscape
in the picturesque tour and developed it into a complex vehicle for
developing character and, more significantly, for promoting
nationalism. British tours such as Gilpin's mentioned historical spots of
interest along the way. But, eager to establish the cultural and political
identity of their young nation, and with the world's eyes trained on
them, American writers of the early nineteenth century developed the

nationalistic implications of such references to the fullest.

In "Childe Roeliff's Pilgrimage" Paulding uses the format of the picturesque tour to reveal his strong sense of pride in America and to argue that Americans ought to feel a similar patriotism, a theme he returns to throughout his career. In his own voice and through the characters Reuben Rossmere and Dibdill, Paulding makes a clear connection between the picturesque tour and nationalism in this tale in two ways. First, the tour offers an opportunity for the author to celebrate American scenery through patriotic characters such as Minerva and Reuben, who admire "the homely charms of an American landscape," while criticizing fops such as Dibdill who disparage it in favor of European scenery (133). During a stop for dinner while traveling in the Hudson River Valley, for example, Minerva suggests that the party walk to a nearby falls. Dibdill disdains viewing an American falls since he has already seen superior ones in Europe, preferring to check into the quality of the dinner fare instead. But Minerva and Reuben are rewarded for their hike with "one of the finest scenes to be found in a state abounding in the beautiful and sublime of nature" (135). With a deft compliment to his native state, Paulding turns an ordinary trip to a local landmark, a conventional element of a picturesque tour, into praise for those who admire America's (here, New York's) scenic beauty and criticism of those who dare to disparage it. Later in "Childe Roeliff's Pilgrimage" the group steams across Lake George, one of the most picturesque lakes in the country as well as one of its most famous in history and legend. The steamboat's slow pace allows the travelers "an opportunity of almost studying the beautiful scenery of the lake," reinforcing their role as picturesque tourists and giving the author the chance to describe that scenery.

More important, though, is Paulding's interpretation of the scene: "It was a rare and beautiful scene, such as seldom presents itself to travellers in any region of the peopled earth, and such as always awakens in hearts disposed to love thoughts, feelings, and associations which cannot fail to attract and bind them to each other in the ties of mutual sympathy and admiration" (159). Reiterating his notion that a sympathetic response to scenery brings people together, the author mentions the scene's unique beauty. As in a classic picturesque tour, he emphasizes not the scenery itself, but the observers' response to it. Among other things, Lake George's picturesqueness engenders "associations" in their hearts, though Paulding does not enumerate those associations. The well read or traveled reader, however, would be expected to fill in the blank here, recalling various historical events associated with the lake.

Travelers could also turn to their guidebooks for help. When G.M. Davison's *Traveller's Guide* recommends an excursion to Lake George, for example, the author suggests that "the interest which is excited from an association of many important historic events" will add to the traveler's enjoyment of the lake's picturesqueness. The *Traveller's Guide* notes some of the events associated with the area. Tourists might visit nearby "Bloody Pond," the site of three different battles between French and British forces on one horrendous day in 1755, or they might plan an excursion to the ruins of Fort William Henry near the lake's southern shore, the site of the Indian massacre of the British commemorated in Cooper's *The Last of the Mohicans* a half-dozen years before Paulding's tale appeared. Other historic attractions recommended by Davison's guide include the popular Ticonderoga, whose importance during the French and Indian War and Revolutionary War is underscored; Diamond Island, once the site of a "military fortification"; and the "mouldering ruins" of Fort George.[22] There is no evidence that Paulding knew Davison's *Traveller's Guide*, but a general reference to "Travellers' Guides" in "Childe Roeliff's Pilgrimage," along with his recommendation of Spafford's *Gazetteer* in *The New Mirror*, argues for the author's knowledge of similar guidebooks of the period that offered advice about where to go and what to see on the American Grand Tour (163).[23] Although Paulding himself does not detail the historic sites located on Lake George, he clearly expects his more sensible and patriotic tourists--Reuben and Minerva--to know them and appreciate their significance, just as he expects his readers to be responsive to the lake's historical associations. The importance of such historic sites in stimulating patriotism in the tourist is explored later in the tale when the travelers visit Lake Champlain.

In "Childe Roeliff's Pilgrimage" the picturesque tour also proves useful as a narrative vehicle for the author's nationalism through Paulding's criticism of Dibdill, who is a foil for the patriotic Reuben Rossmere. Because Dibdill arrogantly believes that his travels on the Continent have fitted him to comment on America's inferiority to all things European, he receives the brunt of the author's satire throughout the tale, just as Stephen Griffen in *The New Mirror* is satirized for similar reasons. In a letter to "Count Rumpel Stiltskin," an imaginary correspondent, Dibdill describes the unhappy results of travel abroad:

"One of the great disadvantages of foreign travel is, that it unfits one
for the enjoyment of any thing in one's own country, particularly when
that country is so every way inferior to the old world." Dibdill
disparages "this vulgar republic," which, he argues, "seems in a fair
way of debauching the whole world with her pernicious example of
liberty and equality" (128). That Dibdill cannot be "bamboozled" into
admiring anything American and, more important, that he disparages
its ideals reveal not only his superficiality, but also the dangers of his
shallow-mindedness. Through the examples of Griffen and Dibdill
Paulding warns readers that when America's native sons travel abroad
their clear-eyed vision may become clouded in the shadowy world of
European culture and morality, or they may become corrupted outright
by Old World immorality. This notion prefigures the fascination of
later writers such as Hawthorne and James with the moral struggles of
young Americans abroad, though Paulding's characters lack the
emotional intensity and intellectual complexity of a Miriam or an Isabel
Archer.

Furthermore, during the critical decades after the
Revolutionary War and the War of 1812, an American's speaking out
against liberty and equality, the keystones of New World freedom, is
equivalent to siding with European restrictions on individual liberties
and setting up a tyrannous king in place of a democratic president.
Thus even the most off-handed of Dibdill's snide remarks about his
native land resonate with meaning for patriotic Americans of Paulding's
day and require careful reading today to recognize their significance.
In a fictional work such as "Childe Roeliff's Pilgrimage," however, the
author maintains his light tone by never allowing Dibdill's remarks to
be taken too seriously by the group. When the ladies of the group look
forward to "banqueting on the picturesque" at Lake George, for
example, Dibdill cries: "I who have seen the Lago Maggiore, and the
Isola Bella-- . . . and I who have luxuriated at the Cafe Hardy on
turbot a la creme et au gratin--I to be bamboozled into admiration or
ecstasy by Lake George and its black bass! . . . forbid it, heaven!"
(131). And no one except Reuben Rossmere, who is a bit of a prig, it
must be admitted, takes offense at Dibdill's posturing.

In addition to using characters' love of native landmarks as a
measure of patriotism, Paulding brings nationalism into the fictional
picturesque tour in a second, more important way by showing that
American scenery is full of associations with past moments of national
glory, contrary to the laments of those writers who claimed that

America lacked the "storied and poetical associations" necessary for literary endeavors.[24] Paulding's linking history and scene in "Childe Roeliff's Pilgrimage" recalls Byron's emphasis upon the historical associations of landscapes in "Childe Harold's Pilgrimage," where, however, the protagonist, who is exiled from his native land, celebrates various peoples' victories over tyranny and commemorates British battles in the ongoing wars against despotism on the continent. Paulding takes his tale to Lake George and Lake Champlain to discover America's own historical sites. Reuben, for example, finds the stagecoach ride between the lakes interesting because they provided an important supply route during the French and Indian War, in which his grandfather had fought. Later, at Lake Champlain, the ruins of Fort Ticonderoga enable the author to explore the connection between scenery and history, with important implications for the nation's future in the latter. "There are few more grand and interesting scenes in the wide regions of the western world than old Ticonderoga," Paulding states, continuing: "Ennobled by nature, it receives new claims and a new interest from history and tradition; it is connected with the early events of the brief but glorious career of this new country." This connection, as the author describes it, provides the associations that make a picturesque scene more than just a pretty picture for the tourist. Ticonderoga's "extensive, massy, picturesque ruins" remind the traveler of the nation's glorious past and, by implication, since the country is so "new," suggest its equally glorious future (161).

A stop at Ticonderoga offered Paulding the sort of iconography any well read tourist of the early nineteenth century would recognize. As Dennis Berthold has demonstrated, Ticonderoga was "an icon of the American past unrivalled for historic significance and scenic beauty." Descriptions of well known views of Ticonderoga, whether of Mount Independence or of the fort's ruins, would be familiar to readers from paintings and engravings by Henry Reinagle, William Guy Wall, and Thomas Cole, and in Dwight's guidebook *The Northern Traveller*. These works appeared before Paulding's tale, one in *The Analectic Magazine*, a popular journal for which the author himself had written.[25] Paulding could rely upon his readers' familiarity with these pictorial images, which gave him a kind of shorthand with which to convey his nationalistic message to the reader. A brief sketch of Ticonderoga alone might have conveyed this meaning successfully, but the author's interpretation of the scene ensures that the reader will follow his reading of it completely.

Paulding makes the most important connection between history and scenery towards the end of the tale when he takes his characters through Lake Champlain to the Bay of Saranac, just before the group enters Canadian waters. With a full moon in the early evening, the setting is romantic, though the author scarcely bothers to describe it in detail. The Bay of Saranac, he states, is "scarcely less distinguished for its beauty, and for more renowned in history" than the city of Burlington, which they had visited earlier. Hence the author focuses on the bay's historic connections rather than its visual beauty, supporting Berthold's argument that visual interest is sometimes subordinated to historic associations in a picturesque scene, particularly in American writing.[26] Since Paulding develops the Bay of Saranac's historic associations in some detail, it is worthwhile to look closely at what he hoped to accomplish in "Childe Roeliff's Pilgrimage" with what becomes, in the tale, a lengthy digression. At first the author simply states: "It was here that the gallant McDonough, now, with his famous contemporaries Decatur and Perry, gone to immortality, won laurels that will never fade while the grass is green on the bank that overlooks the bay, or the water runs in the Saranac River" (172). In highly poetical language Paulding states McDonough's connection to the scene on which his characters gaze. The reader is left to fill in the details that complete the allusion: In 1814, American naval forces under the command of Captain Thomas McDonough, then a lieutenant, decisively defeated the British at the Bay of Saranac and seized control of Lake Champlain. According to an article written by Paulding that appeared only eighteen months after the battle, the American public had feared that a British victory on Lake Champlain would lead to the penetration of enemy forces into the state of New York and possibly to a disastrous loss of the entire state. The unexpected victory "turned their gloomy anticipations into triumphant rejoicings," wrote Paulding, and "Every soul slept in peace that night, and many a prayer . . . was breathed for Macdonough, and his gallant associates, who had thus saved the hopes of the peaceable farmer, and freed his innocent folds from probable plunder and devastation." In addition, the victory "derived a peculiar and picturesque character" from the fact that the naval battle took place "in sight of two hostile armies" and "in the view of thousands of people, who watched in breathless anxiety the result of a struggle that was to decide whether they were to be driven from their homes in beggary, or remain in the peaceable enjoyment of their firesides." With the very hearthsides of the American people threatened, the nationalistic author assures the reader that "the victory was greeted by the shoutings of multitudes."[27] Here is war as spectator sport, with the spoils of war--the lush, productive countryside--in full view of the enemy. Presumably the American navy fought all the harder to protect their native land from despoliation by the British.

What is the intended effect of this reference on Paulding's characters, Reuben and Minerva, and on the reader? Two additional comments in the tale clarify the author's intentions. First, he notes that both characters were known to "these distinguished men" (McDonough, Stephen Decatur, and Commodore Oliver Hazard Perry); Reuben, moreover, knew them "intimately." Second, Paulding develops the brief mention of Decatur, whose military exploits had virtually nothing to do with the Bay of Saranac, into a paragraph-long digression that includes a reference to yet another military hero, David Porter. In the first case, Reuben and Minerva's close acquaintance with these heroes is used to bring in comments on their physique and character, some of which might be known only to intimates of a great man in the days before photography and television. The romantic Minerva cries, "'What a striking figure was McDonough!'" To which Reuben replies, "'And what a sweet, mild, yet manly expression was in the blue eye of Perry!'" These two young men were "united in glory" and "united in death, in the flower of their age," according to the author (172).

What, then, does Paulding emphasize in his characters' description of McDonough and Perry? They were known for the "simplicity" of their character and their mildness, yet both were "manly" too. Both McDonough and Perry were naval heroes who won important victories over the British during the War of 1812. (Perry's victory came during the battle of Lake Erie in 1813.) Sweet, mild, manly, striking: These are heroes for a new age, for a new nation. Paulding makes this point clear in the biography of McDonough in *The Analectic*. Speaking of many of the naval officers who distinguished themselves during the War of 1812, he writes: "They seem, like this country and every thing in it, bearing the stamp of vigorous youth, and promising yet more than they have ever yet performed."[28] Since many of the naval heroes of the War of 1812 were indeed young men, the author's hope of future greatness from McDonough and others was not unfounded; he was not to know then, as his characters state in "Childe Roeliff's Pilgrimage," that McDonough, Decatur, and Perry were all to die young, their future promise unfulfilled.

In short, these three naval heroes could provide excellent role models for young people of the new republic who, by the early 1830s, when this tale was published, had never known first-hand the courage and heroism possible in wartime. Paulding's relatively lengthy dissertation on the merits of Stephen Decatur, whose military exploits had little directly to do with the Bay of Saranac, underscores the importance of these naval men as heroes and role models for Reuben and Minerva and, more important, for readers of the tale. After the high praise accorded McDonough and Perry, the reader is almost surprised to hear that though "'Both were of a high class of men, but they neither of them equalled Decatur.'" Reuben, who "'knew him well,'" had found Decatur's character worthy of study; unspoken until the end is the assumption that the reader may benefit from the character analysis that follows. Decatur, Reuben declares, is "'one of the few-- the very, very few great men I ever met with,'" although, as he avers, "'a truly great man is a rare production.'" Through the first part of Reuben's speech, Paulding's style is worth noting. Reuben speaks in broken phrases set off by dashes that underscore the rareness of the phenomenon that was Decatur. For example, Reuben states: "'He was one of the few--the very, very few great men I ever met with.'" The dramatic pause before the verb complement, along with the use of repeated intensifiers, creates tension in the sentence and in the reader, a tension that is mitigated once during Reuben's speech by the young lady's pleased response to her wooer's addressing her as "'dear Minerva'" (172-73).

The gist of Reuben's comments on Decatur appears in one long, perfectly balanced sentence that reflects the balance Paulding admired in the naval hero's life. He writes: "'Such was Decatur: he was not merely a brave man--I might almost say the bravest of men-- but he was a man of most extraordinary intellect, a statesman as well as a warrior; one who, like David Porter, could negotiate a treaty as well as gain a victory; one who could influence the most capacious minds by his eloquence and reasoning, as easily as he quelled the more weak and ignorant by his authority and example.'" Reuben notes that had Decatur lived longer he would have distinguished himself in a civil career, too (173). The salient feats of Decatur's distinguished military career are all here, but concealed behind generalizations that to a modern audience are obscure. Contemporary articles such as Paulding's own "Biography of Commodore Decatur," which appeared in *The Analectic Magazine* in 1813, highlighted the events of Decatur's career that had made him a hero: during the Barbary Wars he had burned the captured American ship "Philadelphia" as it lay in the harbor at Tripoli, an achievement described as "gallant and romantic"; during an attack on Tripoli he had avenged the death of his brother in single combat with a Turkish commander; he had successfully negotiated a treaty with Algiers; and he had captured a British ship during the War of 1812. Paulding's conclusion to the brief biography underscores the significance of Decatur's character and achievements for Americans in the formative early years of the nineteenth century. Describing his deportment as "manly and unassuming," Paulding praised Decatur's "spirit, enterprise and urbanity." In this man, he said, "the polish of the gentleman" was combined "with the frank simplicity of the sailor."[29]

Paulding admires the courage of the hero in combat, but he also admires the modesty and courteous behavior of the true gentleman. As he states explicitly in "Childe Roeliffe's Pilgrimage," these are the qualities in Decatur that the author wants young Americans to emulate (173). While the tale is less specific about the connection between hero and nation, Paulding's biography of Decatur notes that "the gallant achievements" of the naval officers are "the universal topics of national pride and exultation." He concludes the article with the following comment on the importance of these national heroes: "With the aspiring ardour of truly brave spirits, they pay but little regard to the past; their whole souls seem stretched towards the future. Into such hands we confide . . . our national interests and honour; to this handful of gallant worthies is allotted the proud destiny of founding the naval fame of the nation, and of thus having their names inseparably connected with the glory of their country."[30] Trusting in the honor and courage of these young men, Paulding sees hope for the nation's future in them. America's "Rising Glory" will continue.

How do these comments on the historic associations with the Bay of Saranac and on naval heroes of the War of 1812 connect with "Childe Roeliff's Pilgrimage"? If Dibdill is a negative example of a young American aping the Old World dandies, foppish, imitative, and immoral, then Reuben is the moral exemplum whose character is greatly admired. Even without a war in which to prove himself, Reuben Rossmere exhibits the integrity and honor that Paulding admires in Decatur and other naval heroes. Just before the digressive section on naval heroes, in fact, Dibdill has tried to convince Reuben to elope with Minerva. Here Reuben shows his integrity by his refusal to marry the young woman without her father's permission, and just before the two-page commentary on the Bay of Saranac and American naval heroes he promises Dibdill ("upon my honour") not to act further before they arrive at Montreal. The concept of honor is expanded and clarified through the author's commentary on the integrity of the military men. Reuben does, in fact, live up to those ideals later in the tale and becomes Roeliff's favorite--and future son-in-law--by this display of integrity.

What Paulding achieves, then, in "Childe Roeliff's Pilgrimage" is a tale that successfully integrates the literary form of the picturesque tour into fiction as a vehicle for the writer's patriotic ideals. Certainly this work seems to support Dennis Berthold's contention that "patriotism might have produced the picturesque tour, instead of the other way around," here in a literary rather than literal sense.[31] For the tour offered exactly what Paulding needed in his patriotic campaign to show the world--England in particular--what America had to offer, and to remind Americans of their recent heroic past. The convention of tourists traveling from one scenic vista to another gave him the opportunity to present the usual picturesque and sublime landscapes. But Paulding took Gilpin's occasional references to English history a step further by emphasizing visits to sites where he could recall America's recent heroic past and, often, suggest its future glory. In addition, with references to heroes associated with particular sites he could present positive role models to readers of native courage and integrity. Rather than indulge in "servile imitation" of English writers, a habit he deplored in his essay "National Literature," Paulding took an English form and used it to address contemporary American issues of pride and patriotism[32]. In doing so he showed writers that followed him the potential uses of picturesque travel for both fiction and nonfiction, ranging from the humorous social satire of *The New Mirror for Travelers* to the successful tale "Childe Roeliff's Pilgrimage."

For Paulding the link between landscape and history begins as a relatively minor element of the picturesque tour in an early work such as *Letters from the South*, where the narrator visits York and comments on the American triumph there in the War of Independence. The author's growing sense of literary nationalism may have prompted him to expand his use of this connection in later works. Certainly the essay "National Literature," which appeared three years after *Letters from the South*, demonstrates his sharpened awareness of the need for a distinctively American literature. Admiring the American people's "keen recollection of the past" and "rational anticipation of the future," Paulding calls on writers to produce "Rational Fictions" that use native materials, including history. Although he deplored the "habit of servile imitation," using genres familiar from English literature made good sense and developing these into distinctive American forms was even better.[33]

Paulding's use of the conventions of the picturesque tour, then, evolved during his career. In his early writing, *Letters from the South* featured numerous conventional elements of the tour but scarcely modified its form or contents. The focus in *The New Mirror for Travellers* and "Childe Roeliffe's Pilgrimage" is on the picturesque tour, with the fashionables who make the American Grand Tour satirized sharply. Yet Paulding takes aim at more than just fashionable tourists; in both works he suggests that European notions of individual morality and, more broadly, of national character have corrupted the Americans who absorbed these false ideas while on the continental grand tour. Native-born Americans in these works who have not traveled, thus avoiding potential corruption from abroad, are depicted with more conservative, old-fashioned values than their more traveled counterparts. In place of the superficial values acquired abroad, these Americans retain their native integrity, honesty, and love of country; they stand against what the author viewed as rapid and often wrongheaded change that could, in his view, damage or destroy the young nation. In lieu of foppish Europeans, Paulding presents characters who wouldn't trade the scenic Bay of Saranac, the site of a celebrated American naval victory over the British in the War of 1812, for all the glories of the Rhine River. By advocating native values and offering patriotic role models in his fiction and nonfiction, and by choosing as his format the picturesque tour, a British convention that he borrowed and modified for his own nationalistic purposes, Paulding helped a struggling new nation take pride in its past and in the present-day beauties of its landscapes, and he offered readers of his day hope for its future glory, grounded firmly on the values and ideals on which America had been founded.

Notes

1. Larry J. Reynolds, *James Kirke Paulding*, Twayne's United States Authors Series, 464 (Boston: Twayne Publishers, 1984), p. 10.

2. James Kirke Paulding, *Letters from the South, Written during an Excursion in the Summer of 1816*, 2 vols., new ed. (New York: Harper & Brothers, 1835), 1: Letters #2 (pp. 9-25), #10 (pp. 92-95); 2: Letter #38 (pp. 164-71). All subsequent references to this work will be cited in the text by volume number, letter number, and page.

3. Ralph M. Aderman, unpublished manuscript biography of James Kirke Paulding, ch. 3.

4. J. Hector St. John de Crèvecoeur describes the "middle settlements" in "What is an American?" *Letters from an American Farmer and Sketches of 18th-Century America*, ed. Albert E. Stone (New York: Penguin Books, 1981), p. 71.

5. William Gilpin, "On Picturesque Travel," *Three Essays: On Picturesque Beauty; on Picturesque Travel; and on Sketching Landscape* (London: R. Blamire, 1792), p. 47.

6. See Edmund Burke's *A Philosophical Enquiry into the Origins of our ideas of the Sublime and the Beautiful* (1757) and, for a general study of mountains and aesthetics in English literature, see Marjorie Hope Nicolson, *Mountain Gloom and Mountain Glory: The Development of the Aesthetics of the Infinite* (Ithaca: Cornell University Press, 1959).

7. This fairy story appears only in the 1835 edition of *Letters from the South*, having been added since the 1817 edition. Paulding probably encountered the story after the first edition appeared in print and may have added it to underscore the need for associations--particularly patriotic ones--in the American landscape.

8. Letter to T. W. White, 7 December 1835 (?), in *The Letters of James Kirke Paulding*, ed. Ralph M. Aderman (Madison: University of Wisconsin Press, 1962), p. 171.

9. Duyckinck and Duyckinck, *Cyclopaedia of American Literature* . . .

10. Since Paulding himself reports this nickname in an autobiographical essay for the Duyckincks' *Cyclopaedia of American Literature*, one may assume that he approved of or, at the least, felt flattered by the comparison. Paulding reports that he substantially rewrote the biographical entry on himself for the *Cyclopaedia* in a letter to Evert A. Duyckinck, one of its editors, dated 15 October 1854 (Aderman, ed., *Letters of James Kirke Paulding*, pp. 547-48).

11. James Kirke Paulding, *The New Mirror for Travellers; and Guide to the Springs* (New York: G. & C. Carvill, 1828), [p. 3]. All subsequent references to this edition will be cited in the text.

12. Paulding might have read or read about any or all of the following works: Archibald Alison, *Essays on the Nature and Principles of Taste*, 2nd ed., 2 vols. (Edinburgh: Archibald Constable, 1811); Hugh Blair, *Lectures on Rhetoric and Belles Lettres*, 2nd Amer. ed., 2 vols. (Philadelphia: Mathew Carey, 1793); William Gilpin, "On Picturesque Beauty," *Three Essays*; Uvedale Price, *An Essay on the Picturesque* (London: Robson, 1794).

13. William Gilpin, *Observations on the River Wye* (London: R. Blamire, 1782), pp. 7-8.

14. *Wye Tour*, pp. 8-9.

15. James Kirke Paulding, "A Tale of Mystery; or The Youth that Died without a Disease," *The Atlantic Souvenir* (1826), p. 79. (Subsequent references to this short story will appear in the text.) The guidebook referred to here is Horatio Gates Spafford's *A Gazetteer of the State of New-York* . . . (Albany, New York: B.D. Packard; Troy, New York: The Author, 1824).

16. William Gilpin, "On the Art of Sketching Landscape," *Three Essays*, pp. 67-68.

17. James Kirke Paulding, "A Tale of Mystery; or, The Youth that Died without a Disease" (1826), in Melvin Rosser Mason, "The Uncollected Stories of James Kirke Paulding: An Annotated Edition," dissertation, University of Texas, 1958, pp. 75, 79, 81.

18. William Gilpin, "On Picturesque Travel," *Three Essays*, p. 42.

19. See Reynolds, pp. 2-3, for a brief account of the capture of Major André and its influence on Paulding's writing.

20. John F. Sears, *Sacred Places: American Tourist Attractions in the Nineteenth Century* (New York: Oxford University Press, 1989), pp. 5-6; see also ch. 1 (pp. 12-30).

21. James Kirke Paulding, "Childe Roeliffe's Pilgrimage," *Tales of Glauber-Spa*, ed. William Cullen Bryant, 2 vols. (New-York: J. & J. Harper, 1832), 1: 111. All subsequent references to this edition appear in the text.

22. G.M. Davison, *The Traveller's Guide: through the Middle and Northern States, and the Provinces of Canada*, 5th ed. (Saratoga Springs: G.M. Davison; New-York: G. & C. & H. Carvill, 1833), pp. 183-92.

23. Paulding, *The New Mirror for Travellers*, p. 214.

24. Washington Irving, *The Sketch Book of Geoffrey Crayon*, ed. Haskell Springer, in *The Complete Works of Washington Irving*, ed. Richard Dilworth Rust (Boston: Twayne Publishers), 8: 9.

25. Dennis Berthold, "A Literary and Pictorial Iconography of Hawthorne's Tour," in *Hawthorne's American Travel Sketches*, Alfred Weber, Beth L. Lueck, and Dennis Berthold (Hanover, New Hampshire: University Press of New England, 1989), pp. 124-25. See illustrations #23, #24, #25 (pp. 95-97).

26. Berthold, "History and Nationalism," *Hawthorne's American Travel Sketches*, p. 132.

27. [James Kirke Paulding], "Biographical Sketch of Captain Thomas Macdonough," *Analectic Magazine, and Naval Chronicle* 7 (March 1816): 213-14.

28. [James Kirke Paulding], "Biographical Sketch of Captain Thomas Macdonough," p. 215.

29. [James Kirke Paulding], "Biography of Commodore Decatur," *Analectic Magazine* 1 (June 1813): 503-10.

30. Paulding, "Biography of Commodore Decatur," p. 510.

31. Berthold, "History and Nationalism," p. 134.

32. James Kirke Paulding, "National Literature," *Salmagundi*, second series (New York: Harper, 1835), 2: 270.

33. "National Literature," 2: 268-69, 271.

Chapter 4

The Search for Manliness:
Irving and Parkman in the West

Fourteen years apart, Washington Irving and Francis Parkman headed west to sample the excitement of hunting buffalo and traveling through dangerous Indian territory. Each writer also hoped to see western America before its wilderness landscapes fell beneath the plow and its native tribes were civilized by white settlers. The records of their travels, both journals and published narratives, reveal that Irving and Parkman were attracted to the landscapes through which they traveled: the rolling, green prairies, the long stretches of arid land, and the rugged hills and mountains of the Far West. The attention these writers paid to landscape beauty and the extensive descriptions of scenery in their narratives place their published books in the category of picturesque tours, but their travels came to mean more to them than merely occasions for the appreciation of landscape beauty. From their western tours Irving and Parkman gained a renewed sense of their potential as men, and, with certain reservations, they recommended travel to the frontier as a means of rejuvenation for fellow Easterners who for too long had been cut off from the source of power and strength in America, the land itself. In short, Irving's *A Tour on the Prairies* (1835) and Parkman's *The Oregon Trail* (1849) read like conventional picturesque tours, expanding the geographic territory for picturesque travel in the United States, but at the same time the authors' search for manliness in the American West, particularly for Parkman, transforms the tour into something more than a quest for beauty. For these writers the western tour becomes an opportunity to fulfill a quest for renewed physical and spiritual strength. Ironically, *A*

Tour on the Prairies suggests this in spite of the author's satirizing the other men accompanying him, questioning their motives and his own intentions in the West. In *The Oregon Trail* Parkman does not so much satirize others as present himself and his motives ironically, albeit unconsciously so, by finding adventure not in a physical quest for excitement and new experiences, but in a spiritual quest to conquer himself, a quest that drives him nearly to destroy his body in order to find a renewed spirit on the western trail.

In 1832, wishing to renew his feelings for his country's landscapes after seventeen years abroad, Washington Irving set out on a tour of the eastern United States.[1] After traveling south from New York City to Philadelphia, Baltimore, and Washington, Irving headed back to New York, where he traveled by steamboat up the Hudson River to the Catskills. He was accompanied by the Englishman Charles Joseph Latrobe; a young Swiss, the Count de Pourtales; and a German boy, John Schell (all of whom he had met on board ship during his recent Atlantic crossing); as well as his old friend and fellow Knickerbocker James Kirke Paulding. From Boston he and his companions embarked for the White Mountains of New Hampshire, following a typical route of the Northern Tour, up the Saco River Valley to the celebrated Notch. The eager tourists climbed Mount Washington, but were unable to enjoy the famous view, which was obscured by mist.

The group then separated, with Irving returning to New York; in early August he rejoined Latrobe and Pourtales at Saratoga to begin the western leg of their journey. Avoiding cities struck by the 1832 cholera epidemic, the travelers headed for Niagara Falls, where they admired both the American and Canadian views of the falls and explored Goat Island, typical activities for tourists of the period. In his journal Irving gives his impressions of Niagara in brief, noting the "beautiful transparency of the water," with its "drops like chrystal chandolier . . . and foam . . . like snow."[2] There are few comments in this part of the journal on scenery, though Irving's route includes some of the most celebrated scenic beauty in eastern America. Instead, he describes road conditions, hotels, summer sights and sounds along country roads, and only occasionally mentions a particularly "fine view" or "beautiful scenery."[3] These omissions suggest that his attention was not on picturesque scenery except for the more celebrated spots such as Niagara Falls and the White Mountains. Or, Irving might simply have considered many of the minor attractions of the eastern tour overwritten (as indeed they were at this point) and waited for the novel views of the West to take more detailed notes.

Towards the end of August Irving and his friends headed west to Detroit across Lake Erie. A chance meeting on the steamboat with Henry Leavitt Ellsworth, newly commissioned by the federal government to help pacify Indians west of the Mississippi River, led to their decision to join an expedition to explore what is now eastern Oklahoma, then part of the Far West. In a letter to his brother Peter, Irving stated his reasons for the western portion of the trip: "I should have an opportunity of seeing the remnants of those great Indian tribes, which are now about to disappear as independent nations, . . . I should see those fine countries of the 'far west,' while still in a state of pristine wildness, and behold herds of buffaloes scouring their native prairies, before they are driven beyond the reach of a civilized tourist."[4] With the escort of a dozen or more rangers, Irving and his party, traveling on horseback and well supplied with provisions, were hardly roughing it in the West. They were simply, in Latrobe's phrase, "gentlemen in search of the picturesque,"[5] continuing in the tradition of picturesque travel popularized four decades earlier by Gilpin in England and now carried into the American West by Irving and his fellow tourists.

Washington Irving's western travels, as narrated in *A Tour on the Prairies*, fulfill all the conventions of a picturesque tour. Certainly the author looked forward to seeing the picturesque beauties of the West, as he had written his brother, and he enjoyed discovering such beauty throughout the tour and writing about it afterwards. Throughout the published *Tour* Irving reveals a "picturesque eye" attuned to the landscapes that satisfy his wish for such beauty, and he demonstrates his ability to discover and to present artistically picturesque scenes in the West. For example, early in the book he describes the Arkansas River: "It presented a broad and rapid stream bordered by a beach of fine sand, overgrown with willows and cotton wood trees. Beyond the river the eye wandered over a beautiful champaign country, of flowery plains and sloping uplands, diversified by groves and clumps of trees, and long screens of woodland; the whole wearing the aspect of complete, and even ornamental cultivation, instead of native wildness."[6] Although at first reading the passage appears to be little more than ordinary scene setting, as the narrator pauses here on his way across the country north of the Arkansas, a closer look reveals a consciously picturesque scene drawn in the manner of William Gilpin.

The scene's composition follows picturesque guidelines, featuring unity in diversity. The Arkansas River dominates the picture's foreground. Like a skillful artist, the narrator leads the observer's eye back from the river to the distance, where the "beautiful champaign country," stretches across the scene. Note that the trees here grow naturally in "clumps"; in *Remarks on Forest Scenery*, the only work by Gilpin that Irving definitely knew, the Englishman had written that clumps, or small groupings of trees, serve to diversify the distance in a landscape and to connect the wooded sections of the distance to the plain.[7] Still following Gilpin's lead, Irving describes the woodlands as "screens," or long blocks of trees. Other elements in the scene add appropriately picturesque details: the sandy beach further diversifies the scene, willows contribute a classic picturesque element, and the flowers, according to Gilpin, "add to the richness of the whole."[8] Irving's final comment on the scene establishes it as domesticated, not wild, an interpretation his description has stressed with the use of artistic terms and an emphasis upon its picture-like qualities. The reader is almost surprised to learn, in the passage following this description, that near this cultivated area is "the recently deserted camping place of an Osage war party" (22), reminding the reader that the author is, after all, in the western wilderness, not in a gentleman's park.

Comparing Irving's description of the Arkansas River with the original record from his journal offers a glimpse into his method of converting raw material into literature, here, using the technique Gilpin outlined in *Remarks on Forest Scenery*. The English writer had noted that the traveler's "picturesque eye" constantly reshapes the landscape before him into one of picturesque beauty. The imagination of the observer trained in the picturesque, he explained, forms the rough material before him into pictures. The original description of this river reads as follows: "Resume our route[--]come in sight of the Arkansas river and pass frequently thro rich bottom in sight of it. View beyond of beautiful country--looks as if cultivated. Groves, glades, woody upland, willowd [?] shores, Sandy--beaches--[fine] Sunny Look of The Groves."[9] Irving has taken the details from his notes and added more than the "filligree work" his critics charge him with using to color his prose.[10] He has, in fact, recreated the landscape he saw on the western tour, imagining the scene with his trained eye and reshaping it into a picturesque landscape according to Gilpin's established principles.

References throughout *A Tour on the Prairies* to art and

artists, and the author's frequent use of artistic devices, which he picked up from his knowledge of painting and popular painters, serve a more important function in the book than as mere pictorial devices. Irving often calls attention to the artifice in his landscape descriptions here by noting the "hand of art" that shaped them, though the author's eye for a scene is equally important. For example, in the following scene, the narrator reveals a great deal about his descriptive method and, indirectly, his meaning. The passage is worth quoting in full to watch what happens to the narrator.

> About ten o'clock in the morning we came to where this line of rugged hills swept down into a valley through which flowed the north fork of the Red river. A beautiful meadow about half a mile wide, enameled with yellow autumnal flowers, stretched for two or three miles along the foot of the hills, bordered on the opposite side by the river, whose banks were fringed with cotton wood trees, the bright foliage of which refreshed and delighted the eye, after being wearied by the contemplation of monotonous wastes of brown forest.
>
> The meadow was finely diversified by groves and clumps of trees, so happily disposed that they seemed as if set out by the hand of art. As we cast our eyes over this fresh and delightful valley we beheld a troop of wild horses quietly grazing on a green lawn about a mile distant to our right, while to our left at nearly the same distance, were several buffaloes; some feeding, others reposing and ruminating among the high rich herbiage, under the shade of a clump of cotton wood trees. The whole had the appearance of a broad beautiful tract of pasture land, on the highly ornamented estate of some gentleman farmer, with his cattle grazing about the lawns and meadows. (83-84)

The scene is a classic of picturesque composition: the meadow provides a focus at the center, the trees' "bright foliage" contrasts with the "monotonous" forest, the hills in the background serve as a frame, and various groupings of trees serve to diversify the scene.[11] The "enameled" flowers offer another painterly touch.

But where is the narrator ("we") after the first line? He disappears into a disembodied eye that absorbs and transcribes the scene like Emerson's transparent eyeball. Yet unlike Emerson's eyeball, this eye clearly interprets even as it sees and reports the scene, creating an artful, even artificial landscape that lies frozen on the page like a scene captured on canvas. "The hand of art," as Irving calls it, has been busy here in the West, eliminating the wildness in wilderness even before the author's company rides into the scene he pictures. The scene is static, almost lifeless as a painting; nothing moves except a few horses and buffaloes that graze quietly. The animals add both a picturesque element--Gilpin had recommended animals as suitable objects for the picturesque scene[12]--and a pastoral note, but they are scarcely wild. They do not run, charge, or even look fierce; instead they merely graze, like cows on a farm. Furthermore, when Irving describes the herbage as "a green lawn" and "pasture land," he effectively neutralizes any wildness in the picture and civilizes the scene. His final comparison of the western scene to "the highly ornamented estate of some gentleman farmer" suggests that the author has viewed the scene with his picturesque eye and refashioned it with an imagination trained in European models of the picturesque. In *Tales of Adventurous Enterprise: Washington Irving and the Poetics of Western Expansion* Peter Antelyes also views Irving's references to art and artists as more than just an aesthetic device. Such references, he argues, "provide a literary means to civilize the wilderness itself, transform it into a resource that can be cultivated by the rightly aligned imagination." For Irving, "the principal task of the imagination" sometimes was "the taming of the wildness of the West," a task he undertook in the writing of *A Tour on the Prairies*, and one John Seelye describes as an act of "aesthetic imperialism."[13] Even the act of touring *on* the prairies, as the book's title suggests, was an act of imposing civilization upon the wilderness, just as the author's picturesque eye reshaped the landscape even before he ever took pen in hand to describe it in writing.

E.H. Gombrich, in his influential book *Art and Illusion*, discusses the relationship between seeing a landscape as it is and perceiving it in terms of one's own expectations. Artists, or in this case, writers, may reshape what they see according to their particular cultural background or training. Beginning with a familiar schema--here, the picturesque landscape of William Gilpin--artists or writers try to "match" it with what they see. Washington Irving, for instance, schooled in the tradition of Gilpin's picturesque scenery, might look at a scene in the American West and measure it against the expectations born of that tradition. Instead of seeing prairies and wild animals, Irving's visual imagination reshapes what he sees according to the schema, seeing "lawns" instead of prairies and converting the buffaloes to a harmless pastoral element. The work of art that results does not imitate reality but rather involves a complicated process of matching what the artist perceives against the internalized criteria and imaginatively recreating the landscape according to those criteria.[14] This leads to the very sort of "aesthetic imperialism" Seelye suggests, with Irving asserting his power over the West by his manipulation of its landscapes in *A Tour on the Prairies*, through which he asserts his domination over it aesthetically. For writers like Irving and later, Parkman, the process of recreating the landscape aesthetically leads to the same kind of domination and control over the western wilderness that killing wild animals for sport achieves. Destroying the wild in wilderness, the tourist creates order from chaos, converting the West into a vast park for a picturesque tour and changing its wildlife into objects for casual destruction. Needless to say, this very attitude would lead eventually to the decimation and near extinction of the vast buffalo herds by the end of the nineteenth century and, indirectly, to the destruction of most of the native prairie by another form of territorial encroachment, the increasing hoards of emigrants anxious to bring order with houses and crops planted in what once was the untamed West.

The *Tour* shows evidence of Irving's aesthetic reshaping of his materials in other ways. When scenes lack the proper elements of true picturesque beauty, for instance, Irving simply provides them. In the following example, in an otherwise unremarkable landscape the author not only adds a visual focal point but also the requisite associations for true picturesque beauty. Although Irving's journal notes for this passage are not extant, Ellsworth's comments on the scene provide a useful comparison to Irving's version. Ellsworth writes: "In the midst of our revellings on this day, through the praries, and while conversing upon the beauties of the landscape, we descried at a distance, a perfect resemblance of an old Moorish castle in ruins . . . dame nature in her pranks some way, had so arranged the rocks and stones, as to give the representation, of every part, of an citadel tumbling to ruins, and yet leaving all the traces of ancient magnificence--With leave of Mr Irving Doct Holt named it '*Irvings castle*.'"[15]

While Ellsworth's narrative gives a straightforward description of the view, Irving's account draws on the aesthetic of the picturesque to shape the scene:

> After a toilsome march of some distance through a country cut up by ravines and brooks, and entangled by thickets, we emerged upon a grand prairie. Here one of the characteristic scenes of the Far West broke upon us. An immense extent of grassy undulating, or as it is termed, rolling country with here and there a clump of trees, dimly seen in the distance like a ship at sea; the landscape deriving sublimity from its vastness and simplicity. To the south west on the summit of a hill was a singular crest of broken rocks resembling a ruined fortress. It reminded me of the ruin of some Moorish castle crowning a height in the midst of a lonely Spanish landscape. To this hill we gave the name of Cliff Castle. (61)

The narrator offers an element of surprise and adds drama to the scene by describing the landscape as "breaking" upon the travelers. With its vast extent of prairie and unusual rock formation, the scene is characteristic of the West, containing elements of both the sublime and the picturesque, a combination Gilpin also had found interesting, though he had argued that "the *curious*, and *fantastic* forms of nature" were not "the favourite objects of the lovers of landscape."[16]

The only picturesque element lacking in this landscape is that of association, and Irving, newly returned from Europe, provides this, too, with his suggestion that the rock formation resembles a "ruined fortress." Ruins suggest age and decay,[17] and the Moorish castle is particularly appropriate for a traveler who had spent several months in the Alhambra only three years earlier. The exotic element would appeal to readers, who would also be familiar with Irving's *Legends of the Alhambra* (1832) and might feel from this reference that their native land was equal to Spain in landscape beauty. Perhaps the author's modesty compels him to call this "Cliff Castle," but Ellsworth's version rings truer. Since Irving was the most literary and imaginative member of the group, it is likely that he first noticed the resemblance to a castle and that the group named it after him, not with the uninspired "Cliff

Castle." As reported in the *Tour*, this incident offers another example of aesthetic imperialism in which an outcropping of rocks lacks the aesthetic value of a manmade ruin; therefore the tourist/writer simply provides the missing element, imposing his presence on the landscape by reshaping it imaginatively and leaving his mark permanently by giving the landmark his name, though Irving is too modest to do so himself.

Just as Gilpin advocated reshaping a scene, whether by the artist or writer's suggesting associations that are not present or by adding elements to a sketch or verbal description, and he frequently practiced this technique, so too Washington Irving practiced what Gilpin called "a little imaginary finishing," as in the example above.[18] In the *Tour*, however, Irving frequently does not need to add anything to the existing picture, for anecdotes of his travels, romantic tales of Indian life, and stories about his colorful companions on the tour not only provide associations for western landscapes but also fill out the travel book and entertain readers interested in more than picturesque landscape. For example, at one point Irving and his friends come upon "the remains of an old Indian encampment, on the banks of a fine stream." The "moss grown sculls of deer lying here and there" stimulate his imagination, and, at the suggestion of a fellow traveler, he describes the place as once "the camp of some bold Delawares," whose "brief and dashing excursion into these dangerous hunting grounds" is recorded here by the easterner (47). Irving also relates the romantic tale of a group of Delawares who were nearly massacred on the Great Plains. He describes how the besieged Indians "took refuge on the summit of one of those isolated and conical hills which rise almost like artificial mounds, from the midst of the prairies." They were miraculously saved by an enormous eagle, representing their "tutelar spirit" (50). Linking legend to landscape, as Irving does here, creates romantic landscapes typical of the picturesque tour of this period. Such tales would also stir the imagination of armchair-bound readers and might even inspire some to head west to experience the excitement of exploring this territory firsthand.

Irving's depiction of a legend-rich western landscape in the 1830s indicates that his view of America had changed since the publication of *The Sketch Book* over a decade earlier. Consider how, in "The Author's Account of Himself," the narrator recalls his love of travel and frequent "tours of discovery" in America. He describes the New World in glowing terms that argue its unrivalled beauty: "On no country have the charms of nature been more prodigally lavished. Her mighty lakes, like oceans of liquid silver; her mountains with their bright aerial tints; her valleys teeming with wild fertility; her tremendous cataracts thundering in their solitudes; her boundless plains waving with spontaneous verdure; her broad deep rivers, rolling in solemn silence to the ocean; her trackless forests, where vegetation puts forth all its magnificence; her skies kindling with the magic of summer clouds and glorious sunshine--no, never need an American look beyond his own country for the sublime and beautiful of natural scenery."[19] All the same, the narrator perceives American landscape as incomplete: Only "Europe held forth the charms of storied and poetical association." "My native country was full of youthful promise; Europe was rich in the accumulated treasures of age," he states, and consequently, he longs to explore its storied landscapes and lose himself "among the shadowy grandeurs of the past."[20]

But a different attitude toward the American landscape is evident by 1835. While once only Europe seemed to offer the rich associations that were necessary for picturesque beauty and that fulfilled the longings of the tourist, in *A Tour on the Prairies* Irving demonstrates that American landscapes can also offer treasures for the traveler, reassuring those who criticized him earlier in his career for becoming too European and forgetting his American ties.[21] Ruins of Indian camps, Indian legends associated with prairie or mountain, anecdotes about crossing turbulent western streams--all these give New World scenery the requisite associations. Indeed, in the same *Sketch Book* in which Geoffrey Crayon had lamented the lack of associations in American landscape he had depicted Sleepy Hollow and the Catskill Mountains, specific places that suggested the kind of mystery and romance of which the author's native country was capable. In the early 1830s Irving's western tour confirms the nationalistic implications of his earlier work, arguing implicitly that Americans could find picturesque landscapes rich with associations in the West as well as the East. Just as guidebooks had encouraged tourists to include Sleepy Hollow and Tarrytown on their itinerary in the years following publication of *The Sketch Book*,[22] books such as *A Tour on the Prairies* must have led armchair travelers to view the West not as a blank, unstoried landscape but as a land already rich in history, whether colored by the long presence of Native Americans; by the white explorers, trappers, fur traders, and hunters; or by the soldiers and settlers who followed these groups in the nineteenth century. In different ways each group left its visible or invisible mark on the landscape, and each mark had its own story to tell travelers.

The tour on the western prairies emerges for Washington Irving as a means of learning to know and love America, particularly American landscape. His appreciation of his native country grew, leading him to advocate the western tour in *A Tour on the Prairies* for more reasons than the pursuit of picturesque beauty. In the narrative he strongly recommends the benefits of such a tour over the usual continental Grand Tour: "We send our youth abroad to grow luxurious and effeminate in Europe; it appears to me that a previous tour on the prairies would be more likely to produce that manliness, simplicity and self dependence most in unison with our political institutions" (32). As the author himself states here, these are the very qualities young men will need as future leaders of the new nation. Not surprisingly, they are the same qualities that Paulding had praised two decades earlier, writing about American naval heroes of the War of 1812. In his biography of Commodore Stephen Decatur, for example, he had lauded the military hero's manliness, spirit, bravery, and "enterprise." In the same year Irving traveled west, the tale "Childe Roeliff's Pilgrimage" singled out Decatur and other war heroes for the emulation of aspiring young men.[23]

In addition, Irving points out the "high health and vigour" of the rangers who accompanied his group on the western tour and declares: "I can conceive nothing more likely to set the youthful blood into a flow than a wild wood life of the kind and the range of a magnificent wilderness abounding with game and fruitful of adventure" (32). Peter Antelyes reads Irving's western tour as "a satire of western economic expansion," with the author satirizing his fellow travelers for their misadventures on the prairies, yet it is difficult to read Irving's statements here as anything other than straightforward, though idealistic. Although the rangers' ineptitude is often mocked and Pourtales is pictured as a "self-glorifying adventurer," at the same time the narrator seems sincere in his recommendation of the western tour.[24] Evidence from Irving's letters corroborates this view. He recommends the western tour for putting "both mind and body in a healthful tone" (48) because, as he wrote his sister Catharine, he found that the rigors of frontier life put him in excellent health and spirits for the duration of the tour.[25] For a middle-aged man who may have feared he had gone soft physically and mentally during his long sojourn in Europe, a rousing ride on the western prairie must have reassured

the author of his own manliness and courage, even if he did not
encounter any war-like Indians to test his mettle.

The connection between landscape and character Irving makes
in *A Tour on the Prairies* is by no means accidental. In drafts of a
proposed essay on "National Character" written while he was still in
Europe, he describes the effect of landscape on character. The
"impatience of restraint, . . . the restless spirit, speculative turn and
proneness to hyperbole" attributed to Americans, Irving says, may be
traced in part to "the wild scenes through which they pass and the
grand and indefinite scale on which they are accustomed to see natural
objects." Continuing in this vein, he writes: "He who is brought up
among forests whose shade extends, he knows not whither--whose eye
roves over plains of boundless extent--who looks forth upon inland
seas, where no opposing shore is visible; who sees vast rivers flowing
down from he knows not whence, and rolling a world of waters to the
far distant ocean of which he had only heard. . . . surely it is no
wonder that such a one should be speculative and hyperbolic." Irving
attributes his own love of the beautiful and sublime to the early
memories of the Hudson River that had stimulated his imagination.[26]

The idea that national character is shaped, in part, by the
native landscape was not original with Irving but was voiced by other
writers during the first half of the nineteenth century. The clergyman
and lecturer E.L. Magoon expressed a similar attitude in an essay
entitled "Scenery and Mind," which appeared in *Home Authors and
Home Artists; or, American Scenery, Art, and Literature*, to which
Irving also contributed an essay. "The diversified landscapes of our
country exert no slight influence in creating our character as
individuals, and in confirming our destiny as a nation," Magoon writes.
"National intellect," he continues, "receives a prevailing tone from the
peculiar scenery that most abounds."[27] Irving's belief, then, in the
positive effects of the western landscape, particularly on eastern youth,
reflects his and others' view that the natural environment shaped
national and individual character, and *A Tour on the Prairies* illustrates
his belief that a tour of the frontier and the West would engender
republican virtues such as manliness and independence in America's
young men. For Washington Irving, a picturesque tour of the prairies
revived his own love of the American landscape and had a bracing
effect on his physical and emotional health. The published *Tour*
expressed not only the pleasure he and others could take in western
scenery but also his belief in its positive effect on character. Indeed,

the "manliness, simplicity and self dependence" that Irving argued would result from such an experience would be the very qualities Francis Parkman would seek in the West on his own tour in 1846.

At the beginning of *The Oregon Trail* Parkman gives several reasons for heading west. Although both the author and the cousin who accompanied him, Quincy Adams Shaw, were experienced explorers of the northeastern forests, they had never before ventured into the American West. For Parkman, the journey was "a tour of curiosity and amusement" in a previously unexplored territory with the dual purpose of gathering material on the Plains Indians for a later history and helping his cousin regain his health.[28] Ironically, it was the author who was plagued by ill health throughout the tour (mostly caused by dysentery, but also by eye problems), whereas his companion never suffered from anything worse than a bout with poison ivy.

Yet there were additional, unstated reasons for setting off for the Far West. Parkman had come to feel that the New England aristocracy, inheritors of the Puritan tradition, was becoming weak physically and spiritually. He considered this group, of which he was a member, the natural leaders of America. This view is most clearly expressed several years after the Oregon Trail experience in a review of James Fenimore Cooper's works in which he charges that civilization in America is "nerveless and unproductive" because its writers are "weakened by the want of independent exercise."[29] Parkman felt that these Easterners had to find ways to regain their endangered or already lost masculinity, and according to historian George Frederickson, he believed that "only struggle and hardship could strengthen the backbone of the American aristocracy." Since there was no place in the weakened, emasculate East to develop this strength, Parkman turned to the strenuous life of the West to discover the physical and spiritual strength that he lacked.[30] This results in an interesting similarity between *The Oregon Trail* and *A Tour on the Prairies*, since both trips offer opportunities for the authors to prove themselves as men outside the more comfortable lives they lived in the Northeast or in Europe. Ironically, although Irving did not set out with this motive consciously in mind, he extols the rigors of the western tour for its health benefits in his published work and private letters. Parkman, on the other hand, listed improved health as one goal of his tour, but he suffered terribly on the trip; in spite of this, *The Oregon Trail* speaks enthusiastically about the benefits of western travel. Finally, in the West Parkman also sought out "models of manliness" whose energy and vigor would inspire weak Easterners,[31] and indeed the men he admires most on the trail--particularly Henry Chatillon, his guide--are those who possess manliness and courage.

The journey Parkman and Shaw took to the Far West in 1846, recorded in *The Oregon Trail*, began in St. Louis in the spring. Traveling up the Missouri River by steamboat to the frontier areas of Westport and Fort Leavenworth in what is now northeastern Kansas, they headed west over the Great Plains. The journey culminated at Fort Laramie and what the author calls the Black Hills (actually the Laramie Range), where Parkman alone spent two weeks living with the Oglala Sioux. Rejoining Shaw later, he traveled south to join another company for the journey through dangerous Indian territory back east to the settlements.

Much of Parkman's published narrative reads like a conventional picturesque tour, with the author pausing frequently to enjoy (and to point out for future travelers) picturesque and sublime scenery. He describes landscapes in detail and often uses the familiar terminology of the picturesque traveler. Yet unlike Irving, Parkman generally uses fewer of the descriptive techniques Gilpin popularized-- artistic terms, unified composition, diverse elements--that arrange scenery into a picture for the reader. For example, compare his description of the landscape near the Kansas River with Irving's description of the Arkansas River. Parkman recalls the "farms and cabins of the Delawares" along the roadside; "the little rude structures of logs, erected usually on the borders of a tract of woods, made a picturesque feature in the landscape." "But the scenery needed no foreign aid," he adds, "Nature had done enough for it; and the alternation of rich green prairies, and groves that stood in clusters, or lined the banks of the numerous little streams, had all the softened and polished beauty of a region that has been for centuries under the hand of man." Traveling in the springtime, he also comments on budding maple trees and "flowering shrubs unknown in the East," and he describes with pleasure "the green swells of the prairie . . . thickly studded with blossoms" (20-21). While Irving used the narrator's "picturesque eye" to wander over the landscape, composing the scene into a picture, Parkman simply describes the scene without ordering it in any particular way and without framing it like a picture. This scene contains some of the elements of picturesque landscape: the contrast between prairie and grove, streams of water, flowers, and the rough texture of the cabins. The narrator even uses the term "picturesque" to describe the buildings. Yet the second scene lacks the conscious artistry that makes Irving's landscape read like a verbal picture. This difference suggests that although Parkman is knowledgeable about aesthetics, including the familiar categories of the beautiful, picturesque, and sublime, he merely invokes the terms occasionally as convenient labels for western scenery.

But there is a problem with this reading of his landscape descriptions. The emphasis upon landscape in *The Oregon Trail* suggests instead that the author not only looked forward to picturesque scenery on the trip--a hallmark of the picturesque traveler--but that he also paid attention to such scenes on the trail, described them carefully in his journal, and frequently used landscape as more than just setting in the published tour. The description of the Kansas River landscape in the book, for example, appears to be drawn from several journal entries that include enough details for Parkman to create a brief scene specific enough to suggest an actual landscape. The relevant entries read as follows:

> Travelled only eight miles and encamped in a beautiful prairie--abundance of flowers--the borders of the beautiful oak-openings we had traversed--the shrubbery along the course of a little stream--the occasional rich and sunlit groves--and the emerald swells of the vast plain, made a beautiful scene. . . .
> A beautiful day. Travelled slowly through the country of the Delawares. Fine, swelling prairies. Stopped for nooning . . . Resumed our course--very hot--lines of beautiful woods ran along the bottoms, intersecting our road, with invariably a stream running through them . . .
> All half-civ[ilized] Ind. villages in wooded countries are the same thing--straggling paths through woods and underbrush, with here and there a log house--a creek winding through the midst. . . . Some of the scenery--the rich, sunlit, swelling prairies with bordering hills and groves--was very beautiful.[32]

The scene in the book, culled from these three successive journal entries, summarizes the kind of scenery Parkman observed on the journey to Fort Leavenworth and simultaneously comments upon it.

Note that the "rude structures" of Indian dwellings are picturesque only because they are seen at a distance, from which the poverty of the inhabitants is not evident, and because they are suffused with "the same spirit of Sabbath repose and tranquillity as in some New England village" (20). This sight must have been reassuring to the Bostonian half-expecting to be relieved of his scalp anywhere along the "extreme frontier" which, in his words, "seems full of desperadoes."[33]

Two other descriptive passages in *The Oregon Trail* suggest the significance of western landscapes for both Parkman and his narrative and comment indirectly on the problem of the picturesque tourist in the West. For although the narrator pays frequent attention to landscapes, he is not a typical tourist and explicitly sets himself apart from that species in the following statement, warning future travelers about what to expect: "Should any one of my readers ever be impelled to visit the prairies, and should he choose the route of the Platte . . . I can assure him that he need not think to enter at once upon the paradise of his imagination." Tourists, he cautions, should expect "a dreary preliminary, a protracted crossing of the threshold," before reaching the "'great American desert,'--those barren wastes, the haunts of the buffalo and the Indian, where the very shadow of civilization lies a hundred leagues behind him." For the traveler in search of picturesque beauty, the "wide and fertile belt" beyond the frontier "will probably answer tolerably well to his preconceived ideas of the prairie; for this it is from which picturesque tourists, painters, poets, and novelists . . . have derived their conceptions of the whole region. If he has a painter's eye, he may find his period of probation not wholly void of interest." Possible attractions here, he suggests, are the "graceful and pleasing" scenery, extensive plains, undulating green prairie, and countless streams alternating with woods (34-35).

This passage, which appears early in the narrative, suggests an important theme in *The Oregon Trail*: the difference between the naive tourist's expectations of the prairies, founded upon other travelers' accounts, and the reality.[34] Much of the balance of the book, in fact, seeks to correct mistaken notions about the West as paradise (and, not incidentally, about the Indian as noble savage), just as the rest of this passage lists some of the nuisances of travel in the region west of the Mississippi after describing the picturesque landscape imagined by the tourist. "But let him [the reader] be as enthusiastic as he may," the narrator cautions, "he will find enough to damp his ardor." He lists the wretched conditions of travel in the West: wagons stuck in the mud, lost horses, broken harnesses, "varmints" such as wolves and snakes, and mud everywhere (35-36). Using realistic details to dampen the pretensions of the picturesque tourist, the narrator satirizes the naivete of those who expect the "paradise of their imagination" without its attendant snakes and mosquitoes. Here Parkman offers a realistic corrective to the romance of the frontier and suggests what he himself may have learned from his journey: setting out with a romantic attitude towards touring in the West, he was soon disillusioned by its discomforts and some of the unheroic people and situations encountered there.[35] Joseph L. Tribble suggests that, in this respect, *The Oregon Trail* represents the author's attempt to teach his civilized audience a lesson about "the sterner side of reality" in a harsh world where nature's beauties belie its true function as a testing ground for atrophied easterners.[36] Only later, living with the Oglala Sioux and exploring the hills of the Laramie Range, the narrator confronts the true West for which he had searched, discovering the heroism and wisdom in Indians such as Hail-Storm and old Mene-Seela and discovering his own physical and spiritual strength in the mountains and on the buffalo hunts.

Parkman's caustic comments on the "paradise of the imagination" argue that the West, or at least major regions of it, is unsuitable territory for the casual explorations of the picturesque tourist accustomed to the comforts of the Northern Tour. Yet an intelligent, creative traveler may yet enjoy western scenery and go beyond a conventional tour to discover the unique picturesque beauties found beyond the Mississippi River. One of the challenges of picturesque travel in the West, for both Irving and Parkman, was how to interpret and describe landscapes unlike the conventional beautiful, picturesque, and sublime scenery of the Old World or even of the eastern United States. Irving solved this problem in part with his frequent comparisons between scenery in America and Europe. While Parkman frequently compared western landscapes to eastern ones, and occasionally to European scenes,[37] he was more likely to find new forms of the picturesque and sublime that were unique to the West. For example, the Platte River Valley challenges him to describe a landscape unlike anything he had seen before:

> At length we gained the summit, and the long-expected valley of the Platte lay before us. We all drew rein, and sat joyfully looking down upon the

prospect. It was right welcome,--strange, too, and striking to the imagination; and yet it had not one picturesque or beautiful feature; nor had it any of the features of grandeur, other than its vast extent, its solitude, and its wildness. For league after league, a plain as level as a lake was outspread beneath us; here and there the Platte, divided into a dozen thread-like sluices, was traversing it, and an occasional clump of wood, rising in the midst like a shadowy island, relieved the monotony of the waste. No living thing was moving throughout the vast landscape, except the lizards that darted over the sand and through the rank grass and prickly pears at our feet. (65)

Here is the perfect moment for the picturesque tourist: after a long ride, his anticipation is high. The time of day is dusk, the favorite hour of lovers of the picturesque for the contrasts in light and shadow created by the setting sun. In addition, the narrator views the scene from a hill, attaining a far-ranging prospect of the Platte River Valley. The view itself challenges him as tourist and aesthete, for it is not classically beautiful, picturesque, or sublime. Yet he notes that some of its characteristics are those of grandeur, following Edmund Burke's definition of sublime,[38] and he is struck by its strange beauty. The narrator also calls the reader's attention to the absence of living things in this strange scene. The solitary appearance of the darting lizards suggests a fallen world unsuited even for mankind, and the "paradise of the imagination" tourists dream of is replaced by the wasteland pictured here. Once again Parkman presents a realistic view contrasting with the romantic one envisioned by armchair travelers. Such scenes predominate in *The Oregon Trail*, suggesting that there will be little reward for the tourist expecting conventional picturesque beauty in the West. Instead, there are violent thunderstorms to satisfy a traveler's thirst for the sublime and strange, desert-like landscapes that confound and fascinate the picturesque tourist accustomed to greener scenery back East. Often such landscapes do not merely offer the amusement expected of picturesque travel, but they astound and even terrify the traveler with very real dangers.

In spite of the unconventional nature of many of the western landscapes Parkman describes, *The Oregon Trail* contains many other more conventional elements of the picturesque tour. Anecdotes of western travel, colorful personalities, and Indian life entertain the reader and provide some of the associations necessary for the picturesque tour. The party's frequent encounters with emigrants provide material for anecdotes about the hazards of the long trek west, and encounters with ragged "Kanzas" Indians and the more civilized Shawanoes along the frontier give the author a chance to comment on the fate of Eastern tribes forced into the West (55-60, 86-7, 16-18). From Parkman's own company he draws portraits of low-life characters such as the comical Deslauriers, his muleteer, and of noble ones such as Chatillon (14-15). His two-week stay with the Oglala Sioux provides material on Indian customs and legends, such as the story Mene-Seela tells of the "great black bird" that creates the thunder, a legend associated with the Black Hills (208-09). Several buffalo-hunting expeditions introduce colorful tales of Indian and white bravery into the book (356-66). In this respect, Parkman's narrative is similar to Irving's tour, which also used Indian legends to give western landscapes associations and included buffalo hunts to add excitement to the narrative.

Meanwhile, Parkman's health continued to deteriorate on the journey. At one point, encamped with the Indians on the prairie, he is almost completely debilitated by illness, and he writes: "I sometimes suffered the extremity of exhaustion, and was in a tolerably fair way of atoning for my love of the prairie, by resting there for ever" (166). Harold Beaver identifies the source of Parkman's extreme physical illness on the trail and extraordinary "crack-up" after his return as the result of his simultaneous attraction to Indian savagery, eroticism, and independence and his repulsion for the Indian way of life.[39] More recently, critics such as Kim Townsend and David Leverenz view Parkman as something other than the "heroic historian" admired by earlier generations of American readers and critics. Leverenz argues that Parkman "loves his suffering" on the western trail and "struggles to conquer" himself, particularly his body, through a tremendous exertion of willpower that nearly destroys him. Both critics interpret his illnesses as psychosomatic in nature.[40] Regardless of the origin of his suffering, though, Parkman transcended the pain of endless dysentery and eye problems by keeping his sights focused on his goals: exploring the Black Hills and living with a tribe of Plains Indians, both of which he attained, although at great cost to himself physically. In one sense, then, *The Oregon Trail* truly served as a "survival manual" for anxious patrician men of the mid-nineteenth century, showing them by example how they could conquer their own weaknesses and fears, for the journey that brought him at times close to death paradoxically also healed him.[41] At his lowest point physically on the journey the author recalls how he "used to lie languid and dreamy" by his tent. "When most overcome with lassitude," he writes, "my eyes turned always towards the distant Black Hills. There is a spirit of energy in mountains, and they impart it to all who approach them" (166-67). Later, having heard some of the Indian legends associated with the Black Hills, Parkman and the Oglala tribe are camped at the foot of these mountains, and he experiences the very physical and spiritual rejuvenation he has longed for.

While exploring a glen in the mountains, Parkman catches sight of Mene-Seela, the old Sioux, who is apparently meditating on a large pine tree. Watching him, the author is convinced that the Indian is communing with God through the medium of his "guardian spirit," the pine (286-87). This experience seems to inspire him. Descending into the glen, he looks up and sees a tall peak above him. "Something impelled me to climb," he recalls, and in spite of recent ill health he feels his strength returning. Climbing to the summit, Parkman offers a vision of a picturesque and sublime landscape and speaks in terms that suggest a symbolic reading of his experience: "emerging from the dark shadows of the rocks and pines, I stepped out into the light." Earlier the prairie had been only vast and desolate to the narrator, the mountains frightening and life-threatening. But this experience has brought about a remarkable change both in him and in his perceptions about the landscape. Looking westward--where the search for manliness has brought him--he sees "the pale-blue prairie . . . stretching to the farthest horizon, like a serene and tranquil ocean." The mountains around him are now "striking and impressive," an effect emphasized by the contrast with the softer hues of the prairie. For someone who felt himself close to death a few weeks earlier, he has experienced a remarkable resurgence of strength: "I had not felt for many a day such strength and elasticity of limb," he writes (287-88).

Parkman has found what he sought in the West, for the same land that previously ravaged his body has paradoxically also revived him physically and spiritually. In his experiences with the Oglala Sioux and in the mountains, he demonstrates the power of the western landscape both to soothe the spirit and to rejuvenate the body. The experience on the mountaintop is particularly significant, and it parallels those of other travelers in the West, using what Tribble calls "ages-old symbolism" to convey his meaning.[42] The author gains spiritual insights not only from his fresh perspective in the prospect seen from the summit, but also through his witnessing the Indian's harmony with nature and God. In a larger sense, Parkman's western tour, as portrayed in *The Oregon Trail*, becomes a "redemptive journey" in which he successfully renews himself through an encounter with nature, a "classic American fable," according to Leo Marx.[43] Irving's *Tour on the Prairies* also portrays the author's western travels as a strengthening experience physically. But the narrator's struggles with ill-health in *The Oregon Trail* and his dramatic rendering of his recovery create both a more interesting book and a more convincing argument for the benefits of the western tour. Ironically, while Irving states explicitly that America's young men would acquire manliness and independence on a western tour, Parkman's work speaks more eloquently to the reader, with its extremes of ill health and vitality, arguing that a tour in the West can produce the brave, manly young men who will be the future leaders of the nation. Surely this is the very "independent exercise" (in a literal form) that the author found absent in America's writers three years later.

In the 1852 review of Cooper's works Parkman complained of the "lack of originality" of American writers, lamenting their intellectual dependence upon England and English writers: "Thousands, nay, millions of readers and writers drink from this bounteous source, and feed on this foreign aliment, til the whole complexion of their thoughts is tinged with it, and by a sort of necessity they think and write at second hand." For a moment he imagines America cut off entirely from its mother country and argues that if it were "abandoned to its own resources," the United States would, within a generation, produce an "original literature." "We are weakened by the want of independent exercise," he charges, and warns readers that the dependency of "the most highly educated classes" (including himself, and, presumably, his *North American Review* audience) is producing a "nerveless and unproductive" civilization, while "the vigorous life of the nation springs from the deep rich soil at the bottom of society."[44]

Irving's and Parkman's published tours of the western prairies offer some support for Parkman's charge. Both draw heavily upon the English model of a picturesque tour. While Irving's work successfully transfers the convention of the picturesque tour to the West, featuring conventionalized, highly artistic wilderness landscapes, *A Tour on the Prairies* does not go much beyond the conventional English tour modeled on those of Gilpin except in its opening up of new territory for touring in the United States. Parkman, on the other hand, actually expands the convention of the picturesque tour by making it not only a search for picturesque beauty but also a quest for renewed physical and spiritual well-being. Responding to perceived weaknesses in American young men, he offers himself as an example of a man of heroic will conquering a weak body and suggests the regenerative powers of the western landscape. His encounter with Mene-Seela in the Black Hills and his experiences hunting in the West confirm the spiritual and physical rejuvenation possible on the western tour. As Richard Slotkin has shown, the destructive power demonstrated on a buffalo hunt paradoxically invigorates the hunter even as it kills the buffalo.[45] On his return trip to the settlements, for example, Parkman's mountaintop experiences have brought about sufficient recovery from his illnesses for him to participate actively in numerous buffalo hunts, at one point pursuing a particularly defiant animal until the "stout young bull" is slaughtered (pp. 356-66). In addition, Henry Chatillon, renowned for his prowess as a hunter, provides an excellent example of a common man who, in spite of a lack of education, develops the manly traits of courage and independence that Parkman admires. In the early editions of *The Oregon Trail* the author appended a note praising his guide for his "sincerity and honor and boundless generosity of spirit" (p. 707).[46]

One question that arises is whether the New England traveler read the Knickerbocker's work. In a letter written late in life Parkman lists Irving as one of the three "American writers to whom I owe most," and he knew that writer's western books well.[47] One might speculate on Parkman's opinion of Irving and his tour. Although Parkman admired Irving as a writer who, like Cooper, had successfully used Indian materials in his works since the appearance of *The Sketch Book*, it seems likely that Parkman might have viewed him as part of the weakened Eastern culture that concerned him, particularly since Irving was a full generation older than the younger man. In addition, Irving made light of the dangers he faced from Indians and rough terrain in his published narrative, something Parkman could not have known, while *The Oregon Trail*, in contrast, actually dramatizes such dangers. Parkman's work reads as its author wanted it to be read--as the record of a western tour that was both more challenging physically and more rewarding spiritually than Irving's travels. In writing this kind of book Parkman transforms the picturesque tour and makes a significant contribution to American culture by demonstrating the important gains to be made on such a tour both for the individual and the nation. Discovering the elusive manliness he sought on the frontier, at whatever the cost physically and psychologically, in *The Oregon Trail* he offers to physically and spiritually weakened Easterners the hope of renewal in the landscape and rigors of the American West. To an America looking for clues to its own character and for a reading of its future destiny, Francis Parkman's example reaffirmed the importance of the West in shaping its national identity and suggested the masculine values of courage and independence that would come to be identified with the American character.

Notes

1. Details of Irving's route are described in Stanley T. Williams, *The Life of Washington Irving*, 2 vols. (New York: Oxford University Press, 1935), 2: 37-43. The introduction to *Journals and Notebooks, 1832-59*, ed. Sue Fields Ross, *The Complete Works of Washington Irving*, ed. Richard Dilworth Rust, 30 vols. (Boston: Twayne, 1986), 5: xxi-xxiv, provides further, updated details of the trip.

2. Irving, *Journals and Notebooks, 1832-1859*, 5: 23.

3. Irving, *Journals and Notebooks, 1832-1859*, 5: 14.

4. Washington Irving, *Letters, 1823-1838*, ed. Ralph M. Aderman, Herbert L. Kleinfield, and Jenifer S. Banks (Boston: Twayne, 1979), 2: 733-34.

5. Charles Joseph Latrobe, *The Rambler in North America 1832-1833*, 2 vols. (New York: Harper & Bros., 1835), 1: 15.

6. Washington Irving, *A Tour on the Prairies*, in *The Crayon Miscellany*, ed. Dahlia Kirby Terrell, *The Complete Works of Washington Irving*, ed. Richard Dilworth Rust (Boston: Twayne, 1979),

p. 22. All subsequent references to this edition appear in the text.

7. William Gilpin, *Remarks on Forest Scenery*, 2nd ed., 2 vols. (London: R. Blamire, 1794), 1: 185-87; Washington Irving, *Journals and Notebooks, 1819-1827*, ed. Walter A. Reichart (Madison: University of Wisconsin Press, 1970), 3: 348.

8. Gilpin, *Forest Scenery*, 1: 224-25, 65, 229.

9. Irving, *Journals and Notebooks, 1832-1859*, 5: 107.

10. Originally used by William Hazlitt concerning Irving's writings, the term is cited by Ellsworth to describe the additions Irving made to his original sketches (Henry Leavitt Ellsworth, *Washington Irving on the Prairie, or, a Narrative of a Tour of the Southwest in the Year 1832*, ed. Stanley T. Williams and Barbara D. Simison [New York: American Book Co., 1937], p. 71).

11. Peter Antelyes reads Irving's use of the term "diversity" as a principle opposed to order (*Tales of Adventurous Enterprise: Washington Irving and the Poetics of Western Expansion* [New York: Columbia University Press, 1990], p. 141). But Irving generally uses the term to suggest the kind of variety that was a conventional element of the picturesque, therefore a desirable element of a picturesque scene, even in the American West.

12. William Gilpin, "On Picturesque Travel," *Three Essays: on Picturesque Beauty; on Picturesque Travel; and on Sketching Landscape: to which is added a poem, on Landscape Painting*, 2nd ed. (London: R. Blamire, 1794; repr. Westmead: Gregg International, 1972), p. 45.

13. Peter Antelyes, p. 141; John Seelye, letter to the author, 24 February 1982.

14. Blake Nevius discusses Cooper's picturesque landscapes in light of Gombrich's theory in *Cooper's Landscapes*, pp. 101-02. See also E.H. Gombrich, *Art and Illusion: A Study in the Psychology of Pictorial Representation* (Princeton: Princeton University Press, 1969).

15. Ellsworth, *Narrative*, p. 62.

16. William Gilpin, "On Picturesque Travel," p. 43.

17. Gilpin, "On Picturesque Beauty," *Three Essays*, pp. 7-8; Uvedale Price, *An Essay on the Picturesque* (London: Robson, 1794), pp. 46-48.

18. Gilpin, *Forest Scenery*, 2: 102.

19. Washington Irving, *The Sketch Book of Geoffrey Crayon, Gent.*, ed. Haskell Springer (Boston: Twayne, 1978), pp. 8-9.

20. Irving, *Sketch Book*, p. 9.

21. Antelyes, pp. 46-47.

22. In the fourth edition of *The Northern Traveller*, for example, which appeared a decade after *The Sketch Book*, Theodore Dwight recommends that tourists stop to see Sleepy Hollow, "rendered interesting by Mr. Irving," on the Hudson River route (New-York: J. & J. Harper, 1830), p. 24.

23. [James Kirke Paulding], "Biography of Commodore Decatur," *Analectic Magazine* 1 (June 1813): 503-10, and "Childe Roeliff's Pilgrimage," *Tales of Glauber-Spa*, ed. William Cullen Bryant, 2 vols. (New-York: J. & J. Harper, 1832), 1: 172-73.

24. Antelyes, ch. 3 (pp. 93-147); p. 119.

25. *Letters*, 2: 725, 727, 729, 731.

26. The essay is quoted by Richard D. Rust in "Irving Discovers the Frontier," *American Transcendental Quarterly* 18 (Spring 1973): 41.

27. E.L. Magoon, "Scenery and Mind," *Home Authors and Home Artists; or, American Scenery, Art, and Literature* (New York: Leavitt and Allen, [1852?]), pp. 3-4.

28. Francis Parkman, *The Oregon Trail*, ed. E. N. Feltskog (Madison: University of Wisconsin Press, 1969), pp. 1-2 (subsequent references to this work, a facsimile of the 1892 edition approved by Parkman, will appear in the text); *The Oregon Trail*, ed. David Levin (New York: Penguin Books, 1982), p. 33. Levin reprints the 1849 (first) edition of *The Oregon Trail*.

29. Francis Parkman, "The Works of James Fenimore Cooper," *North American Review* 74 (1852): 161.

30. George M. Frederickson, *The Inner Civil War: Northern Intellectuals and the Crisis of the Union* (New York: Harper & Row, 1965), pp. 33-35. Joseph L. Tribble interprets Parkman's trip with a different emphasis, stressing the "psychological quest" behind what he views as the author's determination to fashion a "paradise of the imagination" out of the hellish landscape he discovered in the West ("The Paradise of the Imagination: The Journeys of *The Oregon Trail*," *New England Quarterly* 46 [December 1973]: 523-42).

31. Frederickson, p. 33.

32. *The Journals of Francis Parkman*, ed. Mason Wade, 2 vols. (New York: Harper, 1947), 2: 421-22.

33. Parkman, *Journals*, 2: 419.

34. Feltskog notes some of the sources of the myth of the "Great American Desert" in contemporary travel literature (p. 460, n. 15). For a commentary on this myth see Henry Nash Smith's *Virgin Land: The American West as Symbol and Myth* (Cambridge, Mass.: Harvard University Press, 1950), pp. 174-83.

35. See Feltskog, pp. 50-51a, 52-53a.

36. Tribble, 531-35.

37. For comparisons between western and eastern scenery, see, for example, pp. 20, 49, 67, 271, and 621, n. 5. For a comparison between the American West and European scenery, see p. 326.

38. The Platte River Valley is sublime or "grand" because of its vastness, the uniformity of the plain ("the monotony of the waste"), the infinite quality of its extent ("league after league"), its solitude, and the terror implicit in its "wildness." Burke cites the example of "a level plain of a vast extent on land" as an example of a landscape evoking the emotion of terror (Edmund Burke, *A Philosophical Enquiry into the Origin of our Ideas of the Sublime and Beautiful*, ed. James T. Boulton [1958; London: Routledge and Kegan Paul, 1967], pp. 57, 71-74).

39. Harold Beaver, "Parkman's Crack-up: A Bostonian on the Oregon Trail," *New England Quarterly* 48 (March 1975): 94-103.

40. Kim Townsend, "Francis Parkman and the Male Tradition," *American Quarterly* 38 (Spring 1986): 98-101; David Leverenz, *Manhood and the American Renaissance* (Ithaca, New York: Cornell University Press, 1989), 224-25. Leverenz states that Parkman tried to conquer himself by escaping into "the gender ideologies of the new middle class," what Leverenz calls the convention of "entrepreneurial manhood" (p. 225). For a typical example of an earlier generation's view of Parkman see Mason Wade's *Francis Parkman: Heroic Historian* (New York: Viking Press, 1942).

41. Leverenz sees Parkman presenting himself as a model for patrician men, advocating "fearlessness, singleness of purpose, and self-control"; in short, Parkman "urges a manly heroism, in which will triumphs over incapacity." Leverenz views *The Oregon Trail* as a survival guide specifically for those heading west, but, in a broader sense, the book offers easterners a model for living anywhere (p. 224).

42. Thomas J. Lyon discusses Irving's portrayal of the protagonist's physical triumph and spiritual insights on the summit of a mountain in *The Adventures of Captain Bonneville* (1837) and argues that the author "is trying to suggest a primordial, mystical harmony with wild nature" that Bonneville acquires from the experience, one interpreted through Indian, not Christian imagery ("Washington Irving's Wilderness," *Western American Literature* 1 [Fall 1966]: 172-74). Feltskog states that Parkman read Irving's western books, although whether Parkman had Bonneville's experience in mind in his portrayal of himself in the Black Hills can only be conjectured (*Oregon Trail*, p. 461, n. 16).

Lyon lists other western writers who have used mountain-climbing and views from the summit for their protagonists to gain spiritual insights ("Washington Irving's Wilderness," p. 172).

Tribble notes some of the symbols and myths Parkman uses: "The parched land under a curse; physical sickness as a symbol of spiritual sickness; water as a healing and regenerative power; the mountains as a source of strength" (p. 540).

43. Leo Marx, *The Machine in the Garden: Technology and the Pastoral Ideal in America* (New York: Oxford University Press, 1964), p. 69.

44. Francis Parkman, "Works of Cooper," pp. 160-61.

45. Richard Slotkin discusses violence and its effect on the hunter in ch. 6 ("The Hunting of the Beast") of *Regeneration Through Violence: The Mythology of the American Frontier, 1600-1860* (Middletown, Conn.: Wesleyan University Press, 1973), pp. 146-79.

46. Parkman dropped this note concerning Chatillon from the post-Civil War editions of the book (pp. 707-08).

47. *Letters of Francis Parkman*, ed. Wilbur R. Jacobs, 2 vols. (Norman: University of Oklahoma Press, 1960) 2: 240. In *The Oregon Trail* Parkman mentions a minor character in *Astoria* as if he knew the book well (p. 132). E.N. Feltskog states that he "had read Irving's western books" (p. 461, n. 16), and Mason Wade cites the records of the Boston Athenaeum as evidence that "Irving seems to have been one of his favorites among American writers" (*Francis Parkman: Heroic Historian*, p. 341).

Chapter 5

Hawthorne's Ironic Traveler

Nathaniel Hawthorne's travel sketches from the 1832 tour of
New England and western New York are full of references to the
American Grand Tour, to the picturesque tourist, and to the guidebooks
that directed tourists on their travels. Both from the author's description
of his intended travels and from later editorial comments on the tour,
it is clear that his format for the original trip was modeled on the
picturesque tour. In a letter written to his college friend Franklin
Pierce, for example, he mentioned his plan for collecting materials
during his travels for a proposed book, which would later become the
framed story-cycle called "The Story Teller," composed of tales and
framing sketches taken from the 1832 tour.[1] Later Park Benjamin, the
editor to whom Hawthorne had submitted his work for publication,
described the first series of "Sketches from Memory" published in
New-England Magazine in 1835 as sketches from the "portfolio of a
friend, who traveled on foot in search of the picturesque over New-
England and New-York."[2] Benjamin's comment astutely pinpoints both
the source of the sketches and their format: the picturesque tour.

Yet references to tours and guidebooks in both "Sketches from
Memory"[3] and other works drawn from the author's travels in the
summer of 1832 do not simply reinforce the idea that the picturesque
tour was popular at this time and that tourists were frequently
encountered at various stops on the Northern Tour. Rather, these
references serve as an ironic counterpoint in the sketches--and probably
in the original "Story Teller" collection--to the narrator's own
increasing experience with the world, its people, and their foibles. As
the narrator moves from innocence to experience, and as he changes
from a naive and often imitative tourist to an increasingly complex and

ironic observer of society--as he matures, in short--such references
serve as more than a simple satire of picturesque tourists and their
excesses, as in "The Notch of the White Mountains" or even in "Our
Evening Party Among the Mountains." Instead, in sketches such as
"The Canal-Boat" and "My Visit to Niagara" Hawthorne's references
to guidebooks and, in general, to others' experiences of the much-
traveled Northern Tour suggest his aesthetic distance from the
superficial and imitative nature of their responses to historical sites,
natural landmarks, and technological innovations. And while sometimes
such comments can result in merely amusing commentary on the foibles
of human nature as evinced in the picturesque tourist, elsewhere
Hawthorne's judgment on this phenomenon is more pointed and more
meaningful for the work as a whole, as in the sketch on Niagara Falls.
Here he effectively contrasts the narrator's experience at the famous
falls with the limited, imitative experiences of other tourists. The
narrator's increasing distance from the others suggests not only his
growing understanding of the meaning of the falls, but also his
increasing maturity, aesthetically and artistically. For in this sketch
Hawthorne neatly presents and deftly solves both the problem of how
to "read" such a masterwork of the American sublime in a fresh,
original way and how to arrange his perceptions into a form
comprehensible by the reader. Herein lie both the beauty and the value
of the sketch, and its extraordinary complexity.

Hawthorne's knowledge of the picturesque tour and its unique
perspective on landscape is evident in several of his sketches drawn
from the 1832 tour of New England and New York. "The Notch of the
White Mountains" and "Our Evening Party Among the Mountains," for
example, serve as a conventional opening for a picturesque tour, with
the traveling storyteller responding like any other tourist to landscapes
and only occasionally indulging in satirical reflections on other
travelers. In "The Notch" he describes himself "loitering towards the
heart of the White Mountains" (28), an appropriate pose for the
fashionable picturesque tourist, albeit a self-conscious one. Adopting
the same sauntering, casual pace that Geoffrey Crayon assumed in
Washington Irving's *Sketch Book*, he takes time to discover and enjoy
the kind of picturesque landscapes advocated by Gilpin and sought by
countless tourists thereafter. For Hawthorne's narrator, though, the
White Mountains hold a special attraction: the "mysterious brilliancy"
of these "old crystal hills," he writes, "had gleamed upon our distant
wanderings before we thought of visiting them" (28).

For their aesthetic value alone, the White Mountains of New Hampshire appealed to any tourist weaned on the scenic attractions of the Old World, whether on a personal Grand Tour or through armchair travel of the sort Hawthorne indulged in during his formative years in the 1820s and '30s. For example, charge-books from the Salem Athenaeum reveal that either Hawthorne himself or Mary Manning (who checked out books for her nephew) read omnivorously in travel literature during this time, ranging from travels in Great Britain, Germany, Turkey, and Africa; to those in his native land, including Bartram's *Travels*; to his compatriot Washington Irving's *Tales of a Traveller*.[4] The White Mountains may have attracted Hawthorne as the closest available territory for a tour through the kind of picturesque and sublime landscapes he had only read of before this; the popular travel guides he used in planning his tours touted the attractions of this "Switzerland of the United States," as the area came to be called.[5] Theodore Dwight's popular tour guide *The Northern Traveller* (1825) highly recommends the scenic beauty of the White Mountains: "Too much cannot be said to the traveller in favour of this delightful region, if he be a man of taste, as all that he especially loves in the varying face of nature is here presented to view, by a country abounding with the most sublime and interesting objects and scenes to be found in the whole circuit of New England, scenes which, while present to the eye, communicate the highest pleasure, and at parting leave a deep and permanent impression on the mind which can never be forgotten."[6]

Hawthorne's travels in the White Mountains impressed him deeply enough for him to use not only the landscape, but also the people and legends encountered there as material for several travel sketches and tales in the next few years: "The Ambitious Guest," "The Great Carbuncle," and "The Great Stone Face," for example. Translating his own experiences into the autobiographical fiction of the travel sketch, he adopts a persona similar to what he himself must have been like in his late twenties and describes the narrator doing things he must have done: appreciating landscape beauty, observing the various types of humanity encountered during a tour, and collecting legends from the local inhabitants.

From what is known of his 1832 tour, both the setting and movement of the narrator in "The Notch of the White Mountains" reflect Hawthorne's own experiences, though some of the incidents and characters may be exaggerated or altered for greater effect. In the opening lines of the sketch, Hawthorne deftly sets the scene with a few phrases, establishing the time as September, the place as the Saco River Valley in New Hampshire, and his narrator as traveling north from Bartlett and heading toward the tourist attraction of the Notch (see Map 3). The traveling storyteller describes his gradual penetration into "the heart of the White Mountains," revealing his increasing knowledge of both the geographical and legendary history of the place. At the same time, he invites the reader to share his growing sense of awe at the secrets to be discovered there. Describing himself in the midst of the mountains, he sketches the following scene from his journey: "Height after height had risen and towered one above another, till the clouds began to hang below the peaks. . . . We had mountains behind us and mountains on each side, and a group of mightier ones ahead. Still our road went up along the Saco, right towards the centre of that group" (28). Aware of the charge that American landscape lacked historical associations, Hawthorne is careful to note the traces of history present in the landscape: the pathways of the slides, avalanches of past and near-present times now nearly "effaced by the vegetation of ages," and the traces of old Indian paths through the mountains, one of which had become the trail taken by the narrator on his tour. Both of these vestiges of the past suggest possible associations with the landscape, a necessary ingredient of the picturesque. The slides recall the recent (1826) disaster of the Willey family, one he would develop later into "The Ambitious Guest." The evidence of Indians suggests the native legends Hawthorne will exploit later in this sketch almost in spite of himself.

The narrator's musings on the legendary or mythological past of the mountains not only become the source of the associations requisite for the picturesque landscape but they also lead him to consider the presence of the divine in the landscape. Introductory remarks prepare the reader for both kinds of associations by noting that the road running through the valley of the Saco River appears "to climb above the clouds, in its passage to the farther region," as if it leads to the dwelling place of the gods, like some New World Olympus.[7] The narrator allows his fancy to consider the origin of the Notch itself and of the old Indian paths that, leading down through the mountains, created the "wondrous path" he now treads. He imagines a demon or Titan "traveling up the valley, elbowing the heights carelessly aside as he passed, till at length a great mountain took its stand directly across his intended road. He tarries not for such an obstacle, but rending it asunder, a thousand feet from peak to base, discloses its treasures of hidden minerals, its sunless waters, all the secrets of the mountain's

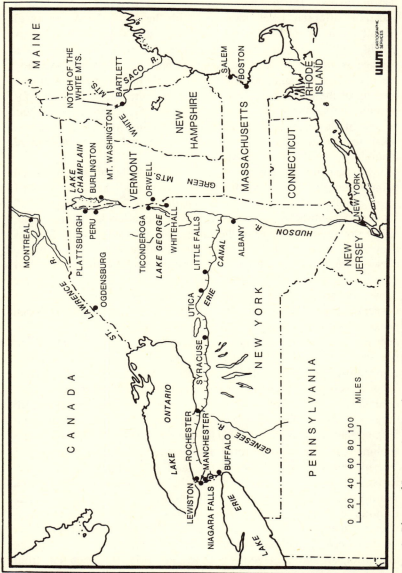

Map 3. Places of Interest in Hawthorne's Travel Sketches.

inmost heart, with a mighty fracture of rugged precipices on each side" (28). Edwin Fussell comments on this remarkable image, suggesting that it "involves Hawthorne's sense of his creative self at the deepest and most primitive level, identified with the gods, the processes of insemination and birth, the concupiscences and traumas of the New World," an image almost sexual in nature.[8] Yet though the tone of the passage is wonder at such an imagined feat, the narrator apparently feels at least some ambivalence if not outright horror at such a violent rending of the earth. Like Roger Chillingworth, who is criticized for probing the secrets of the human heart, the Titan here exposes "the secrets of the mountain's inmost heart," laying its hidden treasures open to the traveler's or explorer's eye--and, later, but more humorously, to the mineralogist's hammer.

Just after this passage the narrator suddenly shifts in mood and berates himself for such thinking: "Shame on me," he writes, "that I have attempted to describe it [the Notch] by so mean an image . . ." Even if Hawthorne were unaware of what Fussell calls the "obstetric, not to say vaginal" nature of the image, his narrator's mixed feelings about the fanciful demon's actions are evident here.[9] The passage closes with a brief return to the sublime imagery the author had originally intended. The Notch, he states, is "one of those symbolic scenes, which lead the mind to the sentiment, though not to the conception, of Omnipotence" (28). In truth, other than the cloud-topped peaks of the opening section of the sketch and the magical way the road appears to lead on to a mysterious "farther region" beyond the horizon, like the distance in a Claude painting, there is not a great deal of the conventional Burkean sublime in the description of the White Mountains or the Notch.[10] One looks in vain for the references to the mountains' grandeur and the traveler's awed response to them that fill other accounts of the White Mountains. In "A Literary and Pictorial Iconography of Hawthorne's Tour" Dennis Berthold argues that the sublime is largely missing from this sketch "because it has disappeared beneath an overlay of commerce and entertainment, two main ingredients of tourism." In "The Notch," he explains, "Hawthorne's visitors to the White Mountains seek comfort and pleasure, not sublime inspiration, and are most content when they feel most at home."[11] Omitting many of the picturesque and sublime scenes that are the object of the conventional picturesque tourist's travels creates an ironic dimension in the protagonist's character early in "Sketches from Memory," a dimension that is developed more fully in later sketches.

This ironic element is reinforced in the second part of "The

Notch of the White Mountains," the focus of which alternates between the sublime setting and the ridiculous characters who enter the scene at this point. Once again the scene is dramatically staged: the narrator enters a narrow passage that seems to have been cut into the mountain by superhuman, rather than natural forces. As he enters the "romantic defile" known as the Notch, whose high granite walls and narrow path suggest the sublimity associated with it, a party of tourists appears out of nowhere.[12] Piled into a rumbling stagecoach, the travelers provide a lively contrast to the narrator, whose search for picturesque beauty has brought him thus far. The description of the party is surely ironic: "To my mind, there was a sort of poetry in such an incident," the narrator states, likening the entrance of stagecoach and tourists to "the painted array of an Indian war-party, gliding forth from the same wild chasm." Hawthorne is well aware that while the latter would be truly picturesque, not to say exciting or even sublime in the frissons it would engender in the traveler, the former is just faintly ridiculous, especially in view of his comments on the tourists and their various activities: a mineralogist, "a scientific, green-spectacled figure in black," wielding a hammer, "did great damage to the precipices," while a foppish young man carrying a gold-trimmed opera-glass in lieu, no doubt, of a quizzing glass, "seemed to be making a quotation from some of Byron's rhapsodies." Other characters from the stagecoach include a trader, a fat lady, and the ubiquitous "fair young girl" of Hawthorne's fiction (29). The traveling storyteller includes these characters both to liven up the sketch, with its emphasis on landscape description, and to introduce those who will play a role in the following work, "Our Evening Party among the Mountains."

The balance of the sketch features the kind of commentary on landscape scenery that was typical of guidebooks of the day, though with Hawthorne's own twist. In his popular *Traveller's Guide*, for example, Gideon Miner Davison effused over the White Mountains, whose magnificence "strikes the traveller with awe and astonishment." According to this guidebook, the emotions aroused by the "grand and majestic scenery" that surrounds Mount Washington are "utterly beyond the power of description."[13] Similarly, the narrator in "The Notch of the White Mountains" stops at dusk at a natural amphitheater and comments on the surrounding group of mountains: "They are majestic, and even awful, when contemplated in a proper mood," a state of mind easily achieved in such circumstances by the man of taste whose eye and mind have been trained to read sublimity into every towering mountain range (29). Mount Washington, in particular, elicits the most comments both from travel guides and the narrator: like Melville describing Mount Greylock in northwestern Massachusetts in "The Piazza" in the 1850s, Hawthorne's tourist personifies the mountain as an old man "as white as snow" who "had caught the only cloud that was sailing through the atmosphere, to veil his head." The narrative is interrupted here momentarily for an aside on the moral value of mountains as "Earth's undecaying monuments" whose names have important symbolic value: "They must stand while she endures, and never should be consecrated to the mere great men of their own age and country, but to the mighty ones alone, whose glory is universal, and whom all time will render illustrious" (29). With a comment on the brisk air, the narrator ends the sketch on a more prosaic note, picturing himself looking forward to a cozy fire and good company at Ethan Crawford's mountain inn, the subject of the next sketch.

The second part of "Sketches from Memory," "Our Evening Party Among the Mountains," is set at Ethan Crawford's inn, a popular stopover for travelers on the Northern Tour. Here the narrator spends two nights, as Hawthorne did, gathering further material for the "Story Teller" framed story-cycle.[14] His comments on Crawford's inn and its guests reinforce the idea that the narrator is on a picturesque tour. Noting the "picturesque group" of local woodcutters, traders, and travelers, the narrator describes the inn as "at once the pleasure-house of fashionable tourists, and the homely inn of country travelers" (30). Although he does not comment on his own motives for travel here, the storyteller might consider himself somewhere in between these two groups since he is no mere "fashionable tourist," yet he travels with a higher aesthetic purpose in mind than the typical country traveler or trader.

The balance of this sketch satirizes various guests at the inn and recalls the numerous local legends the storyteller collected on his tour. Ethan Crawford, the proprietor of this famous inn, provides a colorful character who mixes well with the fictional group described elsewhere in the sketch. As the travelers arrive at the inn, Crawford blows a long tin trumpet whose echo among the hills gives the author an opportunity to embroider fancifully on its sound, in which he imagines "an airy band" playing a "dreamlike symphony of melodious instruments" (31). Their imaginary presence here provides yet another possible legend for these mountains.

The second half of the sketch is dominated by the past, whether in Ethan Crawford's reminiscences about life in the White

Mountains a half-century earlier or in the legends of the earliest inhabitants of the mountains, the Indians. Although the narrator's comment--"I do abhor an Indian story"--near the end of "Our Evening Party" has become famous, his supposed attitude towards Indian legends is belied by the straightforward tone of his recitation of such tales earlier in the sketch. The narrator himself characterizes the general conversation as "animated and sincere." The first legend mentioned here reminds the reader of the Biblical story of the flood. Native tribes of the White Mountains believed, writes Hawthorne, "that the father and mother of their race were saved from a deluge by ascending the peak of Mount Washington. The children of that pair have been overwhelmed, and found no such refuge. In the mythology of the savage, these mountains were afterwards considered sacred and inaccessible, full of unearthly wonders, illuminated at lofty heights by the blaze of precious stones, and inhabited by deities, who sometimes shrouded themselves in the snowstorm, and came down on the lower world" (32-33).

What is significant here is not only that the narrator recounts an Indian legend, but also that he relates it to the present in such a way as to add immeasurably to the romantic associations of the mountains for his contemporaries. A careful reading of this version of the legend reveals that although the parents of the Indian race were themselves saved, and the mountains ever after believed to be occupied by deities, the descendants of that mythical pair "have been overwhelmed, and found no such refuge." As told here, the legend reads as a brief but pessimistic commentary on the status of Indians in Hawthorne's own time. By the 1830s most native inhabitants of the White Mountains were long gone, pushed west by white settlers and by governmental policy. In a few words Hawthorne has given the mountains the requisite associations for them to be truly picturesque or "romantic," in the language of the period. More significantly, he has also implied that the remaining traces of native tribes are, essentially, the ruins otherwise missing from the landscape. Hawthorne links himself with other writers of his time in portraying, if not lamenting, the gradual disappearance of Native Americans from the landscape. Only a few years earlier, for example, James Fenimore Cooper's *The Last of the Mohicans* (1826), *The Prairie* (1827), and *The Wept of Wish-ton-Wish* (1829) had appeared, all of which comment upon the effects of white encroachment on native tribes in the East.

Hawthorne elaborates on his attitude about Indians and

American fiction later in the sketch and comments on the others'
response to these legends:

> The hearts of the pale-faces would not thrill
> to these superstitions of the red men, though we
> spoke of them in the centre of their haunted region.
> The habits and sentiments of that departed people
> were too distinct from those of their successors to
> find much real sympathy. It has often been a matter
> of regret to me, that I was shut out from the most
> peculiar field of American fiction, by an inability to
> see any romance, or poetry, or grandeur, or beauty
> in the Indian character, at least, till such traits were
> pointed out by others. I do abhor an Indian story. Yet
> no writer can be more secure of a permanent place in
> our literature, than the biographer of the Indian
> chiefs. His subject, as referring to tribes which have
> mostly vanished from the earth, gives him a right to
> be placed on a classic shelf, apart from the merits
> which will sustain him there. (33)

Ironically, the White Mountains become a "haunted region" partly due
to the efforts of writers such as Hawthorne who, though he may regret
his "inability to see any romance . . . in the Indian," can through an
effort of the imagination translate Indian material into the stuff of
which literature is made. He demonstrates this himself in "Our Evening
Party" by introducing the Indian tale associated with Mount Washington
and the legend of the "Great Carbuncle," which he would later develop
into a full-fledged story.

Unlike the two preceding sketches, in which the tone remains
fairly straightforward, except when the narrator satirizes other tourists,
in "The Canal-Boat" the tone is more complex, changing from
paragraph to paragraph, and creates a more sophisticated sketch that
ranges from straightforward description to high comedy and low
humor, and from pointed satire to dark irony. Once again the
picturesque tour provides the narrative framework for the story. In this
sketch the youthful protagonist travels in search of the picturesque in
western New York, and as he pokes fun at his fellow tourists and takes
aim at the inflated rhetoric about the Grand Canal itself, the reader
discovers a more complex piece of fiction that culminates in the
narrator's dark vision of a landscape made accessible by technology but

also destroyed by it, concluding in a midnight search for meaning that offers little hope for the future.

In "The Canal-Boat" the wandering storyteller's picturesque tour continues via canal boat on an artificial waterway, the Erie Canal. Completed in 1825, the Erie Canal stretched across western New York, connecting Albany, on the Hudson River, with Buffalo, on Lake Erie. By the time of the author's 1832 tour, the canal had become a standard stop on the American Grand Tour. Spafford's popular *Pocket Guide for the Tourist and Traveller*, for example, focused almost exclusively on the Erie Canal, with brief mentions of scenic attractions along the canal route.[15] Dwight's *Northern Traveller* recommended nearby historic sites from the Revolutionary War and the War of 1812, and landscape scenery, particularly cascades, as well as interesting "manufactories" in the vicinity of the canal.[16] Davison's *Traveller's Guide* gave a detailed description of the canal route, including various landscapes worth viewing on the trip west and the historical attractions of the towns through which the canal passed, though more space was devoted to mills and factories than to historical sites.[17] Davison's comments on the attractions of the canal for the tourist reflect the very considerations Gilpin emphasizes in his essay "On Picturesque Travel" for the picturesque tourist, whose "love of novelty" requires the stimulation of "new scenes continually opening, and arising to his view."[18] Like the celebrated River Wye, in England, whose "gentle, uninterrupted stream . . . adorns, through its various reaches a succession of the most picturesque scenes,"[19] Gilpin, had he lived another half-century and traveled to America, might have equally celebrated western New York's varied views as seen from the deck of a canal boat. In a section entitled "Canal Passage," for example, Davison writes: "Of the sources of gratification to the tourist, during the canal passage, that of novelty is perhaps the greatest." (He admits, however, that canal scenery may be "too little diversified with incident" for the "man of pleasure" to repeat the canal trip, though the "man of business" would not be bothered by such considerations.[20]) The tourist's taste for picturesque beauty along the canal route was whetted by such guidebooks.

In "The Canal-Boat" Hawthorne opens the sketch with the narrator recalling his inflated romantic attitude towards a proposed trip on the Erie Canal: "I was inclined to be poetical about the Grand Canal," he states dramatically in the opening line. He imagines De Witt Clinton, principal sponsor of the canal, as a kind of magician who created an enchanted "watery highway" linking two worlds with one another. More important, he writes, "This simple and mighty conception had conferred inestimable value on spots which Nature seemed to have thrown carelessly into the great body of the earth, without foreseeing that they could ever attain importance" (35). The narrator rhapsodizes about the canal itself not only because it is a major feat of the imagination and of technology, but also because it serves to open up new landscapes for the tourist, the discovery of which was one of the most important goals for the picturesque tour. In "The Canal-Boat" the narrator is, in fact, so enchanted with the canal initially that as he sets forth on his trip he promises himself a second voyage that same summer on the artificial waterway. Of course, since the love of novelty in particular is what draws the picturesque traveler, the tone here is probably ironic, particularly since he may be satirizing Spafford, who recommends "the constantly varying scenery" along the canal and reveals that he traveled the entire canal route two times in one season to gather the information necessary for his *Pocket Guide.*[21]

The opening of "The Canal Boat" describes the narrator's expectations about the proposed tour, and it raises the reader's own expectations. Such highly inflated rhetoric almost begs to be deflated, and this is exactly what happens in later passages. In the descriptive section that follows, the narrator introduces a mythological allusion that is deflated almost immediately: "Behold us, then, fairly afloat, with three horses harnessed to our vessel, like the steeds of Neptune to a huge scallop-shell, in mythological pictures. Bound to a distant port, we had neither charter nor compass, nor cared about the wind, nor felt the heaving of a billow, nor dreaded shipwreck, however fierce the tempest, in our adventurous navigation of an interminable mud-puddle." As for the narrator's--and the reader's--expectations of the picturesque landscapes recommended by Spafford and others, these too are deflated: the Erie Canal, he writes, meanders "through all the dismal swamps and unimpressive scenery, that could be found between the great lakes and the sea-coast" (36).

To be fair, Hawthorne and his peevish narrator almost deserve their ennui: the narrator had, in fact, begun his trip just east of Utica, which is past the sections of the canal generally accounted to be most picturesque, such as the Mohawk Valley. The part he focuses on in "The Canal-Boat" was widely acknowledged at the time to be the most tedious section of the canal route[22]. If Hawthorne had consulted any one of the more popular guidebooks, as seems very likely, he would have read advice such as that in Vandewater's *The Tourist, or Pocket*

Manual for Travellers, which stated: "There is nothing of much interest on the canal for the first sixty miles west of Utica. It is perfectly level and marshy country, without a lock in the whole distance."[23] That the author chooses the most boring section of the canal for his sketch suggests that he plans to put this very tediousness to good use, as indeed he does. For although the narrator acknowledges that "there is variety enough, both on the surface of the canal and along its banks, to amuse the traveller," mostly he emphasizes the "overpowering tedium" that would "deaden [the] perceptions" of even the most eager tourist (36).

By this point no one should expect to see any picturesque landscapes, but Hawthorne continues to tease the reader trained by the conventions of picturesque travel to expect scenic beauty. Beginning a section describing scenes along the canal route, the narrator recalls: "Had I been on my feet at the time, instead of sailing slowly along in a dirty canal-boat, I should often have paused to contemplate the diversified panorama along the banks of the canal." Yet what is the panorama that would repay such leisurely contemplation? Dark, dense forests unrelieved by sunlight and gutted tracts of land covered with "dismal black stumps." And although some of the scenes depicting the urban picturesque--thriving villages and busy cities--may contain the variety essential to a picturesque scene, the lengthy portrait of a poor woman, "lean and aguish," living along the canal, who appears as "Poverty personified," dominates the various views and suggests that the canal has brought at least as much poverty as prosperity to western New York. The narrator peevishly complains that these scenes were "tiresome in reality" and recalls the childish amusements he and his fellow passengers stooped to for entertainment on the canal boat: pelting ducks with apples, shooting at squirrels from the deck, and mocking an unlucky passenger who accidentally fell into the muddy canal waters (37-38). Once again Hawthorne stresses the contrast between the narrator's inflated expectations and the tedious reality of a tour by canal boat.

One way in which the narrator relieves the tedium of his tour is by satirizing his fellow travelers. Observing an Englishman who is "taking notes in a memorandum-book," he indulges his "ill-humor" by imagining the comments on Americans made by the foreigner: the pedantic Virginia schoolmaster, the Puritanical yeoman farmer of Massachusetts, the Detroit merchant who worships Mammon, and the unnaturally modest "western lady" who shrinks from the observer's roving eye (39-40). While other critics have noted Hawthorne's use of the Englishman and his stereotyped Americans, this character's central role in the satire has gone largely unrecognized.[24] In the midst of his comments on his fellow travelers the narrator notes: "I went all through the cabin, hitting everybody as hard a lash as I could, and laying the whole blame on the infernal Englishman" (40). The narrator avoids responsibility for satirizing his compatriots, placing it instead on the much-maligned English traveler, as if Hawthorne dare not admit his own culpability here, though he hints at it. The irony of this passage deepens when the narrator catches a glimpse of his own image in a mirror and realizes that the Englishman's eyes are, in turn, focused on him. In the mirror's reflection, a favorite device of Hawthorne's, the narrator has been caught at what he has accused the Englishman of doing--satirizing fellow travelers--and ironically it is the American, not the Englishman, who later exploits the scene for its literary value by writing this travel sketch.

After an unsuccessful attempt to sleep on the narrow, shelf-like berths of the canal boat, the narrator falls dramatically out of bed, setting off a chain of events that will lead him straight to the symbolic conclusion of the sketch. That the protagonist compares his narrow berth to a coffin does not seem accidental, for the reference introduces a whole series of images of death and darkness. Going on deck at night, the narrator discovers a "darkness so intense, that there seemed to be no world" except the canal boat. "Yet," he remarks, "it was an impressive scene"--an otherworldly scene, one in which references to death, ruin, and destruction occur frequently:

> There can hardly be a more dismal tract of country.
> The forest which covers it . . . is now decayed and
> death-struck, by the partial draining of the swamp
> into the great ditch of the canal. Sometimes, indeed,
> our lights were reflected from pools of stagnant
> water, which stretched far in among the trunks of the
> trees, beneath dense masses of dark foliage. But
> generally, the tall stems and intermingled branches
> were naked, and brought into strong relief, amid the
> surrounding gloom, by the whiteness of their decay.
> Often, we beheld the prostrate form of some old
> sylvan giant, which had fallen, and crushed down
> smaller trees under its immense ruin. In spots, where
> destruction had been riotous, the lanterns showed

perhaps a hundred trunks, erect, half overthrown, extended along the ground, resting on their shattered limbs, or tossing them desperately into the darkness, but all of one ashy-white, all naked together, in desolate confusion. Thus growing out of the night as we drew nigh, and vanishing as we glided on, based on obscurity, and overhung and bounded by it, the scene was ghost-like--the very land of unsubstantial things, whither dreams might betake themselves, when they quit the slumberer's brain. (41)

Unlike the picturesque ruins of the Old World, created by wars or by the ravages of time, these New World ruins were wrought by technology and offer little of aesthetic value other than their symbolic value for the writer. Hawthorne suggests this in the narrator's analysis that follows the lengthy death-in-life description just cited: "My fancy had found another emblem. The wild Nature of America had been driven to this desert-place by the encroachments of civilized man." Building the canal in this area had meant draining the adjacent land, thereby destroying the forests that had previously thrived there. The narrator and his fellow travelers are intruders on this desolate scene, and his final comment on it ironically summarizes the contrast between Old and New World ruins: "In other lands, Decay sits among fallen palaces; but here, her home is in the forests" (41-42). Had he ended his sketch here, Hawthorne's emblem would have spoken clearly enough about the destructive power of technology, exemplified by the canal's destruction of the wilderness in western New York. But the author extends and reinforces his symbolism, widening the meaning and significance of his brief sketch, by developing it further in the conclusion.

When the canal boat's towrope becomes tangled and causes a brief delay, the narrator decides "to examine the phosphoric light of an old tree" in the decaying forest that borders the canal. "It was not," he notes dryly, "the first delusive radiance that I had followed." The fallen tree, "converted into a mass of diseased splendor," throws a "ghastliness" into the atmosphere. "Full of conceits that night," as the narrator describes himself, he calls it variously a "frigid fire" and a "funeral light, illumining decay and death." The fallen, phosphorescent tree is, he says, "an emblem of fame, that gleams around the dead man without warming him; or of genius, when it owes its brilliancy to moral rottenness" (42). These images suggest death and despair. More than this, they remind the reader that this phosphorescent flame burns without consuming, yet without warming either. The source of this light, Hawthorne suggests, is the "moral rottenness" at the core: a physical rottenness for the tree, but a spiritual rottenness for mankind. Is this, then, the "moral rottenness" at the heart of American civilization that, in blind pursuit of material wealth, would wantonly destroy Nature by technological feats such as the Erie Canal? Hawthorne may have been hinting at this earlier when the narrator prostrates himself at the cry "bridge! bridge!", "like a pagan before his idol" (38). Perhaps this also refers to the moral decay in which the narrator himself participated earlier in the sketch when he crudely satirized his fellow passengers in the name of the English traveler. Hawthorne implies that technology creates circumstances in which normally sociable, compassionate people become cruel, though he attributes his narrator's pitiless response to others' misfortunes to mere idleness (38).

At the end of the sketch the narrator, who has been abandoned, appropriately enough, by the callous captain of the canal boat, seizes a phosphorescent flambeau from the decaying old tree and sets out on a "midnight tour" of the dying wilderness. Like an ignis fatuus or a jack-o'-lantern, to use Hawthorne's simile, this flickering, delusive light is an appropriate symbol for the chastened narrator, whose dreams of a picturesque tour by canal boat have fallen victim to reality (43). Setting out on his midnight tour, he might remind the reader of Edgar Huntly, who decades earlier persisted in his own midnight explorations of the wilderness, constantly endangering himself in the process. But the newly chastened narrator of "The Canal-Boat" is not likely to make Huntly's mistakes, nor to suffer from his delusions. The wandering storyteller's midnight tour seems strangely appropriate for the Gothic nether world Hawthorne describes in the sketch.

Reading the conclusion of "The Canal-Boat" on another level, one might interpret the narrator's midnight search for his journey's end as a symbolic search for truth, a common enough metaphor in Hawthorne's writings. In this instance darkness obscures reality, and the narrator's path is lit only by the deceptive light of the decaying, phosphorescent trees that suggest the "moral rottenness" of the writer's world he hinted at earlier. In another work developed from materials gathered on Hawthorne's 1832 tour and published the same year as this sketch, he portrays the traveling protagonist in pursuit of a different goal, metaphorically speaking. In "My Visit to Niagara" the narrator's aim in the story, to comprehend the meaning of the falls for himself alone, becomes a metaphor for understanding the relationship between perception and point of view, between the reflections of others' experiences and the hard-won, original response to experience.

"My Visit to Niagara" serves as the climactic sketch in Hawthorne's series of travel sketches from his 1832 tour, and it may well have originally been intended as the climactic piece of the framework of the proposed "Story Teller" framed story cycle, just as Niagara Falls often served as the climax of the Northern Tour for nineteenth-century tourists. As one critic notes, traveling north on the Hudson River and then west on the Erie Canal, the tourist views scenery that seems designed by nature to demonstrate various kinds of landscape--the beautiful, the picturesque, and the sublime--with the trip culminating in that glorious "icon of the American sublime," Niagara Falls.[25] Whether one is traveling on the American Grand Tour or reading about it in a group of sketches such as these, "My Visit to Niagara" reflects the great expectations felt by the traveler-reader in approaching the falls. The phenomenon of the picturesque tour itself both calls for and reinforces this sense of expectation. Since William Gilpin, the picturesque tourist par excellence, had decreed that the main object of picturesque travel was the discovery of new scenes, a traveler's explorations of scenery as celebrated in literature and painting as Niagara Falls would be bound to evoke a certain measure of disappointment, as Elizabeth McKinsey demonstrates in her work on the falls as cultural icon. Once the falls had been written and rewritten by countless travelers in the eighteenth and early nineteenth centuries, some travelers found they had to account for their disappointment in viewing something they had read so much about or, in other cases, to revile their contemporaries for ruining one of the wonders of the New World with inns, souvenir shops, and mills.[26] This is the context in which Hawthorne writes in "My Visit to Niagara" and, quite likely, the personal experience behind his characterization of the narrator's deeply felt disappointment on his first view of the famous falls.[27]

From the very beginning of exploration and travel in America the falls served not only as a symbol of the sublime, but also, more importantly, as the quintessential symbol of the New World's potential in its enormity, its overwhelming power, and its grandeur. No wonder, then, that it was an essential part of the Northern Tour and that viewing the falls became a goal for every American and European tourist. Added to this, every traveler who scribbled his or her thoughts on the American landscape and its people included a section on Niagara Falls, usually one that hauled in every aesthetic cliche, however redundant, celebrating its sublimity, grandeur, awfulness, and majesty. Hawthorne portrays the narrator of the Niagara sketch as one whose expectations about the falls had been shaped by previous reading and who approached Niagara with the awe and high expectations of a pilgrim who travels to worship at a celebrated and revered shrine. In the opening lines of the sketch, he writes: "Never did a pilgrim approach Niagara with deeper enthusiasm, than mine. I had lingered away from it, and wandered to other scenes, because my treasury of anticipated enjoyments, comprising all the wonders of the world, had nothing else so magnificent, and I was loth to exchange the pleasures of hope for those of memory so soon" (55).

The narrator's use of the pilgrim motif in this opening passage serves the sketch that follows in three important ways. First, it recognizes Niagara Falls as the ultimate in scenic wonders of the American tour and acknowledges the worshipful attitude on the part of the countless travelers who made a pilgrimage to this holyland of the American scene. Second, the exaggerated tone and diction suggest the dual point of view that adds complexity to the Niagara Falls sketch: though the narrator makes his bow to those who have come before him in admiring the falls, his reference to them as "pilgrims" lends a note of irony in its equation of a natural phenomenon with a religious shrine. For Hawthorne, applying the word "pilgrim" to the picturesque traveler had additional significance. As an avowed admirer of James Kirke Paulding, whom he later was to describe as "the admired and familiar friend of every reader in the land,"[28] the author would have read or read about that well known writer's recent work, *The New Mirror for Travellers*, published several years before Hawthorne visited Niagara Falls.[29] He probably was equally familiar with the nickname wags had given Paulding's book, a name that distinguished it from serious guidebooks of the day and established it as satire: *The New Pilgrim's Progress*. The nickname alluded, of course, to Bunyan's famous allegory, Hawthorne's old favorite and one he would later use for an extended allusion in "The Celestial Rail-road." Hence his use of the word "pilgrim" to describe a tourist whose object of devotion was Niagara Falls carries a meaning beyond that of the usual term, and in this case, it foreshadows the satirical tone he adopts frequently in the sketch since Paulding's attitude towards picturesque travel and tourists in *The New Pilgrim's Progress* is largely satirical.

Third, this passage introduces the attitude of anticipation or expectancy on the part of the tourist that had been essential to picturesque travel at least since Gilpin's time. Here, too, exaggeration paves the way for later developments in the sketch. The hyperbole evident in Hawthorne's description of the narrator's "treasury of anticipated enjoyments" and the reference to his future exploration of "all the wonders of the world" ironically prepares the reader for the narrator's disappointment. His statement that he was "loth to exchange the pleasures of hope for those of memory so soon" foreshadows the disappointment ahead and introduces his almost comical efforts to put off the moment when he must confront the object of his longstanding devotion (55).

The balance of the opening section of "My Visit to Niagara" reinforces the reader's sense that Hawthorne is not only satirizing the stereotypical views of others about the falls but is also treating the narrator ironically. Paradoxically, the narrator simultaneously mocks some tourists' approaches to the falls and mimics their ridiculous attempts to discover an original approach to Niagara: hence the mention of the English tourist who traveled thousands of miles to view the falls and then "turned back from the point where he first heard the thunder of Niagara," without having actually seen it (56).

The narrator's response to the falls is unusual but not wholly unexpected, given the mixed feelings with which he has approached Niagara, for he neither rushes to view the falls nor turns back from his journey unfulfilled. Instead, a strange sort of apathy overtakes him, and he writes: "my mind had grown strangely benumbed, and my spirits apathetic, with a slight depression, not decided enough to be termed sadness. My enthusiasm was in a deathlike slumber." Further on, he explains this unusual response: "Such has often been my apathy, when objects, long sought, and earnestly desired, were placed within my reach" (56). Elizabeth McKinsey calls this passage "a strange drama of delayed gratification,"[30] yet the narrator's attitude is consonant with his feelings described earlier in the sketch; he simply does not wish to give up his enjoyment of anticipating the falls. He would prefer to look forward to Niagara and even to continue his journey with the falls unseen rather than risk possible disappointment. He contrasts his own point of view with that of the "French gentleman" traveling on the stagecoach with him who leans forward to gain his first glimpse of the falls from the window and loudly admires the view: "I was glad to think," he writes, "that for me the whole burst of Niagara was yet in futurity" (55-56).

The structure of "My Visit to Niagara" suggests that

Hawthorne's narrator must deal with his own preconceptions and others' views of the falls before he can discover or create his own view. The title, significantly, is not "A Visit to Niagara" but rather "*My* Visit to Niagara," implying the importance of the writer's view as distinct from those of other tourists, writers, and painters. Thus he spends a large portion of the sketch describing and often satirizing the various ways other travelers respond to Niagara rather than establishing his own viewpoint right from the beginning--other than to suggest, as noted above, that his attitude is not going to be the expected one. The balance of the sketch is then taken up with the narrator's many attempts to comprehend Niagara and its meaning for him personally.

The narrator's first view of the falls, with his concomitant attempt to comprehend its meaning, occurs just after the opening of the sketch. First, however, he purchases a walking stick made by a Tuscarora Indian. The "twisted stick" is "curiously convoluted, and adorned with the carved images of a snake and a fish." This "pilgrim's staff," as he describes it, reminds the reader once again that the narrator is on a pilgrimage to the holyland of the American sublime, though his linking himself with the countless "pilgrims" who have gone before him is as ironic as it is self-conscious (56-57).[31]

The narrator's immense disappointment at his initial view of the falls is, then, foreshadowed not only by the hints of impending disillusionment early in the sketch but also by the suggestion here of the meaning of the experience in the symbolic walking stick. Nor are readers themselves disappointed. In spite of the "glorious sunshine" and a glimpse of the "Eternal Rainbow of Niagara," the narrator resists the scene and its conventional impact on the observer. Like the dark rock he spots in the midst of the "river of impetuous snow," unaffected by the churning water, the narrator "resist[s] all the physical fury" before him. And although he wants desperately to respond to the falls and to comprehend its meaning, he fears that he, too, is a "cold spirit" whose resistance prevents him from responding to "the moral influences of the scene" (57).

After a series of initial impressions of the falls, the narrator concludes: "Still, I had not half seen Niagara" (57). What follows is a record of his attempt, instead, to see it *whole*. Moving from one observation point to another, and always descending from a higher viewpoint to a lower one, until he is in direct contact with wind and spray, he tries unsuccessfully to capture the meaning of the falls.[32] At one point the narrator even attempts a panoramic view that, predictably, also fails: "Casting my eyes across the river, and every side, I took in the whole scene at a glance, and tried to comprehend it in one vast idea" (57). Still the sublime scene resists comprehension. In the essay "On Sketching Landscape" Gilpin had considered the very problem facing Hawthorne and his narrator in this sketch. He suggests that the picturesque tourist find "the best point of view" to sketch a landscape, a perspective Hawthorne's narrator cannot settle on, and he warns would-be artists of the problem of reducing the scale of a landscape, particularly an extensive one, to the smaller scale of the paper.[33]

The narrator's initial conclusion comes as no surprise to the perceptive reader[34]:

> Oh, that I had never heard of Niagara till I beheld it! Blessed were the wanderers of old, who heard its deep roar, sounding through the woods, as the summons to an unknown wonder, and approached its awful brink, in all the freshness of native feeling. Had its own mysterious voice been the first to warn me of its existence, then, indeed, I might have knelt down and worshipped. But I had come thither, haunted with a vision of foam and fury, and dizzy cliffs, an ocean tumbling down out of the sky--a scene, in short, which Nature had too much good taste and calm simplicity to realize. My mind had struggled to adapt these false conceptions to the reality, and finding the effort vain, a wretched sense of disappointment weighed me down. I climbed the precipice, and threw myself on the earth--feeling that I was unworthy to look at the Great Falls, and careless about beholding them again. (58)

Between this initial response to the falls and his second attempt to comprehend the meaning of Niagara, the narrator lies awake night after night, listening to the "dread sound" of the falls, a sound heard, significantly, "for ages past and to come."[35] This is the narrator's first hint that he might sometime take his place among the "wanderers of old" who could respond instinctively and immediately, without a screen of received ideas coming between him and the falls. It becomes necessary for him to cast away all secondhand conceptions and respond to Niagara Falls directly and intimately, as Hawthorne states explicitly:

"Gradually, and after much contemplation, I came to know, by my own feelings, that Niagara is indeed a wonder of the world, and not the less wonderful, because time and thought must be employed in comprehending it. Casting aside all pre-conceived notions, and preparation to be dire-struck or delighted, the beholder must stand beside it in the simplicity of his heart, suffering the mighty scene to work its own impression" (59). The man of taste must reflect thoughtfully to comprehend Niagara's impact. Only a simple soul (the young farmer, for example, whose instinctive response to the sublimity of the falls is admired by the narrator later in the sketch) can respond immediately and freshly to Niagara. Although it is not known how many days Hawthorne spent at the falls, his narrator appears to spend at least several days there, until his visit finally culminates on the last day with his fully comprehending the meaning of the falls.[36]

The narrator's final impressions of Niagara Falls appear at the end of his sketch and are interrupted, once more, by other visitors, whose various responses to Niagara he satirizes. Yet in spite of the repeated interruptions, the narrator achieves his long-sought comprehensive impression of the falls: "Never before had my mind been in such perfect unison with the scene," he writes, describing the rare harmony that can result between the receptive observer and his surroundings, which is the ideal of the tourist whose eye is trained in the picturesque and the sublime.

Hawthorne's narrator assumes the position most often recommended by the guidebooks for the picturesque tourist to observe the falls. Taking a seat on Table Rock, which had once projected fifty feet out over the falls but now was truncated from an earlier collapse, he "felt as if suspended in the open air." He recalls, "There were intervals, when I was conscious of nothing but the great river, rolling calmly into the abyss . . ." (59).[37] The narrator communes directly and intensely with the river and falls, and his comments suggest that he transcends this particular moment in time to participate in the eternal time in which Niagara dwells.[38] He compares its "unhurried motion" to "the march of Destiny," suggesting something fateful about the river's course and fall into the abyss, and emphasizes the permanence of its flow rather than its transience: the "eternal storm" of Niagara. Given its existence in a framework of eternal time rather than earthly time, the narrator disagrees with observers who comment on its tumultuous qualities and emphasizes instead its calmness: "It soothes, while it awes the mind" (59-60). Paradoxically, instead of arousing wild emotions in the observer, Niagara calms him.

At last the reader expects to hear the narrator's long-sought view of the falls, but Hawthorne frustrates the reader once more--as he himself must have often been frustrated--by the parade of tourists who periodically block his view of Niagara. Except for the absence of cameras clanking around their necks, these early nineteenth-century tourists could easily be mistaken for their modern-day counterparts. They interrupt the narrator's "contemplations" of the scene, and the reader shares his impatience at their presence and enjoys his satirizing them. With their untrained eyes and clumsy attempts at appreciating nature's sublime, these tourists offer various limited, naive, and sometimes downright foolish means of viewing the falls that Hawthorne contrasts effectively with his own hard-won perspective at the end. First the narrator watches as two "adventurers" descend into the "lower regions" and, accompanied by a guide, disappear behind the falls to attempt to reach Termination Rock, surrounded by mist and spray. Despite the hazardous appearance of the venture, the narrator notes that the passage is actually safer than it seems. Satirizing the adventures of these "children of the mist," he concludes by mentioning the "certificate of their achievement, with three verses of sublime poetry on the back" received by the tourists (59-60). Ironically, Hawthorne had received such a certificate himself when he visited the falls in September 1832, the only proof extant of his stop there.[39]

Then a series of tourists appears, each skewered in turn by the narrator's satirical pen. First John Bull arrives in the person of a "short, ruddy, middle-aged gentleman" and his "robust" spouse. His "broad grin" at the falls, the sort of aesthetically crude response one might expect from an untutored Englishman (particularly when the observer is a patriotic American), contrasts humorously with that of his wife, whose "sweet example of maternal solicitude" concerning her child's safety prevents her from so much as glancing at the phenomenon she crossed the ocean to view. Another traveler, whom Hawthorne characterizes as "a native American, and no rare character among us" pulls out a copy of Captain Basil Hall's famous travel book and "labored earnestly to adjust Niagara to the captain's description, departing, at last, without one new idea or sensation of his own." Once again Hawthorne satirizes the most typical of the American tourists-- those dependent on the guidebook and stigmatized, as Paulding had characterized the species, for their slavish devotion to others' perceptions and interpretations of landscape scenery.[40] "My Visit to Niagara" might even be read as a response to Hall's statement that because the scale of the falls "baffles every attempt of the imagination to paint" Niagara, "it were ridiculous, therefore, to think of describing it."[41] Another tourist pulls out his sketching pad and tries to capture the falls on paper, following Gilpin's dictum that the picturesque tourist must sketch his ideas while still fresh, preferably on the scene. Gilpin's influence is also evident in the narrator's conversation with the sketcher: the would-be artist's suggestion that the position of Goat Island is somehow defective and ought, ideally, to be moved "so as to widen the American falls" recalls the English writer's advice that a scene may be altered by the artist when nature fails to provide exactly the right balance in the composition of a landscape[42] (60).

Two Michigan tradesmen, like countless other businessmen before them, offer the expected commercial viewpoint on Niagara Falls by wanting to harness its power for industry. Their preference for the manmade wonders of the Grand Canal is also the sort of attitude one might expect in businessmen as observed--and stereotyped--by the aesthetically superior narrator. These economically motivated tourists contrast effectively with the young traveler "in a home-spun cotton dress" who succeeds them in Hawthorne's sketch of this little band of tourists. His naive, untutored eye lacks the vulgar qualities of the English visitors, the pseudo-artistic sensibility of the sketcher, and the utilitarian perspective of the Michigan traders. The young man's response to the sublimity of the falls is immediate and fresh: "His whole soul seemed to go forth and be transported thither" as he gazed at Horseshoe Falls (60-61). As McKinsey states, he "has the natural naive capacity for the sublime . . . that the storyteller has had to recover after he arrived."[43]

The narrator achieves his final views of Niagara as he descends from his position above the falls on Table Rock and follows a winding road away from the scene.[44] Here the varying perspectives offered by his changing position are significant, recalling, once again, Gilpin's advice on finding the right point of view from which to view a scene to the best advantage. The narrator writes: "The indirectness of my downward road continually changed the point of view, and shewed me, in rich and repeated succession" the various pictures presented by his changing perspective. Significantly, Hawthorne describes these views in artistic terms: the familiar lights and shadows of his verbal sketching technique characterize the rapids; "the lovelier picture" of Goat Island underscores the artistic quality of the description; and "the long vista of the river" presents an "unrivalled scene." As in a Claude painting, "golden sunshine" colored the whole composition, and "tinged the sheet of the American cascade, and painted on its heaving spray the broken semicircle of a rainbow." Hawthorne suggests a metaphorical reading of this climactic scene in his description of the rainbow, the reminder of God's covenant with mankind, as "Heaven's own beauty crowning earth's sublimity" (61).[45]

As the narrator slowly departs from the scene of his triumphant reclamation of Niagara's sublimity, he "lingers and pauses" as one "who discerns a brighter and brightening excellence in what he must soon behold no more." Since the time of day is sunset, the brightening here could refer not only to the brilliance of the setting sun, but also to the intense clarity of the experience and its newly understood meaning in the narrator's mind. The storyteller has finally captured the meaning of the falls not just for his own time, but within the framework of eternal time in which "the wanderers of old" first stood awestruck at the glory of Niagara: "The solitude of the old wilderness now reigned" over the scene. He concludes: "My enjoyment became the more rapturous, because no poet shared it--nor wretch, devoid of poetry, profaned it: but the spot, so famous through the world, was all my own!" (61). Significantly, like Emerson before him and Thoreau later, the narrator needs solitude for his ultimate experience of the sublime in nature. In the end, undistracted by other travelers, the narrator of Hawthorne's sketch lays personal claim to Niagara Falls. The purpose of "My Visit to Niagara," then, becomes fulfilled, and the picturesque tourist as storyteller can move on to other stops on the American Grand Tour, making them equally his own.

In "My Visit to Niagara" the sketch serves as much more than a vehicle for Hawthorne to satirize tourists and the popular pastime of picturesque touring, and certainly as more than a means to celebrate the sublime wonders of Niagara Falls, both of which countless other writers had done before him, with varying degrees of success. In contrast, "The Notch of the White Mountains" is a more straightforward celebration of the American landscape, though both this sketch and "The Canal-Boat" satirize the absurdities of the picturesque tourist as effectively as the Niagara sketch. Yet like the Erie Canal sketch, "My Visit to Niagara" develops into a sophisticated study that is more than a social satire. "The Canal-Boat" criticizes American technology and its wanton destruction of the landscape in favor of economic progress. The protagonist's midnight travels along the canal offer little light--or hope--in the darkened, morally unsound world he explores. On the other hand, the Niagara sketch is not half so dark in its themes, offering instead of a pessimistic view of contemporary

America an exploration of the artist's quest for understanding and a study of the problem of conveying his conclusions to his readers. Here the choice of a hackneyed symbol of the American sublime is brilliant, since it enables Hawthorne to address the problem of achieving an original view of a much described and interpreted site. Only by presenting and then rejecting the most common views of Niagara Falls can the narrator clear his mental slate and begin to come to terms with it on his own. After this lengthy process of sifting through others' interpretations of the falls he can approach Niagara directly and intimately, capturing its meaning for himself and conveying it to his readers. At last the wandering storyteller can state that this place, "so famous through the world," is his own. In the end Hawthorne's ironic tourist is overcome by the overwhelming sublimity of Niagara Falls, and he abandons satire for his wholehearted embrace of the falls. This cultural and natural icon has brought him a new understanding about himself as tourist and, more important, as an artist and writer.

Notes

1. Nathaniel Hawthorne, *The Letters, 1813-1843*, ed. Thomas Woodson et al., Centenary Edition, 16 vols. (Columbus: Ohio State University Press, 1984), 15: 224.

2. Benjamin's comment is reprinted in Alfred Weber, Beth L. Lueck, and Dennis Berthold, *Hawthorne's American Travel Sketches* (Hanover, N.H.: University Press of New England, 1989), p. 27. Subsequent citations to this edition appear in the text.

3. "Sketches from Memory," First Series, includes "The Notch of the White Mountains" and "Our Evening Party Among the Mountains" and first appeared in *New-England Magazine* in November 1835. "Sketches from Memory," Second Series, includes "The Canal-Boat," "The Inland Port," "Rochester," "An Afternoon Scene," and "A Night Scene" and first appeared in *New-England Magazine* in December 1835.

4. Marion L. Kesselring, *Hawthorne's Reading, 1828-1850: A Transcription and Identification of Titles Recorded in the Charge-Books of the Salem Athenaeum* (1949; repr. n.p.: Norwood Editions, 1976), entries #30, 62, 94, 192, 235, 366.

5. Theodore Dwight, *The Northern Traveller* (New York: Wilder & Campbell, 1825), p. 173.

6. Dwight, p. 173.

7. William Cullen Bryant uses a similar conceit in "Monument Mountain," published the same year of Hawthorne's tour. According to this poem, native tribes of this region believed in the Great Spirit inhabiting the mountaintops. They believed, Bryant wrote, "Like worshippers of the elder time, that God / Doth walk on the high places and affect / The earth-o'erlooking mountains" (ll. 100-102). The poem is collected in *The Life and Works of William Cullen Bryant*, ed. Parke Godwin (New York: D. Appleton, 1883), 3: 253.

8. Edwin Fussell, *Frontier: American Literature and the American West* (Princeton, N.J.: Princeton University Press, 1965), p. 81.

9. Fussell, p. 81.

10. Kesselring lists Burke's *Works*, notably [*A Philosophical Enquiry into the Origins of our Ideas of*] *the Sublime and the Beautiful*, as among the books borrowed from the Salem Athenaeum by Mary Manning and, presumably, read by Hawthorne in November 1828 (entry #66).

11. *Hawthorne's American Travel Sketches*, p. 106.

12. Hawthorne's comment here--"This is the entrance, or, in the direction we were going, the extremity of the romantic defile of the Notch" (28)--is one of several that suggest he has used one or more travel guides both in planning and, perhaps, in writing about this tour. According to Gideon Miner Davison's *The Fashionable Tour: A Guide to Travellers Visiting the Middle and Northern States, and the Provinces of Canada*, 4th ed. (Saratoga Springs: G.M. Davison; New

York: G. & C. & H. Carvill, 1830), for example, most travelers would be moving in a southerly direction here rather than the northerly direction Hawthorne followed on his tour. Thus the entrance, for him, was the extreme end of the Notch for the typical tourist. His first view of the White Mountains, described at the beginning of the sketch, is also similar to that of Davison's *Fashionable Tour*, though not close enough to suggest a borrowing or paraphrase (334-41).

13. Davison, *Fashionable Tour*, p. 334.

14. Hawthorne, *Letters, 1813-1843*, 15: 226.

15. Horatio Gates Spafford, *Pocket Guide for the Tourist and Traveller, Along the Lines of the Canals, and the Interior Commerce of the State of New-York* (New York: T. and J. Swords, 1824), pp. 17-50.

16. Theodore Dwight, *The Northern Traveller, and Northern Tour*, 4th ed. (New-York: J. &. J. Harper, 1830), pp. 47-78.

17. Davison, *Fashionable Tour*, pp. 233-57.

18. Gilpin, "On Picturesque Travel," *Three Essays: On Picturesque Beauty; On Picturesque Travel; and On Sketching Landscape: to which is added a poem, on Landscape Painting*, 2nd ed. (London: R. Blamire, 1794; repr. Westmead, England: Gregg International, 1972), pp. 47-48.

19. William Gilpin, *Observations on the River Wye, and several parts of South Wales, &c. relative chiefly to picturesque beauty; made in the summer of the Year 1770* (London: R. Blamire, 1782), p. 7.

20. Davison, *Fashionable Tour*, p. 236.

21. Spafford, p. 18.

22. Roger Evan Carp, "The Erie Canal and the Liberal Challenge to Classical Republicanism, 1785-1850," dissertation, University of North Carolina at Chapel Hill, 1986, p. 713.

23. Robert J. Vandewater, *The Tourist, or Pocket Manual for Travellers on the Hudson River, the Western Canal and Stage Road to Niagara Falls*, 3rd ed. (New-York: Ludwig & Tolefree, 1834), p. 55. See also Spafford, where little of interest to the picturesque traveler is noted between Utica and Syracuse (36). Vandewater advises tourists to avoid this section of the canal by taking the stage instead (55-56).

24. Leo B. Levy, "Hawthorne's 'The Canal Boat': An Experiment in Landscape," *American Quarterly* 16 (1964): 213-14; Alfred Weber, *Die Entwicklung der Rahmenerzahlungen Nathaniel Hawthornes: "The Story Teller" und andere fruhe Werke* (1825-1835) (Berlin: Erich Schmidt Verlag, 1972), p. 225.

25. See Roger Haydon, *Upstate Travels: British Views of Nineteenth-Century New York* (Syracuse, New York: Syracuse University Press, 1982), p. 10; and Elizabeth McKinsey, *Niagara Falls: Icon of the American Sublime* (New York: Cambridge University Press, 1985). My understanding of the cultural context of "My Visit to Niagara" was deepened by McKinsey's study of Niagara Falls, and I wish to acknowledge that debt here.

26. McKinsey, pp. 189-90 and following.

27. McKinsey points out that Hawthorne's oblique references in *The Italian Notebooks* to his experience at Niagara Falls suggest that he found "the same disappointment and recovery of the sublime" as his narrator in "My Visit to Niagara" (198).

28. Hawthorne, *Letters, 1813-1843*, 15: 468.

29. *The New Mirror for Travellers; and Guide to the Springs* (New York: G. & C. Carvill, 1828).

30. McKinsey, p. 192.

31. Commenting on the symbolism of the walking stick, McKinsey finds the "motif suggestive of a knowledge of good and evil." She argues that the staff "might facilitate a fall from the innocence of anticipation into experience and knowledge," interpreting the narrator's disappointment in Niagara as a kind of fall from his

initial anticipation and his growing understanding of the Falls as his coming to terms with the experience's real meaning for him, rather than simply the stereotypical and rather limited views of other tourists (192-93).

32. Hawthorne appears to have taken the advice of Dwight's *The Northern Traveller* on viewing the falls: "It may be recommended to the traveller to visit this place as often as he can, and to view it from every neighbouring point; as every change of light exhibits it under a different and interesting aspect. The rainbows are to be seen from this [the British] side only in the afternoon; but at that time the clouds of mist, which are continually rising from the gulf below, often present them in the utmost beauty" (85). Note that the narrator in Hawthorne's sketch is indeed viewing the falls in the afternoon--in fact, he has put off his first visit until then--and that he moves from place to place, following Dwight's advice to see the falls "from every neighbouring point" for the best effects.

It is interesting that in the Library of Congress an 1830 edition originally owned by Daniel Ricketson, of New Bedford, Massachusetts, bears the following note on the passage quoted above: "This must be a mistake, for there was a beautiful rainbow there at 9 1/2 Oclock A.M. May 19, 1833. D. R." (handwritten on p. 85).

33. Gilpin, "On Sketching Landscape," *Three Essays*, p. 63.

34. McKinsey states that "the reader expects an affirmative answer" to the rhetorical questions about whether the narrator's hopes had been fulfilled, but I think a careful reader ought to have picked up enough clues by this point in the sketch to be prepared for the "devastating" response that follows (193).

35. McKinsey notes that "the turning point comes at night when he [the narrator] is caught unaware, in a completely passive state of unselfconscious receptivity, no longer haunted by dead conventions and exaggerated expectations" (193).

36. "Night after night," he writes, "I dreamed of it" (59), suggesting anywhere from a few days to a week spent at the falls.

37. Dwight, for example, recommends the view from Table Rock in *The Northern Traveller* (79, 84), and gives an account of its fall (87).

38. Emphasizing the spatial structure of the scene, McKinsey notes that Hawthorne's position here is above the falls, where he "has *risen* to a feeling of perfect unison with the scene." The narrator, she points out, "looks down (literally and figuratively) on others who have not achieved a similar transcendence" (194).

39. James R. Mellow, *Nathaniel Hawthorne in His Times* (Boston: Houghton Mifflin, 1980), p. 51.

40. Paulding, p. 90.

41. Captain Basil Hall, *Travels in North America in the Years 1827 and 1828*, 2 vols. (Philadelphia: Carey, Lea & Carey, 1829), 1: 109.

42. William Gilpin, "On Sketching Landscape," *Three Essays*, pp. 66-70.

43. McKinsey, p. 194.

44. Hawthorne may have followed the route described in Dwight's *Northern Traveller*, which notes the various views seen along the Niagara River and suggests that a "leisurely walk" there "may please the admirer of nature" (83).

45. McKinsey argues that "If his experience on first approaching Niagara was a 'fall,' then it was certainly a fortunate fall," with the rainbow serving as "a sign that he has indeed recovered an authentic experience of the Falls' sublimity" (195).

Chapter 6

Poe's "Picturesque-Hunters"

Scholars have explored Edgar Allan Poe's use of landscape scenery in his tales and longer narratives and have discussed the way his knowledge of landscape aesthetics influenced his work.[1] Yet his interest in the popular pastime of picturesque travel has gone unrecognized, even though it plays a significant role in his most important landscape fiction. The picturesque tour appears as both a structural and a thematic device in two works published at the midpoint of his career: in *The Journal of Julius Rodman* (1840) and "Morning on the Wissahiccon" (1844), and in two important later works, "The Domain of Arnheim" (1847) and its pendant piece, "Landor's Cottage" (1849). Throughout these four works Poe plays on the reader's familiarity with the picturesque tour and its popularity during this period. He expects the reader to recognize the picturesque tourist, whose excesses had already been satirized by writers such as Paulding and Hawthorne, and he assumes the reader is acquainted with popular travel literature in general and with the fashionable tour in particular, as it appeared in numerous contemporary American travel narratives of both the East and the Far West. An understanding of the picturesque tour, then, and of its place in Poe's fiction will lead to a greater understanding of these complex works and will clarify the author's role as both social and literary critic. In addition to using it as a structural device, Poe uses the picturesque tour to satirize both tour and tourist and, occasionally, to parody those writers whose attempts to fuse an essentially European phenomenon with the wild American frontier result, at best, in disjunction and, at worst, in absurdity. Furthermore, in "The Domain of Arnheim" and "Landor's Cottage" the author's emphasis on the picturesque tour as a quest for beauty illuminates the comments he makes in these tales on the artist's role in the creation of beauty and helps to clarify Poe's ideas on nature, beauty, and art late in his career.

Poe's first major work to feature the picturesque tour, *The Journal of Julius Rodman*, appeared serially in *Burton's Gentleman's Magazine* between January and June 1840, while he was working as assistant editor under William E. Burton, and it terminated abruptly when his employment ended over disagreements with the editor-in-chief. Numerous critics have commented upon the problems involved in this unfinished travel narrative, or "travel romance," as Burton R. Pollin has described it.[2] The patchwork quality of the narrative, the unstable character of its protagonist, and the uncertain and changing focus of the work all suggest various critical interpretations: that Poe's intentions changed midway through the narrative; that the piece is simply another example of the author's slipshod work; or even that he intentionally parodies contemporary travel narratives here.[3] However, a close look at *The Journal of Julius Rodman* will reveal that the narrative's odd combination of adventure, exploration, and aesthetic appreciation is more successful than previously thought and, in the context of other travel literature of the period, not that unusual.

From the beginning of *The Journal* comments by the "editor" and Rodman--both of whom, of course, are actually Poe--reflect the notion of the western journey as picturesque tour. In the introduction, for example, the editor describes Julius Rodman as a tourist and calls his trip west a tour. He emphasizes, moreover, that the significant difference between Rodman's narrative and those of other explorers is the "romantic fervor" with which its author traveled--a hallmark of the picturesque tourist--and stresses the unexplored nature of the region through which Rodman traveled. This territory is, he states, "the *only* unexplored region within the limits of the continent of North America" (521-22). Like many other travel writers of his day, the editor echoes Gilpin's ideas on the subject, for as the English writer had argued, it was "the expectation of new scenes" that attracted the picturesque tourist, and unexplored country was the favorite source of picturesque landscapes.[4] Early in the narrative Rodman states clearly that he wishes to make his fortune in peltries on the trip, but he also emphasizes his equal or greater interest in western scenery. Admiring the "majestic appearance" of the Missouri one morning, he looks forward eagerly to exploring unknown regions of the river. As he contemplates the "magnificent works of God" he might soon see, the narrator states: "I felt an excitement of soul such as I had never before experienced, and secretly resolved that it should be no slight obstacle which should prevent my pushing up this noble river farther than any previous adventurer had done" (536-37).

Julius Rodman maintains his perspective as picturesque tourist throughout the narrative. Later in *The Journal* he describes his group as "mere travellers for pleasure," and he points out their loss of interest in the original purpose of the expedition, collecting furs (564). The narrator emphasizes his aesthetic rather than economic motives so often that it is no wonder that some critics have interpreted Poe's tone as satirical. Instead, though, the author might simply wish to stress the noble character of his protagonist and to underscore his purpose on the expedition. In one passage, for example, Rodman describes his increasing wish to "turn aside in pursuit of idle amusement" on the journey. Lest readers misunderstand him, he qualifies the statement: "if indeed I am right in calling by so feeble a name as amusement that deep and most intense excitement with which I surveyed the wonders and majestic beauties of the wilderness. No sooner had I examined one region than I was possessed with an irresistible desire to push forward and explore another" (564).

Although this statement could be read as parodying the picturesque tourist in search of ever greater wonders, it is more likely that Poe is responding here to Gilpin's use of the term "amusement" to describe the pleasures of the picturesque tour. In his essay "On Picturesque Travel" Gilpin uses the terms "amuse" and "amusement" repeatedly to describe the sources of pleasure for the picturesque traveler.[5] Kent Ljungquist has noted that "There is little external evidence that Poe had detailed knowledge of particular British aestheticians of the picturesque such as Gilpin" and others, though he finds Poe's "general familiarity with the movement" reflected in numerous prose works. Examples such as this, however, in which Poe's work reflects Gilpin's theories and even echoes his language, offer internal evidence that suggests Poe either knew Gilpin's work firsthand, or he had read about Gilpin's theories in other people's writings.[6]

In short, there is ample evidence that Poe consciously used the picturesque tour in *The Journal of Julius Rodman* both in the characterization of its protagonist as a picturesque traveler and in his description of the trip as a kind of tour. In addition, the narrator's ongoing quest for picturesque landscapes helps structure the narrative by following Gilpin's established pattern of the pursuit, discovery, and enjoyment of picturesque beauty. The question that remains is whether the author presents Rodman and his aims seriously or satirically, a question that has arisen repeatedly in discussions of this work and one that hinges, at least partly, on the question of authorial intentions. Ljungquist argues that *Julius Rodman* is an unsuccessful attempt to mix the picturesque perspective of the gentleman tourist with that of the rugged explorer in a frontier and wilderness situation. Indeed, earlier travelers such as Washington Irving, in *A Tour on the Prairies* (1835), were more successful in transferring the tourist to the frontier, complete with picturesque descriptions of cliffs as castles and western landscapes as parks. Later travelers such as Francis Parkman, in *The Oregon Trail* (1849), were also more successful in interpreting both prairie and mountain landscapes with the picturesque eye, without the sort of aesthetic disjunctions found in *Julius Rodman*. Both writers also succeeded in combining works of western adventure and exploration with conventions of the picturesque tour. The uneven nature of Poe's narrative, as Ljungquist has recognized, leads readers to question both the author's intentions and the results. Yet when the work is read in the context of other western adventure stories more skillfully blended with the picturesque tour, it is clear that *Julius Rodman* should be considered as part of this hybrid genre and read as the hoax that Poe originally intended it to be.[7]

In fact, I would argue that *Julius Rodman* is more successful than critics have previously considered it. While it remains a flawed work of art, it is moderately successful as a hoax. Although elements of parody exist in it--such as the humorous names of western Indian tribes (551)--overall the narrative reads more like a work imitating travel narratives such as Irving's *The Adventures of Captain Bonneville* and *Astoria* than like a narrative parodying them.[8] Poe may even have used John Jacob Astor as a model for the entrepreneurial Julius Rodman. In addition to the two protagonists sharing an "expansionist imagination," as Peter Antelyes terms it, Poe gave Irving's book on Astor's western enterprise a positive review in the *Southern Literary Messenger* (January 1837), in the same issue in which *The Narrative of Arthur Gordon Pym* first appeared in serial form, three years before *Julius Rodman*'s publication. In short, when viewed in the context of contemporary works of "adventurous enterprise" such as *Astoria* and *Bonneville*, *The Journal of Julius Rodman* reads as an early attempt by Poe to write within the developing tradition of the picturesque tour on

American soil rather than as a satirical commentary on that tradition.[9] This distinction becomes even clearer when *Julius Rodman* is compared to a more obvious satire on the picturesque tourist such as "Morning on the Wissahiccon" or more subtly satirical works such as "The Domain of Arnheim" and "Landor's Cottage."

In "Morning on the Wissahiccon" (or "The Elk," 1844) Poe turns to satire of the picturesque tour and tourists. He focuses on several targets in this sketch, treating some seriously and others satirically. First, he considers the ongoing argument over the superiority of American or European scenery and the role of the foreign tourist. The problem lies in the limited view foreigners acquire of the United States on their visits. Most British tourists "content themselves with a hasty inspection of the natural *lions* of the land," he laments, such as Niagara Falls, the Catskills, New York's lake country, and several western attractions, including the Mississippi River and the prairies. Worst of all are the travel writers who try to meet their publishers' deadlines "by steaming it, memorandum-book in hand, through only the most beaten thoroughfares of the country," returning with an incomplete or even distorted view of the United States and its landscape scenery. But if these tourists were to follow less traveled routes, they might discover some of the lesser-known landscapes of the New World. "In fact," he states, "the real Edens of the land lie far away from the track of our own most deliberate tourists." The "true artist, or cultivated lover of the grand and beautiful" may discover hidden treasures in the landscape. The narrator cites the example of Louisiana, where one might find "a realization of the wildest dreams of paradise."[10] Thus far the sketch reads as a serious discussion of these issues.

The narrator returns to the subject of the American versus the European traveler to suggest how the difference in terrain affects the picturesque tourist, and here he turns to hyperbole and satire to make his point. Since America's finest picturesque landscapes are not to be found on the much-traveled paths of the tourist, but in places inaccessible by carriage, train, steamboat, or even horseback, the true picturesque tourist, he argues, "must *walk*, he must leap ravines, he must risk his neck among precipices, or he must leave unseen the truest, the richest, and most unspeakable glories of the land." In contrast to the daring, adventurous picturesque tourist in the New World, the narrator satirically pictures the traveler in Europe, where "so thoroughly known are all points of interest, and so well-arranged are the means of attaining them" that "the merest dandy of a tourist may . . . visit every nook worth visiting without detriment to his silk stockings" (863).

The balance of the sketch focuses on the beauties of the Wissahiccon, a stream whose glories remain unseen by picturesque tourists and unsung by American writers, thus fulfilling the reader's expectations, which were raised earlier in the work. The "rare loveliness" of this stream, says the narrator, has gone unsuspected by all by a few "adventurous pedestrians" from nearby Philadelphia until, ironically, a European traveler, the English actress Fanny Kemble, pointed out its beauties in her *Journal* in 1835 (864). Writing under her married name of Frances Anne Butler, Kemble recalled her visit to the area on horseback and described the Wissahiccon in hackneyed terms, admiring its "sheet of foaming water falling like a curtain of gold over the dam," "the picturesque mill," and "a most beautiful mass of icicles" that "formed a most enchanting and serene subject of contemplation."[11]

In spite of this publicity, the narrator argues, the "Philadelphian picturesque-hunters" miss the stream's "finest points" by going no farther than the carriage-road takes them upstream. He recommends that "the adventurer who would behold its finest points" pursue the beauties of the Wissahiccon by boat or by "clambering along its banks" well beyond the reach of the road (864). Here is an expedition beyond the reach of the dandy Poe satirizes earlier in the sketch, unless the English traveler exchanges his fine silk stockings for heavy, serviceable boots.

Having established that the Wissahiccon is a worthy goal for the picturesque tourist in search of rare landscapes, the narrator describes its beauties in terms that reveal Poe's knowledge of the picturesque. His description, in fact, recalls that of William Gilpin in *Observations on the River Wye*, which celebrates the English river, just as the narrator celebrates the American one. Like Gilpin, who recommends river scenery--and a route by boat--for its frequent changes of view, the narrator observes that "the windings of the stream are many and abrupt" and comments upon the "endless succession of infinitely varied small lakes" presented to the traveler's eye (865).[12] He suggests that cliffs overlooking the water offer "the most picturesque position for a cottage and garden which the richest imagination could conceive" (864-65). The narrator then takes the reader along on a boat trip on the Wissahiccon, where he floats along with the current, letting his "imagination [revel] in visions of the Wissahiccon of ancient days," the "'good old days'" before the railroads, when the river belonged to no one and when Indians and elk still roamed the riverbanks (865). Wrapped in "half-slumberous fancies," the narrator suddenly glimpses a great elk standing on a precipice above the river, and, amazed at his imagined vision come to life, he responds intensely and sympathetically. He imagines that the elk, too, regrets the changes wrought by "the stern hand of the utilitarian" in recent years. But his fancy is rudely interrupted when a black servant emerges from the thicket and slips a halter over the elk, and the narrator is brought to earth with a bump, realizing that his "noble animal" is actually the pet of an English family living nearby (865-66).

The best clues as to how the reader should interpret the sketch lie both within it, in contradictions made by the narrator himself, and outside it, in other sketches of the Wissahiccon published before Poe's. To cite just a few of the former: first, the narrator insists on the rarity and inaccessibility of this scenery, which qualify it as a worthy source of pleasure for the picturesque tourist, but clearly even the farthest reaches of the Wissahiccon described in this sketch have been traveled before by others. In fact, according to Poe scholar Thomas Ollive Mabbott, the stream's "distinctive charm" had been recognized since the eighteenth century.[13] Second, the narrator disparages English streams of great beauty, whose banks are "parcelled off in lots . . . as building-sites for the villas of the opulent" (863), yet this section of the Wissahiccon has apparently already been subdivided into lots, ironically, for wealthy Englishmen. Finally, just as he extols the Salvatorean character of the scenery and the similar wildness of the elk, both are abruptly domesticated by the presence of the English villa and the servant with halter in hand. These elements undercut any effort to read the sketch in sympathy with the narrator and suggest, instead, that it is actually a satire on the naive expectations of Poe's picturesque tourist/narrator, whose notions of discovering rare, untouched landscapes in the eastern United States are at odds with the heavily traveled, tourist-infested region that it was in the 1840s.

Other travel pieces on the Wissahiccon that appeared in contemporary periodicals reinforce this interpretation of Poe's sketch. For example, "Wissahiccon Creek," a brief sketch that appeared in *The Casket* in 1830, casts doubt upon Poe's premise that the stream was, thirteen years later, still largely undiscovered by picturesque tourists.[14]

In 1835 "The Wissahiccon," by Benjamin Matthias, appeared in the *Southern Literary Messenger* during Poe's tenure on its editorial staff and may have influenced his description of the stream eight years later. Like Poe's sketch, this piece emphasizes the undiscovered nature of the stream, the picturesque quality of its beauty, and the unspoiled nature of its banks and mentions the Wissahiccon as the ancient seat of Indians and elk.[15] The many parallels between these two sketches suggest at least an indirect influence at work here and underscore Poe's satire on the picturesque tourist of the 1840s who expects, more than a decade after the first appearance of this stream in the pages of a popular periodical, that the Wissahiccon will remain untouched by progress and undisturbed by the other fashionable tourists who preceded him in admiring it. Since the Matthias sketch appeared later in the same year of Fanny Kemble's *Journal* and already lamented the incursions of mankind that had driven away its original inhabitants, Poe's work only confirms the eventual domestication of the Wissahiccon that was suggested earlier by Matthias.

After "Morning on the Wissahiccon" Poe did not abandon the notion of the picturesque tourist in the New World, nor did he discontinue his use of the picturesque tour. In two important tales published towards the end of his career these conventions are more successfully used to structure narrative and to develop theme than in his earlier works. In "The Domain of Arnheim" (originally "The Landscape-Garden" [1842] and revised in 1847), and its pendant piece, "Landor's Cottage" (1849), the aesthetic of the picturesque dominates,[16] but, what is more significant, Poe integrates the picturesque tour onto American soil with greater success than before at the same time that he uses it to satirize the artist-creators of picturesque beauty in the New World.

"The Domain of Arnheim" focuses upon the wealthy Ellison's attempt to recreate ideal beauty on earth by designing and creating a landscape garden that would rival the original Paradise and surpass that of present-day nature. The very arrogance of his ambition, which in itself contradicts one of his guiding principles ("contempt of ambition"), suggests the ironic tone that will come to dominate the tale, for although Gilpin, too, had occasionally criticized nature's "composition" as faulty, that clergyman would not have dreamed of suggesting that mankind's humble creations could ever rival God's works, as the narrator speciously argues here.[17]

After a lengthy discussion of the various styles of landscape gardening[18] and a brief description of Ellison's search for the perfect location for his landscape garden, the balance of the tale recounts the narrator's experience in visiting Arnheim. The *trip* to Arnheim, rather than a description of it, is the focus of the second part of the tale. This suggests that, for the narrator, the experience of traveling there was as important as the ultimate achievement of his goal, the revelation of the floating palace of Arnheim, and this is supported by his description of the elaborately detailed waterway created by Ellison as the approach to Arnheim. With his countless millions the landscape-gardener-poet has, in fact, achieved total control over the environment and created a river journey that passes through each of the stages of aesthetic beauty: from the pastoral tranquillity of the "rolling meadows," spotted with grazing sheep; to the picturesque beauty of the twisting turns of the stream, with its banks richly clothed in foliage; to the sublime splendor of the gorge, shutting out the light of day and winding in increasingly intricate turns.[19]

Even at this early point in the tour by water, there are already hints of the ironic reading Poe intends. Although a picturesque stream, such as the Wissahiccon, should contain many curves that enhance a variety of views, this "stream took a thousand turns," with no stretch longer than a furlong, which would surely set the boater's head spinning.[20] Instead of setting free the observer's vision, this landscape cuts it off, for "the vessel seemed imprisoned within an enchanted circle." Even in exploring unknown territory the tourist should retain some sense of where he or she is headed, but here "the voyager had long lost all idea of direction." Perhaps the strangest characteristic of the landscape is its sameness--the "weird symmetry" and "thrilling uniformity" that the narrator admires, contrary to every picturesque traveler before him, who sought novelty, not sameness, in a landscape. Finally, the scene is entirely too tidy--nothing dead or even withered exists; "there is not one token of the usual river *debris*," as the narrator states (1279, 1281). This might have been ideal in an eighteenth-century formal garden, but in a mid-nineteenth-century picturesque garden it sounds ridiculous.

Perhaps one of the oddest characteristics of the narrator on his journey to Arnheim is his strange lack of volition. In an ivory canoe he is swept along by the mysterious current. He drifts without paddle or guide, giving up all will to the unseen force that bears him along. Although landscape gardeners before this had been known--and famed-- for creating scenes that invoked particular ideas and responses in observers, the complete loss of control in Arnheim exaggerates this technique to the extent that the trip becomes a parody of a picturesque tour, with the tourist disoriented by the strange twists and turns of the current; oppressed, not refreshed, by the "strange sweet odor" around him; and distressed, no doubt, by an optical illusion that "wreathe[s] the whole surrounding forest in flames" (1281-83).[21]

At the climax of the tale the narrator's canoe glides between a winged gate and descends rapidly into an amphitheater surrounded by purple mountains "whose bases are laved by a gleaming river," suggesting the original Edenic landscape with its four rivers and surrounding wall. Suddenly "the whole Paradise of Arnheim bursts upon the view," states the narrator. Above this "dreamlike intermingling" of Eastern trees, gaudy birds, and heavy-scented flowers he sights "a mass of semi-Gothic, semi-Saracenic architecture, sustaining itself as if by miracle in mid air," the famed palace of Arnheim (1283). Appropriately for the picturesque tourist in "The Domain of Arnheim," Ellison has designed his palace as the highlight of the long river journey, just as Niagara Falls climaxes the American Grand Tour after the lengthy Hudson River trip and tedious passage on the Erie Canal. Yet the very notion of the long approach to Arnheim as a picturesque tour actually undercuts the final vision rather than highlighting it: if the object of such a tour is the discovery and enjoyment of landscape beauty, then that object is never gained here and, more important, is undermined and mocked by the artifice of the landscape Ellison has created. Likewise, Ellison's secondhand theories and Poe's ironic references throughout the tale lead the reader to question whether Arnheim is an ideal made real. Either Poe is questioning whether mankind can create natural beauty artificially--in itself a contradiction in terms--or he suggests by the narrator's unsuccessful quest for Arnheim (the palace floats beyond reach in midair) that even if the ideal can be imagined by mere mortals it cannot be attained on earth. In "The Domain of Arnheim" Ellison's gaudy, overpowering landscapes and the narrator's disoriented, even distressed response suggest not an ideal come to life, but a tawdry imitation paradise that would make Poe's imaginary earth-angels laugh rather than long to return to earth to dwell in Arnheim.

In "Landor's Cottage" the conventions of the picturesque tour also figure, both structurally and thematically, for the narrator is on a "pedestrian tour," by this date a synonym for a picturesque tour, of New York's Hudson River Valley. This tale does not focus on travel but on the narrator's discovery one evening of an artfully designed landscape leading up to a country cottage. The descriptions of the journey, the landscape, and the cottage all confirm the landscape gardener-architect's knowledge of picturesque conventions, but throughout the tale certain exaggerated elements and questionable references cast doubt upon the narrator's reading of this scene as an ideal world. As with Ellison's Arnheim, the picturesque tourist appears to discover the beauty he seeks at the end of his journey, yet in both tales Poe deliberately undercuts the ideal with comments that suggest artifice rather than art, and excess rather than moderation.

The narrator in "Landor's Cottage," somewhat like the one in "The Domain of Arnheim," proves himself at the outset to be a most unusual picturesque tourist by getting lost and not caring much about the matter at all. Both the river landscape and the smoky, misty day conspire to confuse him, and even after he reaches a path on Landor's estate, its winding, twisting quality bewilders him further. And although he remains naive and uncritical in matters of taste throughout the tale, the narrator comments with some bewilderment on the "*excess* of art manifested" all around him: like the approach to Arnheim, the road here is too artful, with "carefully *placed*" stones at its border, yet without the expected dead twigs and debris; the grass "looked more like green Genoese velvet than anything else"; and the path follows such an exaggeratedly serpentine path (after the ideal of English landscape gardener Capability Brown) that the traveler must be dizzy in walking along it (1329).[22] The pedestrian tourist wonders at the artful scene before him, yet though his attitude remains one of awe, the choice of words undercuts his admiration. He wonders if this is all an "illusion" or a "vanishing picture," and suggests that "the hand of magic" might have created the scenery. In admiring a garish scene of clashing orange, purple, and green, the narrator not only reveals his lack of taste but also his naivete, as Catherine Rainwater argues, for it reminds him forcefully of "the concluding scene of some well-arranged theatrical spectacle or melodrama," and he himself calls it a "monstrosity" (1330-31).[23]

Upon reaching the grounds of Landor's cottage, the traveler unwittingly comments on other jarring elements in the scene. To cite a few examples: he notes that the sheep and deer that appear to roam at will are actually fenced in; a large dog guards the animals; singing birds are caged in "delicate prisons"[24]; and the "picturesque effect" of the house is partially achieved by potted flowers. In short, this is an artfully contrived world where nature is caged and imprisoned, a picture created by the artist, Landor, primarily for effect. Even the narrator in this tale is faintly disturbed by its excessive artifice. The eye of a more sophisticated, experienced traveler would spot such transparent artifice easily and, presumably, scorn it in favor of landscapes that, though shaped by the hand of art, were more natural in appearance.

The question might arise here whether Poe himself preferred the artificial or the natural in a landscape. The answer to this would determine whether the sketch's tone was straightforward or ironic. In a letter written to his fiancee, Mrs. Sarah Helen Whitman, while Poe was composing "Landor's Cottage" he describes his idea for a sequel to "The Domain of Arnheim": "I suffered my imagination to stray with you . . . to the banks of some quiet river, in some lovely valley of our land. Here . . . we exercised a taste controlled by no conventionalities, but the sworn slave of a Natural Art."[25] Any landscape created by mankind involves art shaping nature, but the degree to which the artful dominates over the natural determines whether the resulting scene looks artificial or natural. Poe suggests in his letter that he prefers a "Natural Art," which implies that he would dislike artifice in a landscape. Hence the obvious artifice of much of the scenery on Landor's estate and near his cottage would not appeal to him. Either the author got carried away in describing his dream cottage or, as I would argue, his tone is ironic in the tale.

Since the outcome of the picturesque tours in both "The Domain of Arnheim" and "Landor's Cottage" is the discovery of deceptively ideal worlds, Poe suggests in these tales that although aesthetic pleasures may await the traveler who explores untraveled paths, such pleasures are at best unattainable and at worst deceptive. The conventions of the picturesque tour and tourist in Poe's late landscape tales become a means to convey his doubts about transplanting the picturesque tour to America and, more important, his ambivalence about the achievements of art and the role of the artist, represented by the landscape gardener. In these tales the artist-as-landscape-gardener functions more like a magician employing a few cheap sleight-of-hand tricks rather than like an artist drawing upon truth to present its image in art. Art cannot create beauty as perfect as that of nature, and in these tales beauty created by the artist who relies on superficial effects is not, in the end, a form of truth at all.

Poe's use of the picturesque traveler as protagonist changes over the course of the nine years during which these four works appeared. In *The Journal of Julius Rodman* he began by featuring the picturesque tourist as the central figure in an elaborate hoax on the public, pretending that Rodman was the explorer and discoverer of great tracts of unknown western lands. Although the work is sometimes a crazy quilt of travel narrative and picturesque description patched together with details about the fur trade and Indian life, as a loosely framed picturesque tour it is moderately successful, though not to the degree that Parkman's *Oregon Trail* succeeds in presenting a western tour. And unlike Irving and Parkman, who introduced concerns about the character of American men, particularly easterners, and ideas about the national identity, Poe missed an opportunity to make an original contribution to the developing genre of the combined tour and western adventure story.

In "Morning on the Wissahiccon" the brevity of the sketch enables its author to present a more focused work that succeeds in its more modest aims: to contrast European and American tourism, to argue the superiority of American landscapes, and to question and even mock the picturesque tourist intent on discovering new landscapes in the much-traveled eastern seaboard states. Towards the end of his career Poe's work using the picturesque tour changes direction, employing irony as a key technique to question whether the artist as landscape gardener can create or surpass natural beauty. The picturesque tourists in these works discover the beauty they seek, but it is unattainable, deceptive, or artificial. The only other writer at midcentury to employ the tour in new ways is Henry David Thoreau, whose love of picturesque travel and beauty would carry him throughout New England in pursuit of aesthetic and philosophic pleasures.

Notes

1. See Catherine Rainwater, "Poe's Landscape Tales and the 'Picturesque' Tradition," *Southern Literary Journal* 16 (Spring 1984): 30-43; and Kent Ljungquist, *The Grand and the Fair: Poe's Landscape*

Aesthetics and Pictorial Techniques (Potomac, Maryland: Scripta Humanistica, 1984).

2. Burton R. Pollin, ed., *The Imaginary Voyages: The Narrative of Arthur Gordon Pym; The Unparalleled Adventure of one Hans Pfaall; The Journal of Julius Rodman, Collected Writings of Edgar Allan Poe* (Boston: Twayne, 1981), 1: 508-09, 512. All subsequent references to this volume appear in the text.

3. See Ljungquist, pp. 12-14; Pollin, p. 515; John J. Teunissen and Evelyn J. Hinz, "Poe's *Journal of Julius Rodman* as Parody," *Nineteenth-Century Fiction* 27 (Dec. 1972): 317-38.

4. William Gilpin, "On Picturesque Travel," *Three Essays: on Picturesque Beauty; on Picturesque Travel; and on Sketching Landscape: to which is added a poem, on Landscape Painting*, 2nd ed. (London: R. Blamire, 1754; repr. Westmead, England: Gregg International, 1972), pp. 47-48.

5. The terms "amuse" and "amusement" appear five times on the first page of Gilpin's essay and are used throughout the piece ("On Picturesque Travel," p. 41).

6. Ljungquist, p. 36. Blake Nevius suggests that Poe was more knowledgeable about British aesthetics, stating that Poe had definitely read Burke, "probably" Richard Payne Knight, and possibly others in his review of Ljungquist's book, "Poe's Landscape Aesthetics," in *Poe Studies* 18 (December 1985): 26.

7. Ljungquist, pp. 11-14. Ljungquist argues that Poe recognized the "basic paradox" of trying "to write a story about an eighteenth-century landscape garden in the framework of an American wilderness setting" in *Julius Rodman* and suggests that "the aesthetic contradictions, even absurdities" of this attempt led Poe to drop the work as a result (p. 14).

8. Teunissen and Hinz, pp. 317-38. Burton R. Rollin also argues that *Julius Rodman* is a hoax rather than a parody (pp. 514-15).

9. Peter Antelyes remarks upon Poe's recognition of "Irving's underlying concern for the role of the imagination" in the commercialism displayed in *Astoria* and links this with *The Narrative of Arthur Gordon Pym* (*Tales of Adventurous Enterprise: Washington Irving and the Poetics of Western Expansion* [New York: Columbia University Press, 1990], pp. 199-200). Poe knew *Astoria* well enough to cite a specific passage from it five years later in a review of Cornelius Mathews's *Wakondah*, reprinted in *Edgar Allan Poe: Essays and Reviews*, ed. G. R. Thompson (New York: Library of America, 1984), p. 824. Poe's review of *Astoria* also is reprinted in this edition (pp. 614-41).

10. "Morning on the Wissahiccon," *Tales and Sketches: 1843-1849*, ed. Thomas Ollive Mabbott, *Collected Works of Edgar Allan Poe* (Cambridge, Mass.: Belknap Press of Harvard University Press, 1978), pp. 861-62. All subsequent references to this sketch appear in the text.

11. Frances Anne Butler, *Journal*, 2 vols. (Philadelphia: Carey, Lea & Blanchard, 1835), 1: 66-67. In a review of Kemble's *Journal* an anonymous writer originally thought to be Poe finds "much, very much, to admire and approve, and much also to censure and condemn" in her work, and he praises "the vivacity of its style" and "the frequent occurrence of beautiful descriptions" in it ("Journal--By Frances Anne Butler," in *Early Criticism, Complete Works of Edgar Allan Poe*, ed. James A. Harrison [1902; repr. New York: AMS Press, 1965], 8: 21). The review first appeared in *Southern Literary Messenger* (May 1835).

12. William Gilpin, *Observations on the River Wye* (London: R. Blamire, 1782), pp. 7-8.

13. Mabbott, p. 860.

14. "Wissahiccon Creek," *The Casket* 5 (1830): 505.

15. Benjamin Matthias, "The Wissahiccon," *Southern Literary Messenger* (December 1835): 24-25.

16. See, for example, Sharon Furrow, "Psyche and Setting: Poe's Picturesque Landscapes," *Criticism* 15 (1973): 16-27; Ljungquist, pp. 129-40; and Rainwater, pp. 30-43.

17. In *Observations on the River Wye* Gilpin states, "Nature is always great in design; but unequal in composition" (p. 18), and he suggests that the artist not imitate nature exactly but improve it, using his or her taste as a guideline ("On Picturesque Travel," p. 52).

In an interesting comment on composition and nature, Gilpin suggests in the Wye tour almost exactly what Ellison argues to the narrator in "The Domain of Arnheim." Gilpin writes: "The case is, the immensity of nature is beyond human comprehension. She works on a *vast scale*; and, no doubt, harmoniously, if her schemes could be comprehended" (p. 18). Ellison states that "each alteration of the natural scenery" by the landscape gardener or artist might cause a "blemish" in the larger picture, if one could view the earth as a whole. In this view he echoes Gilpin, though his idea of "earth-angels," for "whose death-refined appreciation of the beautiful" God has created "the wide landscape-gardens of the hemispheres" (1274) would be considered blasphemous by the English clergyman.

The narrator's and Ellison's views here, though they distort Gilpin's ideas, provide another example of Gilpin's influence on Poe's writings.

18. This discussion is taken from an *Arcturus* review of Andrew Jackson Downing's *Treatise on the Theory and Practice of Landscape Gardening*, according to Joel R. Kehler, "New Light on the Genesis and Progress of Poe's Landscape Fiction," *American Literature* 47 (May 1975): 173-76. The first critic to cite Poe's source of the ideas expressed in "The Domain of Arnheim" on landscape gardening as Downing's *Treatise* was Jeffrey A. Hess in "Sources and Aesthetics of Poe's Landscape Fiction," *American Quarterly* 22 (Summer 1970): 179-80. It was Kehler, however, who discovered that Poe apparently gleaned his information from the *Arcturus* review, rather than from a reading of the original Downing book.

19. "The Domain of Arnheim," *Tales and Sketches*, pp. 1278-79. All subsequent references to this tale and to "Landor's Cottage" are to this edition and appear in the text.

20. Rainwater notes the exaggerated nature of the waterway and discusses some of the other qualities at odds with the true picturesque in Ellison's created paradise (pp. 38-39).

21. Rainwater discusses the way the traveler "exerts no power of his own" during the approach to Arnheim, "but is instead controlled by his environment, the creation of the artist, Ellison" and comments on "the traveler's sense of spatial disorientation" on the journey (pp. 37-38).

22. Rainwater discusses the narrator's naivete about aesthetics and comments on Poe's use of Brown's landscape designs in this tale, noting that Poe criticizes the English designer in an earlier *Broadway Journal* review (April 1845). She also discusses the unusual path: "This road sacrifices function almost totally to the exigencies of design" (pp. 31-32, 39-40).

23. Rainwater, p. 40.

24. Ljungquist, p. 136.

25. Mabbott, p. 1326.

Chapter 7

Excursions in New England:
Thoreau as Picturesque Tourist

In the essay "Walking" Thoreau wrote, "I think that I cannot preserve my health and spirits, unless I spend four hours a day at least --and it is commonly more than that--sauntering through the woods and over the hills and fields, absolutely free from all worldly engagements." Walking was Thoreau's favorite outdoor pursuit, and he frequently expressed his delight in this pastime. Like William Gilpin, he felt that "an absolutely new prospect is a great happiness," and in spite of his frequent walks in the Concord area he still found new territory to explore nearby. Indeed, Thoreau argues, "Two or three hours' walking will carry me to as strange a country as I expect ever to see," echoing his famous comment almost a decade earlier in *Walden* that he had "travelled a good deal in Concord."[1] The meditations and images evoked by his favorite pastime were expressed in the literary excursion, which he developed into his most important short prose form. The "romantic excursion," as Lawrence Buell defines it, is a "ramble ('Walking') or trip (*Cape Cod*) or sojourn (*Walden*) which takes on overtones of a spiritual quest as the speaker proceeds."[2] Thoreau combined the structure of the romantic excursion with some elements of the picturesque tour to produce a form uniquely his own.

Like many other nineteenth-century writers, Thoreau's love for landscape beauty and the pleasures of traveling led him to the picturesque tour, but he alone envisioned the picturesque tour as metaphor. Ordinary travel, for this writer, often became a metaphor for exploration of the self. Picturesque travel, more specifically, became a metaphor for moral and spiritual discovery. Transcendentalist philosophy, according to Buell, held that "true travel is spiritual travel, an exploration of one's own higher latitudes."[3] For Thoreau travel, especially picturesque travel, became a means of exploring his inner self, as well as the character of the natural world. In addition, Thoreau presents a clear-cut case of the direct influence of William Gilpin's writings, unlike American writers such as Hawthorne and Parkman, for whom the influence of British aesthetics, particularly Gilpin's work, was indirect and, consequently, difficult to trace. From his journals it is evident that Thoreau not only knew of William Gilpin's writings on the picturesque but also had read them carefully and quoted them frequently. In prose writings from *Walden* (1854) to *The Maine Woods* (1864) and throughout *Excursions* (1863) he shows his familiarity with Gilpin's aesthetic concepts and reveals his love of picturesque travel. While in *Excursions* his comments on the scenery in New England and Canada reveal no more than the ordinary conception of touring as a search for landscape beauty, in *The Maine Woods* Thoreau takes picturesque travel a step further to use it as a search for moral beauty and spiritual discovery. In doing so, he suggests new directions for Americans to pursue in the continuing search for national identity, here, taking the search in a direction that might lead from personal rejuvenation to national revitalization.

According to Thoreau's journals, of all the American writers considered in this book, he was the most knowledgeable about Gilpin, the principles of picturesque beauty, and the idea of picturesque travel. In these volumes Thoreau reveals an interest in Gilpin and the subjects of picturesque beauty and travel in general that began in 1852 and continued intensively for the next two years.[4] In a letter to Daniel Ricketson, who had written him expressing his appreciation for the recently published *Walden*, Thoreau mentions a "list of lovers of Nature" that his correspondent had included in his letter and describes "*Wm* Gilpin's long series of books on the Picturesque" as his own latest "thunder." "If it chances that you have not met with these," he writes, "I cannot just now frame a better wish than that you may one day derive as much pleasure from the inspection of them as I have."[5] From his references in the journals to books read and quotations from others, Thoreau had apparently read seven of the nine Gilpin works he recommended to Ricketson in another letter.[6] These include five of the six major tours (*Observations on the River Wye*, *Tour of the Lakes*, both the *Scotch Tour* and *Western Tour*, *Observations on . . . Hampshire, Sussex, and Kent*), *Forest Scenery*, and *Three Essays*, including "On Sketching Landscape" and "On Picturesque Travel." In fact, according to William D. Templeman, the first critic to examine Thoreau's indebtedness to Gilpin, no other author, other than those personally known to Thoreau, is the focus of so much attention in the journals.[7] Biographer Robert D. Richardson, Jr., summarizes the impact Gilpin had on Thoreau's writing, praising "the great and liberating effect of Gilpin's descriptive genius on Thoreau." "Gilpin had gone a bit further down the road Thoreau was already on," Richardson explains, "and his example could therefore extend Thoreau's range, enlarge his palette, sharpen his vision."[8]

Thoreau also thought more deeply about the moral value of picturesque travel than other writers of his time, certainly more so than Gilpin, who accorded this issue only brief consideration in his essay "On Picturesque Travel."[9] Indeed, he criticizes Gilpin's essay sharply, arguing that to eliminate the moral value of picturesque beauty would be to eviscerate it. Thoreau disagrees with Gilpin, whose view of the picturesque as a purely visual phenomenon he quotes, and implies that true aesthetic pleasure lies instead in the moral and psychological dimensions of a landscape's beauty, not just its surface appearance.[10] Elsewhere he criticizes Gilpin's *Tour of the Lakes* for similar reasons. While admiring the English writer's "elegant moderation, his discrimination, and real interest in nature," Thoreau counters, "I wish he would look at scenery sometimes not with the eye of an artist. It is all side screens and fore screens and near distances and broken grounds with him."[11] As Gordon V. Boudreau has noted, to someone whose vision was "profoundly metaphysical," as Thoreau's was, Gilpin's commentaries on the picturesque seemed "shallow" and "superficial." He argues that Thoreau rejected Gilpin for his "failure of moral vision, penetration, or courage."[12] For example, Gilpin did not admire mountaintop views, commenting only upon their visual value. To Thoreau, this implied that such views were not "deserving of serious attention."[13] In his own work, the American writer would frequently emphasize the moral or spiritual value of the traveler's experiences upon a mountaintop rather than its visual beauty, particularly in *The Maine Woods* on Mount Katahdin. Yet it was only on the issue of the moral value of picturesque beauty that Thoreau would criticize Gilpin; throughout the *Journals* he continued to quote "the great master of the picturesque"[14] extensively and to refer to his work admiringly.

Before a discussion of the major works that were influenced by the picturesque tour, it might be useful to explain why *A Week on the Concord and Merrimack Rivers* is not part of this group. Adapted in part from materials gathered from a trip with his brother John in 1839 and from his journals, *A Week* was published ten years later. An unusual travel narrative that featured an "alternating flow of action and meditation," one of the earlier titles--"Memoirs of a Tour"--implies its connection with the picturesque tour Gilpin and others had popularized.[15] Yet in the decade between the original tour and the book's publication, Thoreau had not yet encountered Gilpin's English tours. In addition, and more important, in spite of *A Week*'s extensive use of the travel narrative, very little of the book focuses on landscape. The author's climb of Mount Greylock in Massachusetts provides one of the few experiences of landscape scenery in the book, yet it is anecdotal in character, for in it the author recalls an earlier mountain-climbing experience, not one from his recent trip.[16] Strongly influenced by Thoreau's ascent of Mount Katahdin in 1846, this section is full of mythological allusions, with only the occasional reference to a prospect or description of a panoramic view.[17] While the book's structure, alternating between straight travel narrative and digressions, is similar to that of a picturesque tour, there simply is not enough sustained interest on the author's part in landscape scenery to justify its inclusion here as an example of picturesque travel.[18]

Thoreau's *Excursions*, on the other hand, reflects his pleasure in picturesque travel and appreciation for landscape beauty, even though most of the outings described in the book are not true picturesque tours. Although their main object is not the pursuit of picturesque beauty but a love of walking and of the wilderness, these excursions are important for the insights they offer into Thoreau's ideas about travel, scenery, and wildness. In addition to *A Yankee in Canada*, three essays deserve special attention in this group: "Walking," for the author's discussion of "the art of Walking" (5: 205); and "A Winter Walk" and "A Walk to Wachusett" as examples of his brief walking tours of the countryside. *A Yankee in Canada*, published in part in *Putnam's* in 1853, records Thoreau's trip to Montreal and Quebec in 1850 with his friend Ellery Channing. The work is a conventional travel narrative of the mid-nineteenth century, with its discussion of historical sites, cities, the local citizenry, anecdotes of the trip, and scenic beauty. While the major object of the trip was not the discovery of picturesque beauty, which disqualifies the narrative from being a true picturesque tour, the author's frequent comments on Canada's mountains and falls suggest his familiarity with the genre and his pleasure in landscape scenery. The tour itself predates Thoreau's recorded interest in William Gilpin and his works, so that few, if any, references suggest any special knowledge of Gilpin's theories or tours.

While some of the narrator's comments on mountain scenery, for example, and the changing colors of autumn foliage reflect no more than the average nature-lover's interest in such beauty, elsewhere his response to prospects and interpretation of landscapes suggests a more knowledgeable interest in picturesque beauty. On Lake Champlain, for instance, he comments on the "impressive" view of the lake, noting that this derives "rather from association than from any peculiarity in the scenery" (5: 7). This implies at least a passing knowledge of associational theory and not just a surface familiarity with landscape appreciation. Although the narrator sometimes gives a "*splendid* view" or an "extensive view" only the most cursory attention (5: 24, 27), his determined pursuit of Canada's many falls suggests an abiding interest in picturesque scenery. To reach the Falls of St. Anne, for example, he and his companion persist in walking through woods and up steep hills to gain a good view of the falls. His description of the falls runs for three full pages, and he concludes with a tribute to the falls' sublimity: "Take it altogether, it was a most wild and rugged and stupendous chasm, so deep and narrow, where a river had worn itself a passage through a mountain of rock, and all around was the comparatively untrodden wilderness" (5: 55). Yet in spite of frequent references to landscape beauty, *A Yankee in Canada* retains its emphasis on that country's many differences from its southern neighbor, and the narrator's pursuit of picturesque beauty remains only secondary.

In other works in *Excursions* Thoreau focuses on his pleasure in touring the local countryside rather than traveling afar, and comments on the meaning of the walking tour for him. In "Walking" he describes his need for daily walks and recommends walking as a means of keeping in touch with nature rather than society, for to him, nature represents "absolute freedom and wildness," essential qualities of his world (5: 207, 205). Though he saunters in no certain direction, he notes that his instinctive direction is always western: "It is hard for me to believe that I shall find fair landscapes or sufficient wildness and freedom behind the eastern horizon," and these are the qualities he seeks on his walking tours (5: 217). Gilpin had noted that the primary source of amusement for the picturesque traveler was "the expectation of new scenes"; assuming the country to be unexplored, he described the tourist's pleasure in pursuing nature "through all her walks."[19]

Similarly, Thoreau appreciated the diversity of views around Concord and loved discovering new views, even where he had walked before. One might, Thoreau argued, discover "a sort of harmony . . . between the capabilities of the landscape within a circle of ten miles' radius, or the limits of an afternoon walk, and the threescore years and ten of human life." "It will," he assured readers, "never become quite familiar to you" (5: 211-12). One important theme in the essay is the author's belief that civilized people lacked the necessary appreciation for "the beauty of the landscape," which would take them into the natural world more often and help them keep the proper balance in their lives between civilization and nature (5: 241-42). This is connected to his discussion of "wildness," a concept Richardson considers central to the essay and to Thoreau's thinking. According to Richardson, Thoreau "understands wildness as the opposite of . . . civilization," while serving as "the ultimate source of the energy that builds civilizations."[20]

In "A Winter Walk" and "A Walk to Wachusetts" Thoreau demonstrates both the pleasure and the meaning one could derive from walking tours, one on a snowy winter's day and the other to a nearby mountain. In the first essay the narrator ventures out at dawn after a night's snowfall. Admiring the snow-laden landscape, he also comments on its meaning for him. For example, he reflects: "Standing quite alone, far in the forest, while the wind is shaking down snow from the trees, and leaving the only human tracks behind us, we find our reflections of a richer variety than the life of cities. . . . In this lonely glen, with its brook draining the slopes, its creased ice and crystals of all hues, where the spruces and hemlocks stand up on either side, and the rush and sere wild oats in the rivulet itself, our lives are more serene and worthy to contemplate" (5: 171). Elsewhere the narrator ascends a hill and comments on the view, at the same time establishing his relationship to the landscape before him:

> We can look over the broad country of forest and field and river, to the distant snowy mountains. See yonder thin column of smoke curling up through the woods from some invisible farmhouse . . . There must be a warmer and more genial spot there below, as where we detect the vapor from a spring forming a cloud above the trees. What fine relations are established between the traveler who discovers this airy column from some eminence in the forest and

him who sits below! . . . It is a hieroglyphic of
man's life, and suggests more intimate and important
things than the boiling of a pot. Where its fine
column rises above the forest, like an ensign, some
human life has planted itself,--and such is the
beginning of Rome, . . . and the foundation of
empires, whether on the prairies of America or the
steppes of Asia. (5: 173-74)

Thoreau's pattern of moving from the actual to the metaphoric,
demonstrated here, would be familiar to readers of *Walden* or any of
his other earlier works.

In "A Walk to Wachusett" he and a companion take a walking
tour in midsummer to explore a mountain whose outline on the horizon
has long beckoned to him. The object of their journey is, to some
extent, the discovery of picturesque beauty, for the narrator comments
frequently on the various prospects he glimpses as he and his friend
ascend the mountain's slopes (5: 137-39). Occasional references to the
mountains as the dwelling place of the gods and symbolic
interpretations of landscape suggest, however, that the picturesque tour
is more than a search for visual beauty for him. Although he notes that
"there was little of the sublimity and grandeur which belong to
mountain scenery" in the prospect from the summit, the view offered
"an immense landscape to ponder on a summer's day." And as he and
his companion ramble along the mountain's upper ridge, he suggests
that in spite of its lack of sublimity, Wachusett might one day be a
Parnassus and offer a home for the Muses: "It was a place where gods
might wander, so solemn and solitary, and removed from all contagion
with the plain" (5: 146, 144). Nearing the end of his trip, the narrator
concludes by interpreting the experience for his readers: "And now that
we have returned to the desultory life of the plain, let us endeavor to
import a little of that mountain grandeur into it. We will remember
within what walls we lie, and understand that this level life too has its
summit, and why from the mountain-top the deepest valleys have a
tinge of blue; that there is elevation in every hour, as no part of the
earth is so low that the heavens may not be seen from, and we have
only to stand on the summit of our hour to command an uninterrupted
horizon" (5: 151). In the essays in *Excursions* Thoreau establishes this
movement from the actual experience of the walking tour and the
traveler's pleasure in landscape beauty to a symbolic interpretation of

both landscapes and tour. Later he develops the technique even further in *The Maine Woods*, where a group of three related excursions reflect the same movement from actual to symbolic, and the traveler's experiences in Maine climax in his ascension of Mount Katahdin.

In all three essays in *The Maine Woods* the narrator emphasizes that traveling through this wilderness terrain is not as simple as walking near his native Concord. In contrast, travel here is arduous. In "The Allegash and East Branch," for example, he exclaims: "Here was travelling of the old heroic kind over the unaltered face of nature."[21] In "Ktaadn" he graphically describes the kind of travel he experienced in the Maine wilderness, where he and his friends "slumped, scrambled, rolled, bounded, and walked, by turns, over this scraggy country" (61). Describing the rough passage to Chamberlain Lake in "The Allegash," the narrator notes the absence of "the larger inhabitants" of the forest except for a dead porcupine: "perhaps he had succumbed to the difficulties of the way," Thoreau notes, with his typically understated sense of humor (219). Elsewhere he complains of the various "insect foes" that besieged them: mosquitoes, black flies, and moose flies (223-23). Travel in the Maine woods is forbiddingly difficult at mid-century; early in "Ktaadn" the author notes that few white men have climbed the mountain and comments that "it will be a long time before the tide of fashionable travel sets that way" (4). This statement confirms Thoreau's awareness of "fashionable travel" and the preference of the fashionable tourists for picturesque vistas that are easily accessible.[22]

Yet travel in the north woods, rough as it was, did not preclude the possibility of aesthetic appreciation of the landscape. The narrator admires the lakes and mountains of Maine as often as he stops to admire the landscape beauties of Massachusetts in *Excursions*. In "The Allegash and East Branch" he describes the sensation of crossing a lake by canoe after being "shut up in the woods" with the lake waters spread before him and the wide sky above: "It is one of the surprises which Nature has in store for the traveller in the forest. To look down . . . over eighteen miles of water, was liberating and civilizing even." Musing on the eternal twilight of the forest, the narrator suggests that the woods' dimness might bring about a similar dimness in its inhabitants, whom Thoreau calls "*salvages*," regardless of their race. In the tradition of the best British picturesque writers, the openness of the landscape has both psychological and political implications. Just as the dim woods engender dullness in the forest-dweller, the lakes, which "reveal the mountains, and give ample scope and range to our thought," are a force that liberates and civilizes the observer (197-98). For a democracy whose future is threatened by people lacking vision, Thoreau offers travel in the wilderness as remedy and restorative. The wildness restores the burning, pagan energy civilized people have lost, and the landscape's openness frees them psychologically and philosophically from the restrictions imposed by modern city life.

In what Thoreau calls the "lake-country of New England," where one lake seems to flow into another, water often attracts the picturesque eye of the narrator, who muses about its isolated beauty. In "Ktaadn," for instance, he describes the "noble sheet of water" of North Twin Lake seen in the twilight. Here there was no "lover of nature or musing traveller watching our batteau from the distant hills," Thoreau notes. He recalls the scene: "At first the red clouds hung over the western shore as gorgeously as if over a city, and the lake lay open to the light with even a civilized aspect, as if expecting trade and commerce, and towns and villas." Through the inlet to the South Twin Lake, he looks across "the entire expanse of a concealed lake to its own yet more dim and distant shore. The shores rose gently to ranges of low hills covered with forests" that had already been culled of their timber (35-36). In a Claudian scene in which the softened distance beckons the observer, the lake "lays open to the light," as if passively awaiting its blessing--and the pen or pencil of the picturesque traveler. Into this luminous, hushed scene Thoreau interjects a disquieting note: for all its wildness, the lake bears a "civilized aspect" that expects, even invites the future settlements and cities that will eventually destroy its isolated beauty. A similar juxtaposition of picturesque beauty with imagined future development occurs later in the same essay when he recalls his descent from Mount Katahdin. Nature offers him a prospect through the shifting clouds: "Occasionally, as I came down the wind would blow me a vista open through which I could see the country eastward, boundless forests, and lakes, and streams, gleaming in the sun, some of them emptying into the East Branch. There were also new mountains in sight in that direction" (65). Moments later a panoramic view opens up before both the narrator and his companions, and they admire the "immeasurable forest" and "countless lakes." Noting the untouched beauty of the view before him, the narrator comments, cryptically, "No clearing, no house." Yet about that same forest he also concludes: "It was a large farm for somebody, when cleared." This echoes an earlier remark on the delicious cranberries he and his fellow travelers found near the mountaintop, when he notes without comment that "these cranberries will perhaps become an article of commerce" (66).

Selling wild cranberries and clearing native forest: How can a writer who would one day say that "in Wildness is the preservation of the World" casually toss away all he believes in and accept the destruction of the north woods as if it were foreordained ("Walking," 5: 224)? Considering his condemnation of the wastefulness and destructiveness of the logging operations in both "Chesuncook" and "The Allegash and East Branch," it is possible that these remarks reflect an earlier, more romantic view of loggers in the north woods.[23] Thoreau's remarks may also exemplify the kind of inconsistency Emerson had in mind when he made his famous comment on the subject, in this case suggesting the range of the younger man's thinking on logging and the wilderness over a period of time. This explanation seems reasonable, given the more than ten years that elapsed between the first draft of "Ktaadn" (1846) and the writing of "Chesuncook" (1853) and "The Allegash" (1858). Significantly, in the intervening years Thoreau also read William Gilpin's work, especially *Remarks on Forest Scenery*, which offers a similar argument for preserving the beauty and extensiveness of the old forests in Great Britain.[24] Comments about the future of a scenic view also suggest the same sort of thinking behind Crèvecoeur's and Paulding's future picturesque; instead of finding associations with the past in a landscape (or in the absence of such associations), the observer imagines future buildings, settlements, even towns on the site, generally viewing these in a positive light as improvements or as least not as detriments to scenic beauty. I like to think, however, that Thoreau would have decried the recent attempt of a developer to build condominiums on a hill overlooking Walden Pond, and that he would have supported modern efforts to preserve as much as possible of the old north woods.[25]

Of the various rivers and mountains explored in his three separate trips to Maine, Mount Katahdin offered the ultimate challenge for Thoreau: not simply the challenge of climbing a difficult mountain but also that of confronting the dark side of nature. Buell defines the excursion ("both in life and as a literary endeavor") for Thoreau as "a succession of confrontations with nature"; "Ktaadn," the essay that resulted from Thoreau's August 1848 trip to the Maine woods, comes closest to being an excursion in both senses. Ironically, "Ktaadn" is also the first of the three excursions in *The Maine Woods*, both according to date of composition (1846-47) and publication (1848), and the only one written before he had read Gilpin.[26]

Although comments on scenery and interpretive analyses of natural phenomena appear frequently throughout *The Maine Woods*, in "Ktaadn" Thoreau's reflections about landscape and his unique understanding of the meaning of travel in this wilderness climax. An early view of Katahdin suggests the author's point of view. "Its summit," he notes, was "veiled in clouds, like a dark isthmus in that quarter, connecting the heavens with the earth" (33). As in similar passages on mountains in *Excursions*, Katahdin occupies a space between earth and sky and serves, he states elsewhere, as a home for the gods (65). Ascending the mountain, the narrator emphasizes the difficulty of his passage, as noted earlier, and he even drops to his knees and crawls on all fours at one point (60), like many a picturesque tourist before him in the American wilderness.[27] Instead of the prospects one would expect, he stresses the lack of visibility during his climb. Throughout the ascension he remarks on the hostility of nature, as if he as man and mortal is invading territory reserved for animals and for the gods. At the summit of a ridge, for example, he finds himself "deep within the hostile ranks of clouds," where "all objects were obscured by them" (63). Here at the top is "vast, Titanic, inhuman Nature" that repels the climbers as if they were invaders (64). In *Thoreau as Romantic Naturalist* James McIntosh describes the author's "personal alienation from nature" in this section of "Ktaadn." According to McIntosh, Thoreau sprinkles his narrative with literary allusions--to Atlas, Vulcan, the Cyclops, Prometheus, as well as to the Titans--"in part to create a saving distance between the writer and his terrific experience."[28] This sense of separation between man and nature persists until the end of the "*Contact!*" passage in "Ktaadn" and is further developed in that section. Sometimes, though, it turns into a meditation on the sublimity of nature, a perception of the world in which the observer is not so much separated from it as in awe of it.

Developing a Burkean interpretation of the mountain and his experiences there,[29] the narrator is deeply impressed with the sublime presence of nature on Katahdin and awed by evidence of the gods there: "Nature was here something savage and awful, though beautiful. I looked with awe at the ground I trod on, to see what the Powers had made there, the form and fashion and material of their work. This was that Earth of which we have heard, made out of Chaos and Old Night. Here was no man's garden, but the unhandselled globe" (70). In *The Maine Woods* and elsewhere Thoreau generally appreciates and even seems to prefer the picturesque in nature, whether wilderness lakes or the rough outlines of the northern forest. Yet at the summit of Mount Katahdin he admires not the picturesque (the "garden" in this passage) but the stark, savage sublime, the raw materials of the world without the softening influence of civilization. Here he can view the world as "the Powers" originally made it, before mankind began to shape and change nature for its own ends. Such a world is both frightening and awe-inspiring to the narrator--even, as he notes, "beautiful" in its own way, though not according to the dictates of picturesque beauty.

Throughout the narrator's climactic experience on the mountaintop, he emphasizes nature's inhospitableness to mankind there and his own awe at treading such sacred ground. He felt there "the presence of a force not bound to be kind to man. It was a place," he writes, "for heathenism and superstitious rites," where the bear and the moose may be welcome, but not people (70-71). As he and his friends walk over the mountain "with a certain awe," the narrator notes that "not even the surface had been scarred by man." Instead, "it was a specimen of what God saw fit to make this world." Finally, standing on the "unhandselled" territory of the mountaintop, he exclaims: "I stand in awe of my body, this matter to which I am bound has become so strange to me. I fear not spirits, ghosts, of which I am one . . . but I fear bodies, I tremble to meet them. What is this Titan that has possession of me? Talk of mysteries!--Think of our life in nature,-- daily to be shown matter, to come in contact with it,--rocks, trees, wind on our cheeks! the *solid* earth! the *actual* world! the *common sense*! *Contact*! *Contact*! *Who* are we? *where* are we?" (71).

Elsewhere Thoreau moves between the physical and spiritual worlds with ease (throughout *Walden*, for example). But in "Ktaadn" he portrays the narrator as mystified not by the spiritual, the unseen world, but by the physical, the matter with which he comes in hard contact on Mount Katahdin. For someone who has consistently idealized nature, he has great difficulty accepting the indifference of the nature he encounters on the mountain's summit. Here Thoreau suggests that his idealized notion of nature as a nurturing force for mankind is not always realistic. Elsewhere the body is "a magnificent expression of the active soul," and nature serves similarly as both expression and symbol of the spiritual world. Yet here on Mount Katahdin the body is "a formless matter that the narrator trembles to inhabit,"[30] and nature likewise has become, for the moment, an impenetrable material world that rejects all links with the spiritual. Both he and the material world are held captive in body and matter and, in the end, nature is terrifyingly indifferent to him and his quest to penetrate its meaning, just as Moby Dick remains coldly indifferent to Ahab's attempts to penetrate "the mask." As Richardson states, Thoreau learned that "on Katahdin nature was at best indifferent to human life." Furthermore, he [accepted] what Ahab could never accept: "Katahdin taught Thoreau . . . that while man is part of nature, he is not the lord of nature. Nature may indeed smile on man in the valleys, but there are also places where man is not welcome. In short, there are limits. Man is still very much a part of nature, but he is only one part; he is not everything. Nature will support and nourish him, but only if he respects and acknowledges the limits."[31]

The evil, then, that Thoreau "fronts" in "Ktaadn" is not just the presence of man in the wilderness, invading a territory that rejects him, but the very indifference of nature to his presence and to his quest. The picturesque tour has clearly become not only a physical quest, but a spiritual one too: throughout the essay the traveler has emphasized the difficulty of his journey--the roughness of the territory and the arduousness of his passage through it. He frequently refers to the superiority of his own philosophical and spiritual pursuits in the wilderness over the more mundane and destructive pursuits of hunters and loggers.[32] At the summit of Mount Katahdin he celebrates the unfathomable nature of the physical world: that though the traveler may enter into the very heart of nature, he still may be denied access to its meaning. Yet of all the invaders of the wilderness described in *The Maine Woods*--hunters, loggers, and travelers like the narrator--he may come closest to understanding and appreciating nature without destroying it. Like the poet in "Chesuncook" "who makes the truest use of the pine," the narrator on Katahdin's summit makes the "truest use" of the "mysteries" he discovers there, plumbing them for what knowledge he may be permitted and finally acknowledging his own limitations in penetrating the mysteries of the physical (pp. 71, 121).

In succeeding passages in "Ktaadn" and in its conclusion, the narrator returns to his usual benevolent relationship with nature, as McIntosh points out. The drama of the "*Contact!*" passage may, indeed, cause critics to overemphasize its importance for "Ktaadn" as a whole.[33] After the narrator descends the mountain his comments return to more mundane matters: the terrain, meals, provisions, and another traveler's comments on the area.

Although Thoreau returns to a generally more romantic view

of nature after the "*Contact!*" passage in "Ktaadn," he does not completely abandon the grim vision he achieved momentarily on the mountaintop. McIntosh suggests, in fact, that "the two passages were consciously designed to balance each other," both sections having been added at a later date to the original draft of the essay. The author, he argues, is "juxtaposing extreme statements to express both sides of a mixed truth" about nature, presenting both its "grim and tender" sides.[34] Certainly the conclusion of "Ktaadn" supports this interpretation, for Thoreau seems to wish to remind the reader of both the romantic and realistic views of the Maine wilderness he has portrayed in the essay. In the final paragraphs Thoreau writes: "What is most striking in the Maine wilderness is, the continuousness of the forest . . . It is even more grim and wild than you had anticipated, a damp and intricate wilderness, in the spring everywhere wet and miry. The aspect of the country indeed is universally stern and savage, excepting the distant views of the forest from hills, and the lake prospects, which are mild and civilizing in a degree" (80).

To reinforce his message that the Maine landscape is as savage as it is beautiful, with the grim forest counterbalanced against the beautiful (and, once again, "civilizing") lake views, the narrator compares these forests with those of England in what can only be a reference to Gilpin's descriptions of the English forests in *Forest Scenery*, which Thoreau had read: "These are not the artificial forests of an English king--a royal preserve merely. Here prevail no forest laws, but those of nature. The aborigines have never been dispossessed, nor nature disforested" (80). Thoreau reminds the reader that the New World wilderness is not like the "artificial forests" of the Old World nor, one might add, is travel here like a picturesque tour in the tame "preserves" of England. In Maine the beauty of the lakes exists side by side with the savagery of forest and mountaintop. Though one might find the beautiful and the sublime coexisting in Great Britain, here the two come to symbolize the "two faces of nature"[35] that the traveler may discover on a tour in the American wilderness. In Maine, Thoreau writes, the traveler discovers the "inexpressible tenderness and immortal life of the grim forest." Though the author may stress the "perpetual youth" of "blissful, innocent Nature" towards the end of "Ktaadn," one cannot and should not forget the grimness that is also present.[36]

In the essay's conclusion the narrator actually emphasizes the grimmer view of the New World landscape he discovered and expressed near the summit of Mount Katahdin, rather than its milder beauties. Writing of his native country, he asks: "Have we even so much as discovered and settled the shores?" "Tell me," he challenges the traveler along the coastline, "if it looks like a discovered and settled country, and not rather, for the most part, like a desolate island, and No-man's Land" (82). The rhetoric of the conclusion underscores the narrator's emphasis on the unexplored nature of the New World and on the dark reality of its wilderness. "We have advanced by leaps to the Pacific," he writes, but we have "left many a lesser Oregon and California unexplored behind us." Bangor stands "like a star on the edge of night," bordering the "howling wilderness which feeds it." Only sixty miles from this city "the country is virtually unmapped and unexplored, and there still waves the virgin forest of the New World" (82-83).

In describing the land as a "howling wilderness" Thoreau echoes the words of a stern old Puritan like William Bradford, and not accidentally. As "Ktaadn" demonstrates, the author does not subscribe single-mindedly to a romanticized view of the New World landscape, nor does he consider it only in a darker light. A traveler in the Maine wilderness will discover both picturesque beauty that one can simply admire--in its lakes, the forest, and even on the mountaintop--and the grimmer side of nature that repels and frightens the traveler. While an earlier American writer such as Charles Brockden Brown depicts his protagonist, Edgar Huntly, discovering the dark side of human nature and the world only at night or while sleepwalking, Thoreau shows his narrator confronting this reality in broad daylight on Mount Katahdin, and not forgetting the discovery upon his descent. The author never completely abandons this view of nature, as McIntosh points out, for although Thoreau maintains a romantic point of view overall, the grimmer side of nature surfaces occasionally in later writings.[37] The picturesque tour of the wilderness, then, may lead to the beautiful and even to the sublime, but it could also lead to the discovery of a dark reality that at times supersedes a romantic view of nature. What Edgar Huntly chooses to ignore at the end of his journeys about the dark side of human nature and of nature itself, Thoreau readily acknowledges at the conclusion of "Ktaadn," balancing nature's grimness against its tender beauty even as he prepares to set forth again on another journey into the Maine wilderness.

The political implications of Thoreau's discoveries about himself and nature in *The Maine Woods* are not as clearly stated as his thematic intentions in the three excursions. Yet they are there.[38] What Frederick Turner concludes about *Walden* in *Spirit of Place: The Making of an American Literary Landscape* applies as well to *The Maine Woods*. Thoreau, he argues, "tells all who will listen that America, the New World, is first and last a grand spiritual opportunity. And wherever we confront the facts of our place so steadily that we see them glimmer on both their sides--physical and spiritual--*there* America is the New World still."[39] In *The Maine Woods*, "fronting the facts" of his existence on "the unhandselled globe," Thoreau transforms the physical journey of the picturesque tour into a metaphor for a spiritual quest for truth. "Talk of mysteries!" he had exclaimed on Mount Katahdin. Journeying into the "unmapped and unexplored" country of the New World, he discovers there the "grand spiritual opportunity" that is America and inspires others to make that journey themselves.

Notes

1. *Excursions and Poems*, *The Writings of Henry David Thoreau*, Walden Edition, 20 vols. (Boston: Houghton Mifflin, 1906), 5: 207, 211 (further quotations from this volume are cited in the text by volume number and page); *Walden*, ed. J. Lyndon Shanley, *The Writings of Henry D. Thoreau* (Princeton: Princeton University Press, 1971), p. 4.

2. Lawrence Buell, *Literary Transcendentalism: Style and Vision in the American Renaissance* (Ithaca: Cornell University Press, 1973), p. 188.

3. Buell, p. 197.

4. William D. Templeman discusses Thoreau's interest in Gilpin and his knowledge of the Englishman's writings in "Thoreau, Moralist of the Picturesque," *PMLA* 47 (1932): 864-89.

5. *The Correspondence of Henry David Thoreau*, ed. Walter Harding and Carl Bode (1958; repr. Westport, Conn.: Greenwood Press, 1974), p. 341.

6. Thoreau, *Correspondence*, p. 389.

7. Templeman, pp. 880-86. Gordon V. Boudreau lists the specific dates on which Thoreau borrowed these volumes from the Harvard College Library ("H. D. Thoreau, William Gilpin, and the Metaphysical Ground of the Picturesque," *American Literature* 45 [1973], pp. 358-59, n. 4-5).

8. Robert D. Richardson, Jr., *Henry Thoreau: A Life of the Mind* (Berkeley: University of California Press, 1986), p. 263. Richardson offers a brief but perceptive analysis of Gilpin's influence on Thoreau in sections 71 and 72 in his biography (pp. 259-66).

9. William Gilpin, "On Picturesque Travel," *Three Essays*, 2nd ed. (London: R. Blamire, 1794; repr. Westmead, England: Gregg International, 1972), pp. 46-47.

10. *The Journal of Henry D. Thoreau*, ed. Bradford Torrey and Francis H. Allen, *The Writings of Henry David Thoreau*, Walden Edition, 20 vols. (Boston: Houghton Mifflin, 1949), 6: 59.

11. Thoreau, *Journal*, 4: 283-84.

12. Boudreau, pp. 365-68.

13. Thoreau, *Journal*, 4: 283-84.

14. Templeman, p. 871.

15. The complicated history of Thoreau's composition of *A Week on the Concord and Merrimack Rivers* is discussed in Linck C. Johnson's Historical Introduction to *The Illustrated A Week on the Concord and Merrimack Rivers* (Princeton: Princeton University Press, 1983), pp. xvi-xxxi. Johnson discusses the book's structure on pp. xxiv-xxvi.

16. Buell emphasizes the ascent of Mt. Greylock as anecdote and discusses the episode (pp. 220-21).

17. The Saddleback section in *A Week* is found on pp. 180-90. Johnson discusses the relationship between *Maine Woods* and *A Week* on pp. xxvii-xxviii.

18. Buell discusses *A Week* as a transcendentalist travel narrative in *Literary Transcendentalism*, pp. 203-07 and ch. 8 (pp. 208-38).

19. Gilpin, "On Picturesque Travel," pp. 47-48.

20. Richardson, pp. 224-25. Thoreau's ideas about wildness in "Walking" and other works are discussed in sections 60 and 62 (pp. 224-27, 230-33).

21. Henry D. Thoreau, *The Maine Woods*, ed. Joseph J. Moldenhauer (Princeton: Princeton University Press, 1974), p. 235. All subsequent references to this edition appear in the text.

22. In more recent times "the tide of fashionable travel" has nearly overwhelmed Mt. Katahdin. In "Ktaadn Revisited" Margie Whalen describes the contemporary scene in the summertime, when "the mountaintop is covered by camera-laden hikers" (*Thoreau Quarterly* 13 [1981]: 29-33).

23. See, for example, Thoreau's comments in "Ktaadn" on the "exciting," "arduous," and "dangerous" life of driving logs (p. 42), and compare with his remarks later in "Chesuncook" and "The Allegash" on logging, loggers, and the destruction of the Maine woods (pp. 121-22, 153-54, 228-29).

24. Thoreau read *Forest Scenery* in 1852 and commented on it extensively in his journals, describing it as "a pleasing book, so moderate, temperate, graceful, roomy, like a gladed wood" (Templeman, pp. 872-73).

25. "Battling Over Walden Woods," <u>Newsweek</u> 115 (30 April 1990), p. 27; "Forests at Risk: Shifting the Fight to the Maine Woods," *Los Angeles Times*, 7 July 1991, pp. M2, M6.

26. Richardson calls the ascent of Mount Katahdin the "central experience" of both Thoreau's first trip to the Maine woods and of "Ktaadn"; he discusses the trip and Thoreau's first draft of "Ktaadn" in detail (pp. 179-83). See also Buell, p. 202; and Moldenhauer, *Maine Woods*, pp. 358-60. According to Moldenhauer, Thoreau may have worked on "Ktaadn" after 1851 or 1857, complicating a close analysis of the text since Thoreau read Gilpin's works in between those years. Since I do not find any significant differences in the writer's attitude towards travel or in his landscape descriptions among the three *Maine Woods* essays, I would argue that "Ktaadn" was revised at some point after his initial encounter with Gilpin (1852), but probably not before this date.

27. Compare Thoreau to Parkman in the Black Hills or to Edgar Huntly in the cave.

28. James McIntosh, *Thoreau as Romantic Naturalist: His Shifting Stance toward Nature* (Ithaca: Cornell University Press, 1974), p. 201.

29. See Ronald Wesley Hoag's "The Mark on the Wilderness: Thoreau's Contact with Ktaadn" for a close reading of Thoreau's experience with the sublime in "Ktaadn" (*Texas Studies in Literature & Language* 24 [1982]: 33-35).

30. McIntosh, p. 206.

31. Richardson, p. 181.

32. In "Chesuncook" Thoreau writes: "What a coarse and imperfect use Indians and hunters make of nature! No wonder that their race is so soon exterminated." Contemplating a pine tree in the Maine wilderness, he considers its various purposes for the lumberman and the tanner, asking who "understands its nature best?" "It is the poet," he responds, "he it is who makes the truest use of the pine--who does not fondle it with an axe, nor tickle it with a saw, nor stroke it with a

plane; who knows whether its heart is false without cutting into it; who has not bought the stumpage of the township on which it stands" (pp. 120-22).

33. McIntosh, p. 207.

34. McIntosh, pp. 209-10.

35. McIntosh, p. 210.

36. In *Dark Thoreau* Richard Bridgman interprets the conclusion of "Ktaadn" as a reflection of "the strain existing between his [Thoreau's] desire to render the experience positively and attractively, and his actual feelings" and suggests that the author was "trying to neutralize unwelcome discoveries" at the end of the essay (Lincoln: University of Nebraska Press, 1982), pp. 203, 205. I would argue, however, along with McIntosh, that Thoreau presents a dual view of nature in "Ktaadn," and in the conclusion he expresses both sides of the wilderness honestly and without any particular tension in the narrator.

37. McIntosh, pp. 211-12.

38. Bruce Greenfield takes a broader view of the political implications of "Ktaadn" in "Thoreau's Discovery of America: A Nineteenth-Century First Contact," reading Thoreau's work in the context of earlier explorers of the New World and nineteenth-century American explorers of the Far West (*ESQ* 32 [1986]: 81-95).

39. Frederick Turner, *Spirit of Place: The Making of an American Literary Landscape* (San Francisco: Sierra Club Books, 1989), p. 39.

Chapter 8

Conclusion

The conventions of the picturesque tour offered an ideal vehicle for American writers seeking to establish a separate identity for the new nation during the period of political evolution, cultural development, and territorial expansion that followed the Revolutionary War. At first, writers interested in picturesque travel modeled their own works on William Gilpin's tours, importing the British convention to establish it on American grounds. With a nation in search of its own identity and with the special considerations necessary for travel in the United States, duplicating the picturesque tour was often unsuccessful, producing jarring incongruities. Charles Brockden Brown, however, did not use the tour uncritically; instead, he criticized would-be American tourists, questioning the notion of blind acceptance of European imports. Later writers such as Paulding and Irving transferred the tour to American soil more successfully by using it to demonstrate the superiority of landscape scenery in the New World, to satirize the European-corrupted dandies who practiced this form of travel, and to promote nationalism with visits to historic sites that commemorated American military glory and independence. Developing the expression of nationalism in the travel sketch in a different way, Hawthorne contributed an ironic, implicitly critical element that was previously missing in picturesque discourse. Later, Thoreau transformed the convention itself by taking it in a new direction morally and philosophically.

In a general sense, the travel narrative as a genre gave writers (and their protagonists) an opportunity to explore the United States, whether well known regions such as the White Mountains or generally untraveled areas such as the Maine wilderness. Within this larger genre, the picturesque tour's focus on landscapes allowed authors to showcase one of America's greatest assets: its natural beauty. From the beauty of New York's lake country to the picturesqueness of the Hudson River Valley and the sublimity of Niagara Falls, travelers and writers demonstrated that the United States equalled or surpassed Europe in offering tourists landscapes worthy of their attention. Furthermore, for travelers who were willing to risk the dangers of Indians, wild animals, and rugged terrain, the Far West offered landscapes unique to the United States--the prairies, for example, and the extraordinary Rocky Mountains. This literary use of picturesque travel helped to define and highlight America's uniqueness in its landscape beauty.

In addition, the tour's focus on picturesque beauty, with its need for associations in the landscape, encouraged comments on the historical or legendary significance of landscapes that could also serve the nationalistic aims of a writer. Authors as different as Silliman, Paulding, and Hawthorne recalled America's past triumphs on the battlefield by including stops at historic sites on their picturesque tours. Reminiscences about the French and British fight over Fort Ticonderoga and the later American victory there, for example, gave historical significance to the New York landscape and, more important, reminded readers of the new nation's strength. Even a brief comment such as Paulding's mention of a British general taking refuge in a cave added luster to the Pennsylvania scenery he described, recalling the American triumph over a more powerful foe in a past war. Though less blindly nationalistic, Hawthorne probes Americans' relationship to the past, present, and future in travel sketches such as "Old Ticonderoga" and "The Canal-Boat." As Dennis Berthold observes, "Even while they follow many of the prescribed patterns for evoking nationalistic sentiments, Hawthorne's travel sketches come to question the significance of the American past and the promise of the American present." There is, he notes, "an ironic opposition between the beauties of the landscape and the realities of history and politics" in the American travel sketches.[1] With their admixture of autobiography and fiction, these sketches also enable the author to create more sophisticated prose than Paulding's earlier light satire in *The New Mirror* and more successful tales such as "Childe Roeliff's Pilgrimage," combining fiction with the picturesque tour.

America's westward expansion created new territory for the picturesque traveler and offered new directions for the published tour.

Instead of celebrating America's past and present, as in the typical eastern tour, the western tour often celebrated the future of a landscape lacking a historic past or present, whether in western Pennsylvania in Crèvecoeur's "On the Susquehanna" or in Thoreau's "west," the wilderness of the Maine woods. Here was the direction of future settlement by easterners and immigrants, and here history was being made as Indian tribes were resettled, new territories and states were established, and wars were fought over possession of land. For writers like Irving and Parkman, the challenges of western travel also offered a testing ground for the American male. Their tours of the West became a quest for what was missing in the East, and the rugged, independent character fostered by such travel encouraged them to believe that the western tour could produce the kind of men who could best lead the new nation. Parkman took this quest for physical strength a step further and found spiritual rejuvenation on the western trail, transforming the picturesque tour in the process.

Later writers such as Poe, Hawthorne, and Thoreau expanded the tour's generic boundaries by using one or more conventions of the picturesque tour metaphorically. Hawthorne employed a traveler's search for the right perspective on Niagara Falls as a means of reflecting on the artist's search for perspective in his art. For Poe, the search for picturesque beauty in a landscape offered the artist an opportunity to explore the possibility of creating ideal beauty on earth through the metaphor of the landscape designer creating a garden. Thoreau employed the picturesque tour throughout his travel books, using its conventions to probe the relationship between his own nature and that of the natural world. For him, the pursuit of landscape beauty became a metaphor for a search for spiritual knowledge. The travel works of all three writers suggest not only the diverse tonal qualities possible in picturesque discourse but also the intellectual and philosophical sophistication that American writers had achieved by mid-century. Grounding their writing in the nation's soil also helped to refute charges that American literature was derivative, establishing instead its literary independence.

In the 1850s, however, when Thoreau's interest in Gilpin and the picturesque tour peaked, the genre underwent an ironic inversion that would culminate in Melville's *The Piazza Tales*. During these years Thoreau traveled to Canada and throughout New England, writing and eventually publishing the travel books that featured the conventions of picturesque travel even while reflecting a growing awareness of the flexibility of these same conventions. But in more general terms, the literary picturesque tour was largely exhausted by this time. These years marked the waning of literary interest in the tour as a form of travel writing, though later writers such as Mark Twain (in *Roughing It*, for example) continued to express a conventional interest in picturesque beauty on their travels. By this time American cultural identity, especially in terms of differentiating from Great Britain, was more secure than in the early part of the century. Westward expansion was nearly complete, since by 1853 most of the continental territory had been acquired. Given these changes, it is hardly surprising to find writers turning to other literary themes and forms, even while Thoreau continued to expand the borders of picturesque travel in works like "Ktaadn" in *The Maine Woods*.

To understand how and why the literary use of the picturesque tour declined during the 1850s, consider Herman Melville's use of picturesque travel. *The Piazza Tales* (1856) signals the end of the literary tour with the author's persistent ironic treatment of its conventions and his deeply pessimistic parody of the tour itself, particularly its assumption that the traveler could attain picturesque beauty. In "The Piazza" the narrator sets up his tale within a picturesque framework, calling the countryside around his farmhouse a picture, describing the prospect as "a very paradise of painters," and suggesting that the surrounding mountains are a picture gallery for the observer.[2] Furthermore, he sets off on a picturesque-like tour in mid-story in search of the elusive golden light he sees in the distant mountains. Interestingly, most of the journey is described in terms of a sea voyage, a new twist Melville brings to the picturesque tour that culminates in "The Encantadas." Yet the major portion of the tale, particularly its ending, undercuts any sense the reader may have of this journey as a conventional picturesque tour or of the golden light as an ideal. When the narrator reaches the light's source and discovers Marianna, the light is revealed as deceptive and Marianna as deluded. Paradoxically, at tale's end the narrator can sustain his illusions only by day. At nightfall, "truth comes in with darkness," and it becomes clear that since his journey resulted in the loss of his illusions, the narrator will venture no more from his piazza in search of an elusive, perhaps nonexistent ideal (12).

In "The Encantadas" Melville undercuts the conventions of the picturesque tour more dramatically by moving the scene from land to sea and by making the search for beauty so unsuccessful that the narrator is thoroughly disillusioned about both the nature of mankind and the nature of the world. Instead of the paradise he might expect to find in a place called the "Enchanted Isles," Melville's narrator discovers a desert-like hell on earth occupied by "tortoises, lizards, immense spiders, snakes, and that strangest anomaly of outlandish nature, the *iguana*." Inhabited by such people as the Chola widow and the hermit Oberlus, the islands oppress the visitor with an atmosphere of desolation and even malignancy. Disillusioned and despairing, the narrator is haunted ever after by the "lasting sorrow and penal hopelessness" of life as he saw it symbolized in the Galapagos tortoise (127, 129).

The narrator's travels in the Encantadas parody the picturesque tour as it was practiced in the half-century before Melville wrote these sketches. Richard S. Moore has observed, "The death-ridden landscape of the Galapagos is repeatedly connected with such American centers of picturesque interest as the Erie Canal and Adirondack Mountains." He concludes that Melville intentionally parodies "the conventional picturesque tour-book" in "The Encantadas."[3] Yet the narrator's description of the islands and their inhabitants, and the pessimism that prevails in the sketches combine to produce a work that is more an anti-picturesque tour than a simple parody. Melville took a conventional form--the picturesque tour--that emphasized landscape beauty and turned it in upon itself to produce a tour that discovers a wasteland instead of a paradise and that produces depression, not astonishment or pleasure, in the disheartened traveler. Whether such a depiction of the Galapagos and of picturesque travel reflects the author's own increasing despair about the reception of his work or about the nature of mankind and the world in general is not clear. What is clear, however, is that the sort of relatively superficial satire Paulding achieved in *The New Mirror* nearly three decades earlier has been transformed into a much darker and certainly more despairing parody of the same travel and literary conventions at mid-century.

Although the picturesque tour as a literary phenomenon was largely exhausted by the 1850s, this does not mean the tour is unimportant to literary history. This study reveals how American culture was shaped and defined by looking at how a British convention is imported, satirized, and eventually transformed by American writers as part of the new country's developing cultural independence and national pride. With such a perspective, minor travel works acquire new significance. Hawthorne's travel sketches, for example, have generally been ignored as works of little interest or relationship to his more important fiction, the tales and novels. Yet these sketches consider serious issues (the role of the artist in "My Visit to Niagara," for example) with as much seriousness as a longer work such as *The Scarlet Letter*. Though not with such depth and complexity, their craft is often fairly sophisticated and interesting.[4] For a writer such as Thoreau, the travel narrative as genre is even more important. Although most critical attention is directed at *Walden*, Thoreau's love of travel and preference for the travel narrative is evident in all his other works, except for the political writings, from *A Week on the Concord and Merrimack* to *Cape Cod* and *The Maine Woods*. Several of his travel works depend in varying degrees on the conventions of the picturesque tour, making an understanding of this phenomenon and its use in literature necessary for a full understanding of Thoreau and his work.

During this formative period for American literature, then, the nation's unique landscapes and geography were an integral part of its identity, distinguishing it from England and anywhere else in the Old World. Picturesque travel particularly suited the developing national literature and influenced it in four major ways, transforming the imported conventions of the tour at the same time. First, the picturesque tour encouraged writers to explore the American landscape and enabled them to celebrate its unique qualities. In addition, the tour's emphasis upon associations and landscape scenery focused attention on the nation's history, including the past triumphs on the battlefield that established the United States as an independent nation; here the various tones achieved by different authors suggest the diversity possible in picturesque discourse, ranging from light satire to darkest parody and despair. Third, picturesque travel in the West highlighted American expansionism and enabled writers to suggest the future growth and glory of the country. Finally, what originated in England as largely a tour of landscape scenery became transformed into a spiritual and intellectual quest that broadened the scope of picturesque travel and deepened its meaning for both traveler and reader. In these ways the picturesque tour played a significant role in enabling American writers to establish a national identity during the formative period between the War of Independence and the Civil War.

Notes

1. "History and Nationalism in 'Old Ticonderoga' and Other Travel Sketches," in Alfred Weber, Beth L. Lueck, and Dennis Berthold, *Hawthorne's American Travel Sketches* (Hanover, N.H.: University Press of New England, 1989), p. 133.

2. Herman Melville, "The Piazza," *The Piazza Tales, and Other Prose Pieces, 1839-1860*, ed. Harrison Hayford et al., *The Writings of Herman Melville* (Evanston: Northwestern University Press; Chicago: Newberry Library, 1987), 9: 1-2. All subsequent references to "The Piazza" and other works in *The Piazza Tales* are to this volume of the Northwestern-Newberry Edition.

3. Richard S. Moore, *That Cunning Alphabet: Melville's Aesthetics of Nature*, Costerus, n.s. vol. 35 (Amsterdam: Rodopi, 1982), pp. 195-96.

4. For further reading on Hawthorne's travel sketches from the early 1830s, see Weber, Lueck, and Berthold, *Hawthorne's American Travel Sketches*.

Index